# Th

# Anstruther
# &
# St Andrews
# Railway

*by*
*Andrew Hajducki, Michael Jodeluk,*
*& Alan Simpson*

# THE OAKWOOD PRESS

British Library Cataloguing in Publication Data
A Record for this book is available from the British Library
ISBN 978 0 85361 687 0

Typeset by Oakwood Graphics.
Repro by PKmediaworks, Cranborne, Dorset.
Printed by Cambrian Printers, Aberystwyth, Ceredigion.

'B1' class 4-6-0 No. 61340 passes Kingsbarns with a summer Saturdays working from St Andrews to Glasgow, 11th July, 1964. *C.C. Thornburn*

*Title page*: This reversed photograph shows the original company seal of the Anstruther & St Andrews Railway - note the Saltire cross, the anchor, the garlands of thistle and oak and the early locomotive. *Glasgow City Council Museums*

*Front cover*: North British 'J37' class 0-6-0 No. 64629 on a Crail to Thornton local drifts in to Anstruther for Cellardyke on a sunny afternoon in May 1959 with the tower of the Waid Academy clearly visible in the background. *G.Hunt/Colour-Rail*

*Rear cover, top*: A Dundee to Glasgow train in the capable charge of 'B1' class 4-6-0 No. 61278 crosses a down working at Crail, May 1959 in the presence of signalman Sam Myles and Mr McQueen, the porter. *G.Hunt/Colour-Rail*

*Rear cover, bottom*: 'D34' class 4-4-0 No. 62467 *Glenfinnan* with a mixture of Gresley and Thompson stock, trundles towards Stravithie with a local from Leuchars on a cold Spring day in the 1950s. *Nigel Dyckhoff*

Published by The Oakwood Press (Usk), P.O. Box 13, Usk, Mon., NP15 1YS.
E-mail:    sales@oakwoodpress.co.uk
Website:  www.oakwoodpress.co.uk

# Contents

The handsome lines of 'B1' class 4-6-0 No. 61344 are displayed to full effect at Crail on the last day of services between there and St Andrews, Saturday 4th September, 1965 - note the burgh sign in the background.

*Norman Turnbull*

# Foreword

During World War II my mother was granted just enough petrol to get us children into school in St Andrews in the morning and home in the afternoon. In between she bicycled the four miles uphill home and the four miles back into town in the afternoon. The route crossed the Anstruther & St Andrews Railway at the Allanhill bridge. Mother used to complain that her five-year-old required her to stop and wait every day for a train to pass under that bridge. Not often did a train turn up but that bridge was my first direct contact with the Anstruther & St Andrews Railway.

Much of one's life in the 1940s and 1950s revolved around comings and goings at the delightful railway station in St Andrews with its line of horse-drawn hansom cabs, its grand staircase to the platform, its beautifully-tended flower displays and the smell of steam and oil. Often I would accompany my father to Stravithie station to collect items for the farm or for his wine cellar. I recall herding a flock of sheep, bought earlier that day in Aberdeen, from Mount Melville station the three miles to our farm. Whenever I had an opportunity in the 1960s I would travel to Edinburgh 'round the coast' - if possible in the very front of a diesel multiple unit. In my biased view it was the most beautiful of railway journeys.

On that sad day in 1965 I was by chance at home from my job in Italy. I took the silver spade, with which my great-grandmother dug the first sod of the Anstruther & St Andrews Railway, on the last train from Anstruther to St Andrews. The spade now hangs on the wall in my home as a reminder of what we have lost. Most days I still drive over the Allanhill bridge. Strangers to the district enquire why there is this hump-backed bridge in the middle of nowhere. As I explain, memories flood back for me while the stranger finds it extraordinary that a railway ever passed this way.

This book about the Anstruther & St Andrews Railway is surely overdue, but therefore all the more welcome. Alan Simpson and his co-authors, Andrew Hajducki and Mike Jodeluk, have researched in great depth the background to how these railways came about, how they operated and why they faded away. I have found it fascinating and not only because of my family's involvement with them. It just shows how the determination and enterprise of our Victorian forefathers, in spite even of their mistakes, are an example to us. This was just one link in the chain of innovative infrastructure, which provided for the biggest economic and social revolution our country has ever experienced. Can our present generation match them?

This book is nostalgic, but it is also more. It is a major contribution to the history of East Fife and to an understanding of the depth and extent of the Victorian industrial revolution and its socio-economic impact. It is a reproach to our own generation for its short-sightedness in letting go of something which would now, 40 years later, be coming right back into its own. It is a labour of love by its authors for which I and many others will certainly be most grateful.

*John Purvis CBE,*
*Gilmerton,*
*St Andrews,*
*Member of the European Parliament,*
*Scotland Constituency*

A classic view of Kingsbarns looking towards Crail on 11th May, 1964; signalman James Anderson walks back to the box with the token for the long section from St Andrews while the Metro-Cammell dmu departs for Edinburgh.

*C.C. Thornburn*

# Authors' Preface

In *The St Andrews Railway* the authors set out the history, from inception to closure, of the pioneering branch line that connected the ancient university and golfing town of St Andrews to the outside world. This book continues the story of the East Fife Railways and deals with the fascinating and often tortuous history of one of the least prosperous and most ill-fated of all of the small companies that struggled to complete the coastal loop from Thornton to Leuchars, the Anstruther & St Andrews Railway. Opened in two stages between 1883 and 1887, this rather wandering 16 mile-long single track linked the terminus of the Leven & East of Fife Railway at the busy fishing port of Anstruther with the genteel burgh of Crail and, turning north, served the villages of Kingsbarns and Boarhills, although in the case of Kingsbarns the station was a long walk away from the village it purported to serve. From Boarhills (or, more accurately, from a point somewhere near to Boarhills) the line then swung through a great arc and, passing through nowhere in particular, had remote stations at Stravithie and Mount Melville before beginning a fearsome descent to St Andrews where its flower-decked and spruce station was the meeting point with the branch from Leuchars. In an astute move the shareholders of the Anstruther & St Andrews eventually sold out to Scotland's largest railway company, the North British (NBR), and thereafter the line rose to new heights under the NBR and the London & North Eastern Railway (LNER), even carrying a named train, the fabled 'Fife Coast Express'. The combined effects of an economic recession and bus competition caused the four intermediate stations between Crail and St Andrews to close to passengers as early as 1930 and this section survived a threat of complete closure to serve the wartime airfields at Crail, Dunino and Stravithie. The post-war boom ended with rapidly falling revenues and even the dieselisation of the passenger services could not stop local people from turning their back on the line. When, in the 1960s, the line was finally closed many regretted that Crail was no longer on the railway map and that it would never again be possible to sit at the front of a diesel unit and trundle through a beautiful rural landscape interspersed with sea views, farmland and the four mysterious stations that seemed to have fallen asleep under a wicked spell.

*The Anstruther & St Andrews Railway* is as self-contained as the authors can manage and the branch from Leuchars, the line from Anstruther to Largo, Leven and the west and the various branches leading from it are all dealt with in the companion volumes. The authors, however, have to apologise for the fact that, by a quirk of railway geography, the Royal Burghs of Anstruther Easter and Anstruther Wester, fall to be split between two separate railway companies and thus separate volumes in this series and the full story of fish and holidaymakers and the heroic struggle to reach Anster from the west all properly belong to our forthcoming work, *The Leven & East Fife Railway*. To those who remember the slow trains that trundled their way around the East Neuk, the Anstruther & St Andrews Railway was possibly the most fascinating and least visited part of the whole system and it is still held in great affection by those who knew it. It is therefore with great pleasure that, once again, the authors invite you to take your seats and await the green flag and whistle.

*A.H., M.J. & A.S.*
*Cellardyke, Edinburgh, Stirling and Kirkcaldy*
*October 2008*

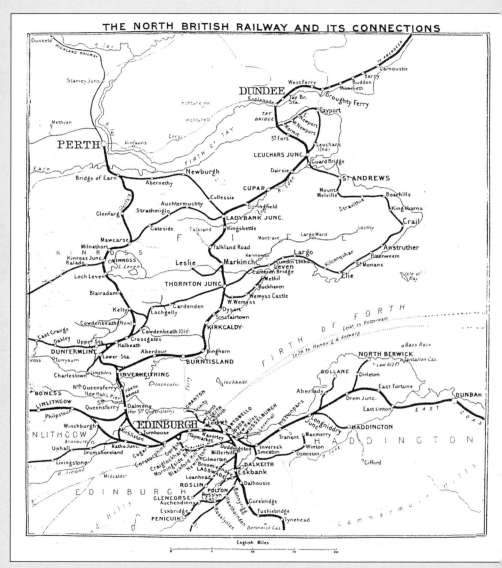

North British Railway (Eastern Area) official map, 1900.

# Chapter One

## A Coastal Peregrination:
## From Anstruther to St Andrews

*'Such a quest is best made under grey skies, and in a nipping and an eager air.'*
John Geddie, 'The Fringes of Fife'

### *The East Neuk and Beyond*

As the county and kingdom of Fife reaches its easternmost end and the Firth of Forth emerges into the cold North Sea, the rocky coastline encircles an area of great beauty known as the East Neuk; a beauty, however, that is tempered one moment by howling gales and another by the long hours of sunshine peculiar to this part of the country. Composed almost entirely of calciferous sandstone, the East Neuk is a land of rich soils and prosperous farms and its small but safe harbours were for many years busy with a fishing industry that was second to none. From Kirkcaldy eastwards a string of small seaside burghs, many of them with a royal charter, traded with the Low Countries and with the rest of Scotland in an era when roads were impassable and, with the advent of the railway, many of these little places enjoyed a new lease of life as tourist haunts and resorts for those who eschewed the more obvious pleasures of the holidaymaker at large.

As one travelled eastwards, passing by the delights of Elie, St Monance* and Pittenweem were reached. Here the twin burghs of Anstruther, or 'Anster' in the local parlance, where, contemporaneously with the construction of the Leven & East of Fife Railway, plans were launched for a new harbour to rival that of many a busy port on the east coast and the town became, in time, the undisputed centre of the winter herring trade in Scotland. Beyond Anster lay the genteel Crail, the most easterly and windiest of the East Neuk burghs and for long the haunt of crab-catchers, amateur painters and keen golfers. Beyond Crail lay nothing but Fife Ness - in the words of John Geddie in his entertaining work *The Fringes of Fife* 'the Ultima thule of the Kingdom, beyond which there is no land until you come to Denmark'. Here at the Ness, where the inhospitable

Fife Ness.

---

\* The favoured spelling in North British Railway days although now largely supplanted in modern times by St Monans.

9

coastline now abruptly turned northwards, the winds blow strongest. Continuing round by Kingsbarns and Boarhills, the only two settlements of any significance in the area, one reaches St Andrews, the ultimate goal upon which the ambitions of any self-respecting local railway would be fixed. But all of this is anticipating the journey that we have not yet made, the peregrination of this stormy coast - a journey which John Geddie held was best done in winter 'when cold weather and easterly haar resume their reign … and the last of the bathers and holiday-makers have fled with the leaves' for it is only then, in his words, that 'Fife is itself again'.

### Of Fisher Lassies and Princesses

Anstruther, whose Gaelic name *An struthair*, refers to the small streams which flow through the town, is in reality an amalgam of the Royal Burghs of Anstruther Wester and Anstruther Easter, two twin municipalities divided from each other by the Dreel Burn and a sense of local rivalry and which survived a combination in December 1929 with its neighbours Kilrenny and Cellardyke to become the local authority area with the longest title in Scotland, namely, the United Burghs of Kilrenny, Anstruther Easter and Anstruther Wester. Having a population of just below 2,000, the town was, in Victorian times, a busy local centre with, in the words of the *Ordnance Gazetter of Scotland*,

Anstruther in Edwardian times with St Adrian's parish church in the background. The Dreel Burn, the boundary between Anstruther Wester and Easter, runs across the middle of the picture but the famous stepping stones across the burn are hidden by the high tide. This scene is still instantly recognisable today but had the railway line from the station to the harbour been built this landscape would have been very different - fortunately it was not!
*Authors' Collection*

a post office with money order, savings bank and telegraph departments, branches of the Clydesdale, Commercial and National Banks, a gasworks, hotels, a custom-house, a town hall (1871; accommodation 800), a Masonic lodge, several insurance offices, a library and reading room, a lifeboat station, and a fishery office. Friday is market day; and the industrial establishments are rope and sail, net, oil and oilskin and fishing-gear factories, and a brewery.

As this description clearly points to, the main occupation of the inhabitants of Anstruther was fishing and fish-curing and, by the mid-century, the town was one of the busiest fishing ports on the east coast and 'the head of all the fishery districts between Leith and Montrose'. Even now, when the fish have long since departed, Anstruther is still the commercial capital of the East Neuk and has a new and prosperous air far removed from that of, in the words of Robert Louis Stevenson, 'a grey, grim, sea-beaten hole'.

A short distance to the east, and physically joined to Anstruther, lies Cellardyke, whose name in its original version Sillerdyke reflected the offshore reefs and plentiful fish. Cellardyke possessed a harbour, known as Skinfasthaven, and was the ancient port for Kilrenny, but by the 19th century was home to seafarers and fishermen, fisher lassies and to the captains of the great China tea-clippers as well as to coopers, cod-liver oil merchants and those who worked in a myriad of small fish-related industries. Rarely in the news, on its own account Cellardyke maintained a proud and separate existence from Anstruther (whose station nameboards, lest there should be any confusion about the matter proclaimed 'Anstruther for Cellardyke') and this distancing remains to the present day.*

Inland from Cellardyke is Kilrenny, an ancient settlement centred around its church and mill and whose name seems to have been the cause of some controversy - is it really derived from *Cill Reithneach*, the church of the bracken or was it once *Cill Righinn*, the church of the princess? - perhaps the latter derivation is more fanciful but then it has to be admitted that princesses were more easily found in those days than now. By the end of the 19th century Kilrenny's fortunes had been eclipsed and although the railway was to pass close to the village, no station was ever provided for its inhabitants.

### Rock and Herring

Following the rugged coastline along from Cellardyke one passes by the Caiplie caves, reputedly the home of St Ethernan, an Irish missionary who supposedly lived there in solitude until he was murdered by a band of Vikings. Eventually, after an invigorating walk, Crail (Gaelic *carr* and *ail*, meaning the boulder rock in an apparent tautology) is reached. This small seaport, the most easterly of all Fife's harbours, was tucked in to the coastline at the point where it was most exposed and provided a welcome last haven before the full storms of the North Sea were encountered.

---

* In an brief moment of fame, Cellardyke became the focus for the world's media when, in 2006, a dead swan infected with avian flu turned up in its harbour and the press were politely informed that this was Cellardyke, not Anstruther!

Crail harbour in about 1910 - note the tall chimney belonging to the sea-served gas works and the potato boat waiting to load its export cargo.          *Alan Brotchie Collection*

A picturesque little town of golden sandstone walls and red pantile roofs hugging the sandstone cliffs, Crail was a place of considerable antiquity, having a venerable town hall and market cross, being and by far the oldest of the five Royal Burghs of the East Neuk proper. Recorded as Caraile in 1153, and with the dangerous Carr Rocks three miles offshore, the town was once an important port and herring fishing centre. In the 14th and 15th centuries the burgh traded with many countries bordering the Baltic. Even as late as the 17th century the trade through Crail harbour was known to include exports of herrings, salt and cloth to Danzig, Stockholm, Memel, Konigsberg, Stettin and Riga while imports included Swedish bar iron, Polish flax and timber from Sweden and the Baltic. Trade had dwindled by the 19th century and by then Crail harbour saw only a small amount of coastal traffic consisting principally of potatoes and locally dug ironstone bound for the Tyne ports; by 1860 even this latter traffic had ceased and Crail remained only as a small fishing centre specialising in locally-caught partans (crabs) and lobsters, its fish trade being greatly overtaken in importance by the neighbouring burghs of Anstruther and Pittenweem. All was not lost, however, for a golfing society was founded in the town in 1786 and the Golf Inn was opened three years later but Crail's fortunes were slow to revive, so much so that in 1827 Robert Chambers described its main streets as being 'half-covered with rank grass and weeds' and the town 'as a venerable and decayed burgh which possessed no trade', while another contemporary guidebook, *The Traveller's Guide to Scotland*, commented that 'the burgh bears evident marks of having seen better days'.

Even as late as 1880 Crail was still very much cut off from the rest of Scotland and, in a late Victorian guidebook, Jackson's *Guide to Crail*, it was said that:

CRAIL CROSS.

Until the opening of the railway … Crail's isolation from the outer world was proverbial. The story is told of a gentleman in Glasgow who enquired of a friend there if he had ever been in America. 'No', he replied. 'I was never in America, but I'll tell you what - I've a brother who was once in Crail'. In these pristine days, the arrival of Edmond's coach from Anstruther was the event of he morning – an event duly heralded by the blast of Robbie Kirkcaldy's horn, which, as he beat his drum and cried, 'Notiz', was heard from one end of the burgh to the other. A visit to St Andrews then meant perforce an entire day. Leaving Crail at eight in the morning the journey took two hours. You then had to wait on till five in the afternoon to be taken back again. And with the chance, you might think, of not getting a place! Yet the risk of that was slight. Though the vehicle was a small one, the amount of packing it was capable of, outside and in, was extraordinary, and wonder now is, how it could have been done.

Within half a century Crail was to develop as a centre for genteel holidaymakers and as a haven for 'retired persons of the better class', notwithstanding the fact that according to Stewart Dick in his 1910 *Pageant of the Forth* 'for all the windy towns on the shore of the Forth, it has the distinction of being the coldest'. To properly serve the genteel holidaymakers and retired persons, however, Crail would have to eagerly await the somewhat belated arrival of its railway. But even this trade would be a strictly seasonable one for 'during winter or early spring this easterly region, when the bitter blighting east wind is in full blast, attains to a sublimity of bleakness'.

### The King's Barns

North of Crail lay the parish of Kingsbarns, a somewhat sparsely populated area straddling the main road from to St Andrews and whose eastern boundary was formed by a rocky and much eroded coastline.

The only settlement of any note in this parish was the eponymous village at its centre, its name showing that the area had once contained royal granaries or barns probably related to Falkland or nearby Crail rather than St Andrews. Kingsbarns was, in 1837, described in a guidebook as 'a thriving little place and carries on a considerable manufacture of Osnaburgh shirtings and other linens for the Dundee market. The largest and best flag-stones in the country are to be found a short distance from the village and along the shore marble of a fine quality is met with occasionally'. By the latter half of the century, however, the textile trade had migrated to the larger centres of Leven, Kirkcaldy and Cupar and the economy of Kingsbarns had reverted to being almost wholly based on local farming and the settlement clustered around its handsome church, water pump and broad square was suffering a slow decline in population. The small harbour, which had been built in 1810 by the Earl of Kellie for the export of potatoes, grain, locally-dug coal and drainage tiles made from the products of neighbouring clay pits, had been eclipsed, the harbour was in decline by the 1850s and not many years later was completely derelict and never used again. Kingsbarns was not, however, devoid of recreational facilities for a golfing society was founded here in 1815 and, as sea-bathing became increasingly popular, the Cambo sands, a mile from the village, attracted some interest from the more adventurous tourist. There were two principal landowners in the parish the Moneypenny family, who owned the Pitmilly estate north of the village, and the Erskine family, who owned the Cambo estate to the south, and members of both of these families were to feature in the story of the local railway.

### Swine and Seed

A couple of miles north of the village the coastline turned westwards towards the mouth of the River Eden and the public road also swung westwards crossing first the Pitmilly Burn and then the larger Kenly Burn or Water before reaching the secluded settlement of Boarhills. Allegedly part of the run of wild pigs granted by Angus I, King of the Picts, to the monastery of Kilrule, the latter-day St Andrews, Boarhills remained a rather out of the way place. Described in *The Buildings of Scotland* as a 'hamlet of vernacular rubble-built and pantiled cottages [in] a winding street squashed between farm steadings', the hamlet in 1890 possessed a mission church, post office and public school but little else. In the gorge of the Kenly lay the mansion house of Kenly Green and the busy meal mills of Park and Pitmilly, but of the wild boars that had given the place its name, there was no trace. To the south-west of Boarhills were the parishes of Cameron and Dunino, whose sparse population was to be found in scattered farmsteads and in a handful of settlements large enough to merit the designation of hamlet. Formerly a moorland area, the parishes became predominantly agricultural in the mid-19th century but their populations began to decline thereafter and by the 1880s, when the railway was to cross their northern borders and build stations at the isolated railheads of Strathvithie and Mount Melville, there seemed to be little prospect of a burst of prosperity in either parish.

### The Pilgrim City

Beyond this long stretch of exposed upland lay St Andrews,* the ancient city which became the chief bishopric of Scotland a thousand years ago and where, in 1411, Scotland's first university was founded. A place of great pilgrimage in medieval times via the often rough sea link between North Berwick and

---

* A fuller (and perhaps more balanced) account of St Andrews is given in the companion volume, *The St Andrews Railway*.

Earlsferry, and the scene of much change and tumult in the Reformation, St Andrews gradually lost its dominance as a local market town to Cupar but managed to foster one of the chief pillars of its present prosperity, Golf. Originally played on the town's sandy links, golf in St Andrews achieved an exalted height when the Royal & Ancient became the governing body of the game in much of the world and people flocked all through the year to play on its courses, to watch its tournaments and generally to bask in the atmosphere of this mecca of the game. And yet there were other attractions, too. The sandy beaches had begun, in Victorian times, to attract holidaymakers and tourists and those with an antiquarian bent enjoyed the Cathedral ruins and other ancient buildings of the town. The University eventually recovered from the doldrums and regained a position of academic and social excellence. Schools, most notably St Leonards school for girls and the pioneering Madras College added to the academic attractions of the city. Perhaps all that was missing was the weather for, as the *Ordnance Gazetteer of Scotland* somewhat delicately put it 'The situation is somewhat exposed, but the climate is healthy and bracing'. By 1881 St Andrews parish had a resident population of 6,400, almost double that of 80 years before. But, as the *Third Statistical Account* put it a couple of generations later:

> St Andrews … emerges as a town that enjoys many advantages. It is prosperous, comfortable and a place of appearance, though the shortage of work for men is a serious handicap, not entirely compensated for by the absence of industry as a despoiler of beauty. And, in the main, the residents are conscious and proud of their heritage and good fortune. Yet it must be admitted that the sense of community is scarcely as strong as it might be hoped and expected, and St Andrews remains an imposing and picturesque, rather than a friendly, town, one in which the rules of etiquette and orders of precedence at times appear to be thought more important than warm or hospitable action.

Whether these words, penned more than half a century ago, are still true today is, of course, a matter for the reader to judge for him or herself.

St Andrews, *c.*1900 showing children playing on the West Beach, the world-famous Old Course, the R&A Clubhouse, the University's Hamilton Hall and, in the background, buildings on North Street and The Scores.          *Alan Brotchie Collection*

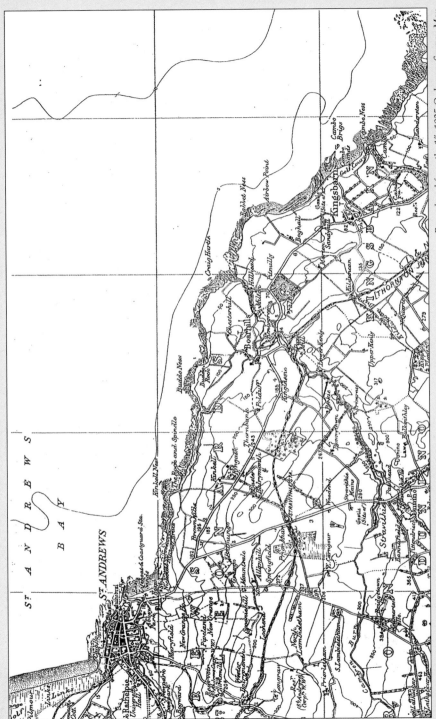

The northern section of the Anstruther & St Andrews Railway

*Reproduced from the 1", 1925 Ordnance Survey Map*

# Chapter Two

# A District Unsurpassed:
# The Anstruther & St Andrews Railway 1865-1880

*'A district unsurpassed in Fife for the fertility of its soil or the ability
and enterprise of its agriculturalists.'*

Letter to the Fifeshire Journal

## A Main Line Through Fife

In 1845 the Edinburgh & Northern Railway company came into being, with powers to construct and operate a line that would stretch across Fife and eventually link Edinburgh with Dundee and the north. The line began from the low-water pier at Burntisland, to where steam ferries regularly plied from Granton, and followed the coast to Kirkcaldy before heading inland towards Markinch and the village of Ladybank, where one branch headed westwards through Newburgh to Perth and the other followed the valley of the Eden to reach the county town at Cupar.

In 1847 trains began running between Burntisland and Cupar and by May of the following year an extension to Leuchars was opened. Soon a further extension to Tayport (or Ferryport-on-Craig) was in use and this, coupled with a regular river service over the Tay to Broughty Ferry, constituted a new and important route from the capital to the north-east.

A Prospectus for a branch line from Leuchars to St Andrews, following the estuary of the Eden, came to naught but, with the arrival on the scene of the ill-fated Thomas Bouch and the era of 'cheap railways', another attempt was made to link St Andrews with what had by now become the Edinburgh, Perth and Dundee Railway. This time the proposal was for a locally-financed branch line that was to be basic in its design and economical to construct and so rapidly was the line built that, within a year of the St Andrews Railway receiving Parliamentary approval, the first trains traversed the five miles of line between Leuchars, Guardbridge and St Andrews on 29th June, 1852.

Operated on behalf of the St Andrews company by the Edinburgh, Perth & Dundee, the line was gradually brought up to more modern standards although the original terminus, situated adjacent to the Old Course and links, was picturesquely placed but something of a long trek from the town centre. Nevertheless  the line proved popular with the public and the shareholders received good dividends; and, as the line prospered, so did the town. In 1877, after more a quarter of a century of independence, the St Andrews Railway was absorbed by the North British and, with the completion of the Tay Bridge a year later, the St Andrews branch appeared to have an assured future.

Reproduced from the 1", 1925 Ordnance Survey Map

The southern section of the Anstruther & St Andrews Railway.

## All Stations to Anster

By 1863, Anstruther had become the terminus of the Leven & East of Fife Railway, a locally-owned branch line some 19 miles in length which ran in a generally eastern direction from the North British main line at Thornton, half-way between the towns of Kirkcaldy and Markinch and close to the junction with the Cowdenbeath and Dunfermline line. Although originally planned as far back as 1845 as a single entity to run along the whole of the coastline to Anstruther under the title of the East of Fife Railway, sufficient money could not be raised to make the project come to fruition and in its place a line was built in three stages starting with the Leven Railway. The six mile-long Leven Railway was a mirror-image of the St Andrews Railway and was designed and built under the supervision of Thomas Bouch as a 'cheap' railway. It followed the valleys of the Rivers Ore and Leven on easy gradients down to the terminus implied by its name. An intermediate station was provided at Cameron Bridge, close to the distillery of that name and to the village of Windygates. Leven was an attraction in itself, being not only the largest town on that stretch of the coast but also a burgeoning centre of industry and commerce and, somewhat incongruously, a holiday and golfing resort of increasing fame.

The Leven Railway was opened in 1854 and originally worked by the Edinburgh, Perth & Dundee Railway (EP&D), but, after the two companies fell out with each other in the summer of the following year, it was thereafter operated by the Leven company independently of the EP&D, using a locomotive and stock bought by the Leven company with its own resources. In 1857 a 6½ mile eastwards extension was opened to Lundin Links, Largo and Kilconquhar by an associated company which operated under the revived name of the East of Fife Railway and, although the Leven and East of Fife companies were nominally separate concerns, the two companies ran a single through passenger and goods service between Thornton, Leven and Kilconquhar, pooling their stock and locomotives.

Kilconquhar was, however, only intended as a temporary terminus and in 1861 the two companies merged to form the Leven & East of Fife Railway (L&EoF) which, with some vigour, commenced building a further eastward extension of some six miles from Kilconquhar to Elie, St Monance, Pittenweem and Anstruther. The Leven & East of Fife company opened its line to Anstruther on 1st September, 1863 and thereafter settled down to a prosperous and largely uneventful period where through trains were run between Thornton and Anstruther, using its own passenger and goods stock and a locomotive stable which eventually rose to five in number. In 1877, the L&EoF finally sold out to the North British, being taken over by that company on the same day as the St Andrews company.

## Enumerating the Benefits

The Leven & East of Fife fulfilled a need but there was still no direct railway from the East Neuk to the main administrative and cultural centre of the region, St Andrews. The journey by rail via Thornton, Cupar and Leuchars, was roundabout, time-consuming and expensive and the direct horse-bus connections were both slow and, if a report which appeared in the *Fifeshire Journal* of 18th October, 1863 was anything to go by, hazardous.

COACH ACCIDENT – One of the two omnibuses at present running in opposition between Anstruther and St Andrews, that belonging to Mr Thomas Smith of Pittenweem, was just starting from the railway station on Monday morning when one of the hind wheels of the omnibus gave way by reason of breakage in the spokes. It being a large four-wheeled omnibus it did not come down, and the horses were fortunately stopped in time to prevent further damage. There were a good many passengers in it at the time, but none were hurt by the accident; and after the passengers had all been extricated, they transferred their patronage for the time being to Mr Donaldson's omnibus, and proceeded to St Andrews.

For many, a line that ran no further than Anstruther was not enough and, within months of the opening of the extension to that town, a move was afoot to have a line built to serve Crail and beyond. In February 1864 a letter, signed rather unimaginatively by 'X', appeared in the *Fifeshire Journal*. This seems to have been virtually the first time that such a proposal was seriously mooted:

RAILWAY COMMUNICATION TO THE EAST NEUK

Sir, - As the local exponent of the wants and requirements of that time-honoured district of Fife called the East Neuk, perhaps you will allow me, through your columns, to suggest to the landlords, farmers and others likely to have an interest in the matter, the importance of a subject deserving, it appears to me, their best consideration. It is doubtless a matter of congratulation to the good folks of Anster that they have, partly at least, by their own energy and enterprise, succeeded in getting the facilities of carriage afforded by the railway so far east as themselves, and I hope that they will be able to do so more, in the way in which human nature most readily appreciates a benefit, on the declaration of the next dividend. At present, however, no inconsiderable portion of one of the most productive districts of Fife is still in want of the facilities alluded to, namely the rich country as far as Boarhills, a district unsurpassed in Fife for the fertility of its soil, or the ability and enterprise of its agriculturalists; and I think a line of railway running along the coast from Anstruther, via Crail, to St Andrews, beside being of incalculable benefit in developing the resources of the country and conferring a great boon on the inhabitants, would in all likelihood prove a profitable investment - the proposed route presenting no great engineering difficulties, which in these days of cheap railways could be constructed at no great expense. There is no harbour between St Andrews and Crail where vessels can load potatoes or grain, and to cart these is in many instances, both inconvenient and expensive; besides these, large quantities of artificial manures have now to be carted long distances - often at a time to when this delay can be ill spared. But I need not enumerate the many benefits which such a line of railway as I have proposed would confer on this district of country, the practicability and usefulness of which require no demonstration.

Local opinion apparently agreed with the anonymous letter writer for, in September of the following year, the same newspaper reported that:

> We understand that a line of railway from Anstruther to St Andrews has been surveyed by Mr Coyne, C.E., Edinburgh, and that the tracings of the line have already been in the hands of several parties interested, and highly approved of. It is understood that the landed proprietors and farmers in the district are very favourable, and that subscriptions to a considerable amount have already been promised. This is as it should be, for there is nothing which increases the value of land and its produce more than a line of railway passing along or through any district. We learn that there are no special engineering difficulties, and from the tracings of the line and section, it would seem that the making of the line should neither be difficult or expensive – the earthworks being very light, and the gradients excellent, the bridges are neither numerous or heavy. The traffic prospects of the district are very encouraging, especially when we consider the agricultural wealth of the district and the large amount of coals that must necessarily be brought into the district, from Anstruther round the line, and to St Andrews, as has been verified in the case of the East of Fife line. The passenger traffic by the east coast route from the south to St Andrews will be much more considerable than may at first sight appear; and the fact that from Thornton to St Andrews there will be no lost time either by waiting or by change of carriages, and the station being close to St Andrews, and so near the centre of the city, will make this line more agreeable to passengers than any other. The whole line will form a beautiful drive, and the visitors round the coast of Fife during summer will doubtless avail themselves of its attractions, and in this way the line will prove attractive to visitors, and thereby, and by other traffic, produce a fair return to the shareholders.

## Routes and Disputes

Within a week a Prospectus was published and a glowing account was given of the proposed traffic over the new line, so optimistic that a lively debate was conducted in the local newspaper columns for some time on this subject. What was interesting was the route of the proposed railway in that it was to run along the same path as the later Anstruther & St Andrews line as built between Anstruther to Crail but thereafter it would take a more easterly route passing closer to Kingsbarns and crossing the Kilduncan to Morton road roughly at a midway point. Crossing the Kenly Burn near to the existing road bridge the line was then to pass through Boarhills and take a north-westerly path through Kittock's Den, thereafter following the sea coast for two miles or so adjacent to the rocky coastline before terminating at Maggie Murray's bridge at the foot of Bridge Street in St Andrews. There was to be no connection with the St Andrews Railway, whose inconveniently situated terminus at the links was some three-quarters of a mile to the west. The total length of the line was 13½ miles and the estimated cost of construction was £65,625; stations were to be provided at Crail, Kingsbarns, Boarhills and St Andrews. Perhaps the most prescient comment was that made by a correspondent to the *East of Fife Record* of 29th September who caustically pointed out that:

> For the passenger traffic, the Prospectus states that the income per annum at £4,969. As many shillings would more likely be nearer the mark. Does the writer believe that

passengers will go round the East of Fife just for a *ride* by rail when they can have a coach from Anstruther at less cost, and which will set them down in the middle of the town as soon, if not sooner, than they can get there by the circuitous route of railway.

On Tuesday 2nd October, 1865 a public meeting was held at the Cross Keys Hotel, St Andrews, presided over by Sir Thomas Erskine, Bart, of Cambo, near Kingsbarns. In Sir Thomas' words:

> All [were] aware of the object of the meeting. He was not a compromising supporter of the proposed scheme of railway. He personally would suffer many disadvantages from it, but he supported the scheme because he considered the eastern district would derive great advantage from it. There was certainly one great drawback in its not joining the St Andrews Railway Station, and also by its running into a bad line at Thornton Junction
> ...

One speaker, a Mr Coyne, stated that he had gone carefully over the ground and 'that he could not conceive that a more economical line could be built' and he compared the St Andrews Railway with the present scheme in most unfavourable terms. Philip Oliphant, the Anstruther solicitor who had been a prominent figure in the Leven & East of Fife company's extension to his hometown, said that the cost could be reduced to £45,000 'if landowners would rent rather than sell the land required' but this suggestion was recognised as being impractical.

A tide of enthusiasm in favour of the proposed line prevailed and a Provisional Committee was appointed, consisting of Alexander Hill of Stoneywynd, Thomas Duncan of Boghall, William Duncan of Pittern, David Brown of Pinkerton and Provost of Crail and George Fortune of Barnsmuir. A subscription list for shares at £19 each was then opened, and those present at the meeting subscribed for them to the extent of £8,000. However, the project went into abeyance as there appeared to be some difficulty in raising the remainder of the capital required. In December 1866 it was announced that it had been deemed advisable to postpone the application for a Bill, but that, in the meantime, a fresh survey had been undertaken and that several alterations and improvements had been made to the scheme.

### Interest Revived

In September 1874 a further Anstruther and St Andrews Railway proposal was being championed in the local press. The *East of Fife Record* carried details of the proposed new line which was largely similar to the previous scheme but included an additional station at Balmungo, a mile and a half south of St Andrews. On 22nd October, 1874 a meeting of proprietors, tenants and others interested in the proposed railway was held once more in the Cross Keys Hotel, St Andrews with Sir Thomas Erskine again in the Chair but it came to naught and the scheme was again placed in abeyance. However, within three years the scheme was revived, this time successfully, at a meeting in Crail Town Hall on 24th August, 1877 followed by a meeting of the Provisional Committee of the proposed company in St Andrews. As the local press reported:

We are glad to learn that the prospects of this undertaking are now most favourable. At the meeting of the Provisional Committee in St Andrews last week, Mr Oliphant reported that shares to the amount of £13,000 had been subscribed, but since that date £8,000 additional have been taken up, making fully the half the capital required. With three exceptions, the whole of that sum has been subscribed in the East of Fife, and a number of proprietors and others have not yet been waited upon.

## Within a week the capital subscribed had amounted to £25,000,

... and the remaining £15,000, it is hoped, will soon be taken up. We learn that there will be held, in the town hall of Cellardyke ... a meeting to take the matter into consideration and seeing that the railway to Anstruther did so much good, it is hoped that the fishermen and others will come forward now, as formerly, and lend a helping hand to the carrying through of this line, which will be of great advantage to the neighbourhood.

In August 1878 it was noted that 'the prospect of this line being shortly proceeded with is now bright' and the apparently unstoppable Philip Oliphant had ascertained from the North British that they would be willing both to assist with the construction of a joint station at Anstruther in addition to building a new station at St Andrews, which would be closer to the town centre and thus capable of being linked to the Anstruther & St Andrews line. Ten months later it was clear that matters were now sufficiently advanced to justify taking further steps, the share subscription now amounting to £43,500, another £500 being promised and 'only £1,000 requires to be raised in order to apply for parliamentary sanctions'.

A public meeting of the subscribers to the stock of the Anstruther & St Andrews Railway was held on 28th July, 1879 in the Council Chamber at St Andrews with the intention of taking initial steps in preparation to seeking Parliamentary approval for the scheme in the next session. Major Moneypenny, Younger, of Pitmilly was in the Chair with Philip Oliphant being appointed Secretary. The remainder of the Provisional Committee consisted of Sir Thomas Erskine of Cambo as Committee Chairman, Dr Cleghorn of Wakefield,* W. Douglas Irvine of Grangemuir, Robert Duncan of Kirkmay, George Fortune of Barnsmuir, Bailie McGregor of St Andrews, George Downie, Senior, of Balcomie, A. H. Russell of Kenly Green and John Anstruther Thompson of Charleton.

Philip Oliphant, after advising those present as to the difficulties which he had encountered in raising the capital required, said that:

He had not the least doubt that the line would pay very well. When the East of Fife line was projected, all the communication they had between Anstruther and Leven was an old horse and a still older bus - (laughter) - and they scarcely ever made a journey with it but there was a break-down . (Renewed laughter) But the line that had taken its place now paid 5 per cent. (Hear, hear) What now was the number of communications between Anstruther and St Andrews? They had a large double-horse bus from

---

* The Wakefield referred to is not its more famous namesake in West Yorkshire but the house of that name situated by the Wakefield Burn close to Dunino; the house was also known as Stravithie House.

Anstruther direct to St Andrews and back again every day; they had another from St Andrews round by Crail to Anstruther, and back again at night, and so far as he could see they were always quite filled. Then they had one which went direct from Crail to St Andrews and beside these, there was the post conveyance (a wagonette) from Crail to St Andrews. They had three trips between Anstruther and Crail and he thought that if one horse communication with its passengers could produce sufficient traffic to yield no less than five per cent, surely all the communications he had just mentioned could produce much more.

It was emphasised that the line was to run through the best agricultural district in Fife and that there were several quarries along the proposed route which would be bound to provide a considerable traffic for the line. When one prescient objector pointed out that it was a pity that the station at Kingsbarns was to be so far from the village which it purported to serve, Philip Oliphant replied that it was so sited 'so as to avoid cutting up valuable land'; a local minister, the Reverend Tod, then added that by placing the station at its location the result would be that few Kingsbarns folk would use the train to travel to Crail.

### Half a Loaf

Notwithstanding this criticism, the meeting was judged a success and a further meeting held at the same venue on 9th September, with the aim of taking the project further. The estimated cost of the line was now said to be £67,283 and it was resolved that shares to the value of £57,000 would be issued and the rest raised on loan. It was announced that the North British had approved of the proposed new station at Anstruther. It had voted the sum of £1,000 towards the expenses of promoting the line on the twin conditions that the Anstruther & St Andrews promoters applied in the next session for Parliamentary authority to proceed with the construction of the line and that the plans for the proposed junction were to be drawn up to the satisfaction of the NBR engineers. The North British would contribute a further £1,000 towards the construction of the line from Anstruther Junction (the meeting point of the old Leven & East of Fife line just outside of its original terminus station) and the new Anstruther station on the basis that the North British was to have free use for passenger trains of that station in perpetuity; the expenses of working the new station would be borne by the two companies in direct proportion to the use which they made of it. The final plans, by the consulting engineer John Buchanan of Edinburgh, were then drawn up to accompany the Parliamentary application but there was opposition to the Bill, mainly from those who thought that the line should physically join up with the St Andrews branch - opposition which was strongly expressed at a public meeting held at St Andrews Town Hall on Monday 26th January, 1880, and chaired by Provost Milton.

The meeting had been called by the Town Council to consider the proposals as to where the terminus of the line was to be situated. Oliphant tried to placate those who were against the scheme by saying that he hoped that the NBR would support a line to link up with its branch line from Leuchars but that, in the meantime, the Anstruther & St Andrews line would be temporarily terminated at Cairnsmill, a mile and a half south of the city (a little past where the future Mount Melville station would be built) pending a resolution of the matter. From Cairnsmill two railways were proposed - Railway 'A' to Argyle, on the outskirts of the town and Railway 'B' from Argyle to the existing St Andrews station on the North British branch line. He emphasised that any station at Argyle would be only a temporary one until the North British built its link line and that a preferred terminus would be 'close to Mr Woodcock's house at the west end of the town'. There would be no station at Argyle, where the line would be situated in an 18-foot deep cutting and he added that 'no man who had an eye in his head or a piece of brains about him' could have thought otherwise; brains or otherwise this was, in fact, where the station was eventually constructed!

Baillie Welsh commented that:

> The proposal to have a terminus without a railway station is the most extraordinary thing I ever heard of. You arrive and you have no platform. You are to have no means of which you can either get in or get out of a carriage. If they are [not] going to open that railway the length of Argyle they had better not open it at all, for it won't pay. If it is proposed to go under Argyle and on to Mr Woodcock's park why not openly say so?

The *Fifeshire Journal* pithily summed up those against the scheme by saying that:

> Some people in St Andrews are of the opinion that unless they can have the entire loaf, they will have no loaf ... They will not have a railway from Anstruther to St Andrews unless the junction is made at once in the scheme with the city terminus. They will continue to go the humdrum Crail coach road first, as their sleepy forefathers did before them. It is an odd choice, and one for which on rational grounds, there is no accounting.

There can be little doubt, however, that Philip Oliphant's assurances that a joint station would eventually be built carried the day and the opposition to the scheme 'suddenly collapsed' in February 1880.

### Agreement, Arbitration and an Act

It was now necessary for the Provisional Committee to enter into an arrangement with the North British in relation to the operation of the line since the promoters had no intention of operating the service over the new line themselves. Accordingly on 5th March, 1880 a Minute of Agreement* between the Committee and the NBR was entered into whereby for the six months following upon the opening of the line 'the railway, works, stations, offices, conveniences, permanent way and other structures' would be maintained by and at the cost of the Anstruther & St Andrews Railway to the satisfaction of the North British; thereafter the line would be maintained by the latter company.

* The full text of the Minute of Agreement appears as a schedule to the 1880 Act.

On completion of the line to the satisfaction of the Board of Trade the NBR would enter into possession of the line for a period of 10 years during which it would 'work the said railway and manage and regulate traffic upon the same in an efficient manner and so as to fully develop the traffic of the district and shall provide the necessary locomotive power, rolling stock and plant of every kind for the purpose of effectually working the traffic coming to or on to the said line'. In return the NBR would receive 50 per cent of the residue of the gross revenue arising from the goods and passenger traffic after the payment of certain dues and taxes. If the residue was less than £12,000 per annum then the proportion of the receipts payable to the NBR for working expenses would be restricted to the actual cost to the company 'as the same shall be ascertained by arbitration failing agreement'. It was further agreed that it would take two years to compete the line and a Joint Committee was to be set up to fix or determine any matter in relation to rates and charges for traffic and, in relation to any disputes which might arise between the parties, an arbiter was 'to be named by the Sheriff Principal of the County of Fife'. When it became clear that the Bill for the line would be passed, a further meeting of the Provisional Committee, held on 23rd July, 1880, decided that tenders for the permanent way would be sought immediately, due to the rising price of rails and, at the same time, the working plans for the line were approved.

On 26th August, 1880 the Anstruther & St Andrews Railway Act (43 & 44 Vict., cap. clxxx ) was given the Royal Assent. The Act gave effect to the agreement with the North British and authorized the share capital of the company at £57,000 in 5,700 shares of £10 each and the route of the line to be built described in Section 5 as:

> A railway, fifteen miles long, three furlongs or thereabouts in length, commencing in the parish of Anstruther Wester by a junction with the Leven and East of Fife branch of the North British Railway, and terminating in the Parish of St Andrews at a point on the south side of the road or street leading from the West Port of South Street, St Andrews and through the district of St Andrews called Argyle, to Ceres, one hundred and three yards or thereabout, measured in a westerly direction along the said road or street, from the archway of the said West Port ...

The route, however, differed from that of the previous proposal in that instead of following the coastline, which would have been good for views but likely to generate little traffic, it now turned inland from Kingsbarns in order to serve the scattered farming communities lying to the south of St Andrews. Thus it would be able to exploit a prosperous agricultural area, albeit one which was still suffering from the prolonged trade depression of the 1870s. There was, however, a potential downside for, in taking the landward route, a further couple of miles were added to the already indirect path between Anstruther and St Andrews, the two principal places served by the line, giving the direct road an advantage of some six miles over the steeply graded and circuitous railway.

Philip Oliphant was appointed Secretary of the company and his firm, Oliphant & Jamieson, their solicitors. At the last meeting of the Provisional Committee the following tenders were accepted for the permanent way:

| | £ | s. | d. |
|---|---|---|---|
| *Rails:* Moss Bay Hematite Iron & Steel Co., Workington | | | |
| 2,100 tons @ £6 14s. 6d. per ton | 14,122 | 10 | 0 |
| *Bolts & Nuts:* Phoenix Bolt & Nut Co., Handsworth, Birmingham | | | |
| 16 tons @ £10 10s. per ton | 168 | 0 | 0 |
| *Fish plates:* North British Railway Co. | | | |
| 62 tons @ £6 15s. 0d. per ton | 418 | 10 | 0 |
| *Spikes:* North British Railway Co. | | | |
| 85 tons @ £8 7s. 6d. per ton | 711 | 17 | 0 |
| *Chairs:* 986 tons @ £3 6s. 0d. per ton | 3,234 | 0 | 0 |
| | 18,654 | 17 | 0 |

On 30th September, 1880 the local press reported that Mr Buchanan, the Engineer, had already commenced work in marking out the line, that he had secured the fencing off of most of the land required between Anstruther and Kingsbarns and that he would shortly be preparing the specifications for the works.

A few weeks later the first General Meeting of the new company was held at the Town Hall, Anstruther on Friday 19th November, 1880 at 12 noon with, Sir Thomas Erskine declining office, Colonel Moneypenny in the chair. Dr Cleghorn and John Purvis of Kinaldy were formally appointed as Directors and Mr Purvis was duly appointed as Chairman of the company. The shareholders were informed that matters were all now in hand and that an agreement had been concluded between the Anstruther & St Andrews and the North British companies for the management and regulation of traffic on the new line. Sir Thomas went on to say that he hoped that an agreement could be reached between the two companies for a joint station at St Andrews but that, in the interim, a temporary stop would be made to the line at Cairnsmill.

Thereafter matters moved rapidly and on 3rd December it was noted that:

In response to an advertisement which appeared in several of the daily newspapers, nearly thirty contractors arrived in Anstruther on Tuesday morning, and accompanied by Mr Buchanan, C.E., made an inspection of the proposed line. The contracts, we notice, are to be received by Wednesday next, and as soon as the Directors have decided which offer they will accept, a commencement will immediately thereafter be made to the construction of what cannot fail to prove a most beneficial public undertaking.

Anstruther Junction, where the Anstruther & St Andrews Railway physically met the Leven & East of Fife line - this view, looking towards Leven, was taken in May 1965.

*Michael B. Smith*

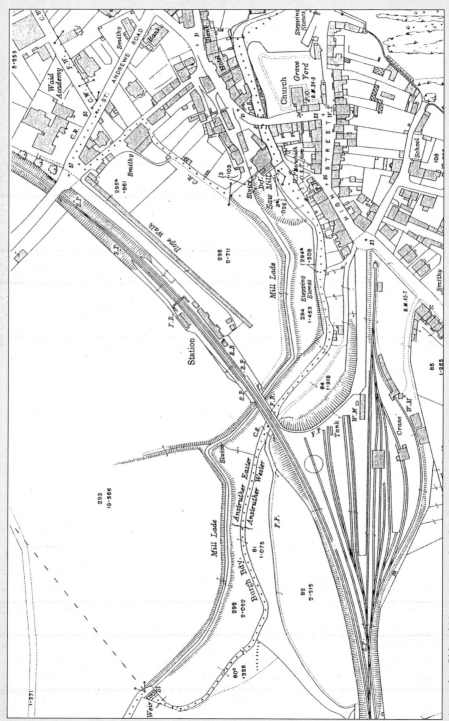

Anstruther Old and New stations after the 1901 alterations (see page 101).

(see page 101).

*Reproduced from the 25″, 1914 Ordnance Survey Map*

'B1' class No. 61401 approaches Anstruther Junction with the 5.48 pm Summer Saturdays service from Anstruther to Thornton, 27th July, 1963 - the lines to the right lead to the Old station while the smoke from the engine obscures the New station behind.                    *Roy Hamilton*

Anstruther Old station, *c*.1955 showing (*left*) the Anstruther & St Andrews New station and (*right*) the original terminus of the Leven & East of Fife Railway (later the goods station) and the two-road engine shed.                    *NBRSG Hennigan Collection*

Ex-LMS Stanier 'Black Five' 4-6-0 No. 45304, a Bolton engine which previously worked a Manchester to Glasgow service, has been pressed into action on a Glasgow to St Andrews summer special and is seen here crossing the Dreel Burn viaduct and entering Anstruther station on 22nd August, 1964.
*C.C. Thornburn*

A busy scene with enthusiasts and locals present as No. 61330 prepares to leave Anstruther via the Dreel Burn viaduct on 1st May, 1965 - note the bracketed footbridge added in the 1901 alterations.
*Michael B. Smith*

The Dreel Burn viaduct from below, October 2007; the left-hand arch carried the line over the burn itself while the right-hand arch housed the lade for Anstruther corn mill and a public footpath. *Alan Simpson*

Anstruther in the late 1930s - note the buffer stops at the down platform. *R.W. Lynn Collection*

A rare view of the roadside elevation of the original Anstruther & St Andrews Railway buildings at Anstruther New shortly after closure.          *Authors' Collection*

NBR 'J37' class 0-6-0 No. 64602 in the up platform at Anstruther waits with an enthusiasts' special on 1st May, 1965. Note the original Anstruther & St Andrews station on the right with its bookstall and weighing machine and on the down side the NBR waiting room. *G.M. Staddon*

A handful of passengers await the arrival of a Crail service hauled by 'B1' class No. 61401 on 24th August, 1963.                                                                                  *C.C. Thornburn*

The down platform buildings at Anstruther - a typical NBR structure from around the turn of the century.                                                                                              *Authors' Collection*

'B1' class 4-6-0 No. 61103 prepares to leave Anstruther with the 5.48 pm Thornton local on 4th July, 1964 - the unusual presence of a 'B1' at each end of the train is not indicative of a push-pull service but the authors can only guess that the incoming 4.51 pm Thornton to Anstruther service was running late and No. 61103 was available for use.      *C.C. Thorburn*

Looking across towards the down platform from the up at Anstruther with a Metro-Cammell dmu on a Crail to Thornton service in June 1959 - note the curious arrangement of the sleepers set into the surface of each platform.      *Roy Hamilton*

A Leven-bound service stands alongside 'B1' class No. 61101 on a recently arrived down service terminating at Anstruther, 13th July, 1963.                                    *C.C. Thornburn*

The east end of Anstruther station looking towards Crail with Stanier 'Black Five' 4-6-0 No. 44970 preparing to depart with the 9.30 Saturdays-only Glasgow Queen Street to St Andrews service on 13th July, 1963. Note the ex-LMS brake coach, the overbridge carrying the Anstruther to St Andrews via Dunino main road and the Waid Academy buildings.                *C.C. Thornburn*

# CHAPTER clxxx.

An Act for making a Railway from Anstruther to Saint Andrews in the county of Fife; and for other purposes.

A.D. 1880.

[26th August 1880.]

WHEREAS the construction of the railway herein-after described from Anstruther to Saint Andrews in the county of Fife would be of public and local advantage:

And whereas the persons herein-after named, with others, are willing at their own expense to construct the said railway, and it is expedient that they should be incorporated into a company, and that the powers herein-after contained should be conferred on them for that purpose:

And whereas it is expedient that the Company herein-after incorporated and the North British Railway Company should be empowered to enter into and carry into effect the agreements by this Act authorised:

And whereas plans and sections showing the lines and levels of the railway by this Act authorised, and also books of reference containing the names of the owners and lessees, or reputed owners and lessees, and of the occupiers of the lands required or which may be taken for the purposes or under the powers of this Act, were duly deposited with the principal sheriff clerk for the county of Fife at his office at Cupar, and are herein-after respectively referred to as the deposited plans, sections, and books of reference:

And whereas the purposes of this Act cannot be effected without the authority of Parliament:

May it therefore please Your Majesty that it may be enacted; and be it enacted by the Queen's most Excellent Majesty, by and with the advice and consent of the Lords Spiritual and Temporal, and Commons, in this present Parliament assembled, and by the authority of the same, as follows:

1. This Act may be cited as the Anstruther and Saint Andrews Railway Act, 1880.

Short title.

[*Local.–180.*]    A

# Chapter Three

## Boarhills or Bust:
## The Anstruther & St Andrews Railway 1881-1883

*'The shareholders and the general public in the district have every reason to be satisfied with the arrangements made ... in their interests'*

East of Fife Record, 1882

### A False Start

The successful contractor, appointed on 7th January, 1881, was William Orr Coghill of Greenock, trading as Messrs John Coghill & Sons. Coghill, having been vouched for by the Caledonian Railway and others as being 'most respectable and responsible men', seemed to be a man of substance and it was perhaps a measure of the extent that those tendering had undercut the prices of each other which eventually led to his downfall. His estimate for the works was £37,698 (adjusted after an earlier underestimate), exclusive of the costs of supplying the permanent way and he undertook to complete the construction to Boarhills within a timescale of 18 months. If this surprisingly low quote was not enough, Coghill offered to take £5,000 in stock and the balance in cash - a considerable saving to the beleaguered Board. Coghill subsequently acquired on hire purchase a 5 ton double-jib Derrick crane and a double-cylinder portable engine from Butters Brothers, engineers of Glasgow and, later, a locomotive on the same hire-purchase principle. Simultaneous with his appointment, the components for the permanent way, ordered by the Board in the previous year, began to arrive and, in one typical week in February 1881, seven truckloads of track parts were delivered. In the same month it was announced that not only had most of the components been delivered but that the lands required were now either in the course of being acquired or had already been acquired; the sole exception in relation to the acquisition of lands were those required at Kirkmay and the dispute concerning these resulted in unpleasant litigation in the Court of Session and the making of what were described as completely unfounded allegations of fraudulent behaviour on the part of Philip Oliphant.* Notwithstanding this difficulty, the main contractor was now ready to commence operations and this necessitated an immediate call on the shareholders of £10,000.

### Denting the Spade

On 13th April the ceremony of the cutting of the first sod took place 'in a field lying a little to the north-west at Anstruther station. A contemporary newspaper account stated that the ceremony was:

---

* A full report of the proceedings in the case of *Duncan v Anstruther & St Andrews Railway Company* appears in the *East of Fife Record* of 30th March, 1883.

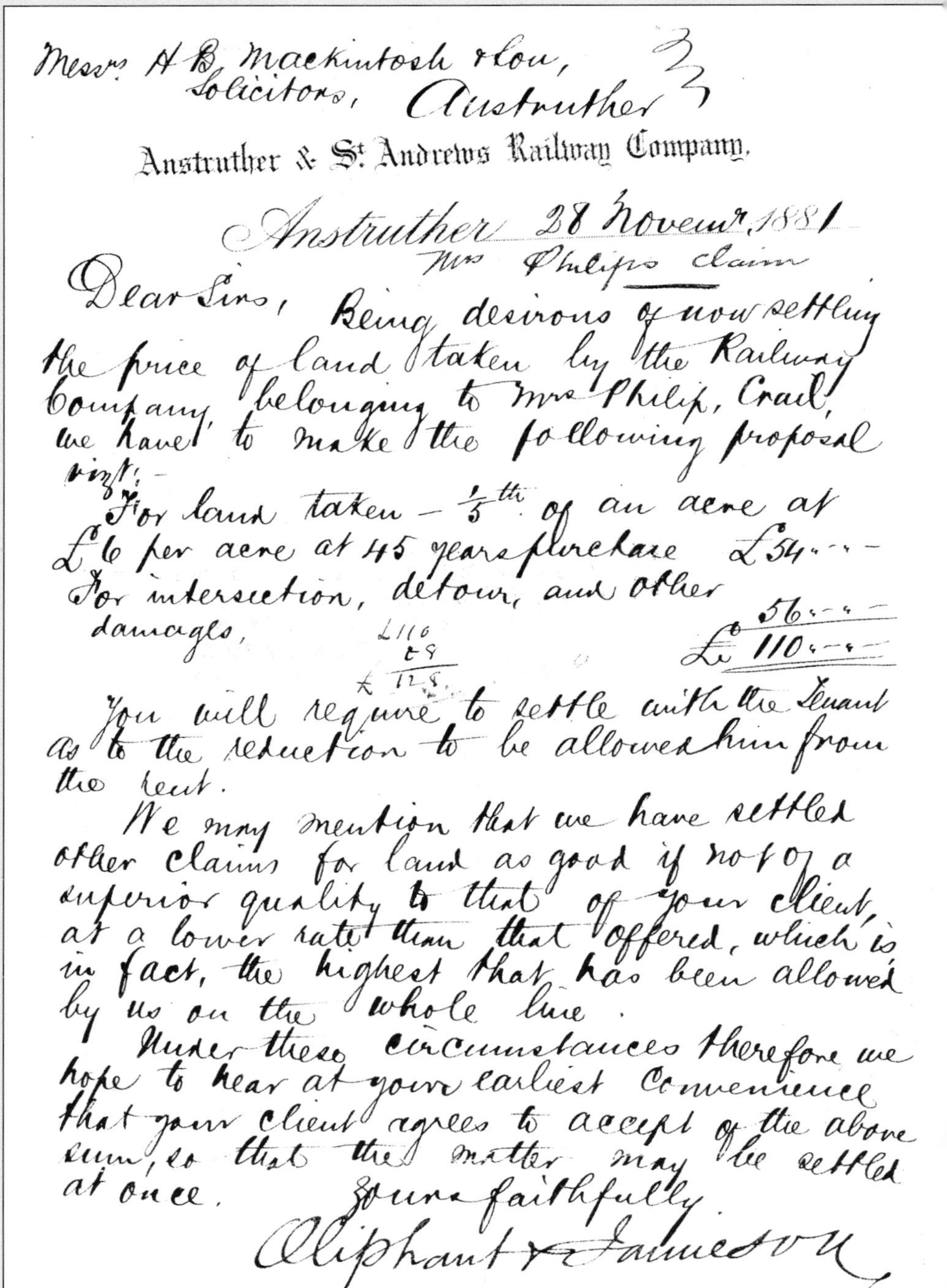

Messrs H.B. Mackintosh & Son,
Solicitors, Anstruther

**Anstruther & St Andrews Railway Company.**

Anstruther 28 Novemr. 1881

Mrs Philips claim

Dear Sirs, Being desirous of now settling the price of land taken by the Railway Company, belonging to Mrs Philip, Crail, we have to make the following proposal vizt:—

For land taken — ⅕th of an acre at £6 per acre at 45 years purchase £54 ...

For intersection, detour, and other damages,
£56 ... —
£110 ... —

£110
£9
£128

You will require to settle with the Tenant as to the reduction to be allowed him from the rent.

We may mention that we have settled other claims for land as good if not of a superior quality to that of your client, at a lower rate than that offered, which is in fact, the highest that has been allowed by us on the whole line.

Under these circumstances therefore we hope to hear at your earliest Convenience that your client agrees to accept of the above sum, so that the matter may be settled at once.

Yours faithfully,

Oliphant & Jamieson,

The company's solicitor communicating to a fellow solicitor with regard to the valuation of land belonging to a Mrs Philip of Crail.

The dented silver spade used by Mrs Purvis to cut the first sod on the line now in the ownership of the Purvis family.                                         *Alan Simpson*

... in the presence of a large crowd of spectators, who evinced the utmost interest in the proceedings. In honour of the occasion a half-holiday was observed in the town, and the road leading to the station was profusely decorated, flags of all sizes and descriptions being suspended from a rope put up for the occasion ... By the time the Chairman of the Company (Mr Purvis of Kinaldy) and his lady arrived, the site selected for the cutting of the sod was surrounded by a large number of representative gentlemen from Anstruther, Pittenweem, St Andrews &c.

The proceedings commenced by Mr W. Orr Coghill calling on the Revd Mr Murray, minister of Anstruther Easter, who offered up an impressive and appropriate prayer. Thereafter an oaken spade, silver mounted and bearing a suitable inscription, was handed to Mrs Purvis, who in the most graceful and dexterous manner at once lifted a sod amid the loud cheers of the spectators. Mr Coghill, in requesting Mrs Purvis to accept the spade as a memento of the occasion, expressed his belief that the manner in which the first sod had been cut was a good omen that the undertaking would prove a success as well as a benefit to every one interested in the district. (Cheers)...

A less prescient omen was the size of the crowd, which was such that Mrs Purvis was prevented from reaching the specially prepared sod and instead she had to dig into an area of hard and unprepared ground elsewhere with the silver spade causing it to become dented.* Notwithstanding this, Mrs Purvis remarked that she 'confidently predicted that the undertaking would materially contribute to the prosperity of the district through which the line would pass'.

---

* For a period thereafter the oak-handled silver spade was displayed in the window of Messrs Duncan & Sons, jewellers of South Street, St Andrews before being held by the family. On the closure of the line 84 years later her great-grandson took this spade on the very last train between Crail and St Andrews and he proudly displayed the dented spade to his fellow passengers.

Further speeches took place followed by a banquet of cakes and wine in the Municipal Buildings in Anstruther Easter at which 200 ladies and gentlemen were present. After much merriment, the Provost of Anstruther proposed the toast of 'Success to the Anstruther and St Andrews Railway' (A&StAR) amidst much applause.

On 27th April the company's Engineer submitted plans for the new stations at Anstruther, Crail and Kingsbarns but was told to modify the cost of the same. At the same Board meeting it was announced that the Board of Trade had allowed a temporary dispensation of the obligation to provide turntables until the link with the St Andrews branch had been completed, provided that the trains were run 'at a low rate of speed'. Matters were now beginning to move when the contractor had brought his equipment on site including a steam crane and, later on, his own locomotive. By July of that year 120 men were at work in the Anstruther area and a large squad of men were employed at Crail, where it was noted that 'the quiet town ... will soon yield to the embracing power of the railway'. At the beginning of September it was reported that:

> The wet weather experienced of late has to some extent interfered with the operations in connection with the new railway. The bridge across the Dreel Burn at West Anstruther, and another across the turnpike road near the Museum, are amongst the greatest difficulties; and although there are a good many men employed at these two branches, the progress is seemingly slow. Across the burn the supports for the arches of the bridge have now all been founded and built up a good height, so that in a few weeks, if the weather holds good, the embankments on each side of the burn will be connected by a handsome stone bridge. The bridge at the turnpike road is also well advanced but there is on each side of it a pretty deep cutting which will take some time to excavate and remove. From Cunzie Parks eastwards through Kilrenny to Crail, where the ground is more or less of a level nature, the works are almost ready for the rails, as few cuttings or embankments require to be made. A good few men are emplaced between Crail and Kingsbarns. Immediately after harvest, when the crops are all off the ground, much greater progress will be made along the whole line.

A fortnight later it was stated that the keystone on the first bridge on the line, that which carried the St Andrews turnpike road over the line at Anstruther, had been laid in a small ceremony conducted by Philip Oliphant. After making a short speech Oliphant commented that he hoped that the works would progress at a faster rate than they had done up to now and that it would only be a short time before the keystone on the last of the 20 bridges on the line would be laid. There was, however, to be a considerable delay before the line was completed. At first work progressed satisfactorily marred only by an incident on 4th January, 1882 when:

> On Friday morning, while the foreman and some of the men employed on the Anstruther & St Andrews Railway were proceeding to their work, they found the lifeless body of a navvy near the bridge at the Museum. It was identified as that of Michael Mulhorn, an Irish man, aged 45 years, who had been drinking heavily. In his pockets were found 14s. 10d. in money. He leaves two or three of a family, who are said to reside in Dundee.

This, unfortunately, was not destined to be the last navvy death caused by drink. However, construction continued and contracts were now signed for the more minor works on the line - that for Anstruther station and the railway cottages at Thirdpart and Kirkmay went to Alexander Wallace, an Anstruther builder, the station costing £817 8s. 1½d. and the two cottages £214 11s. 8d. each. Thomas Harris of St Andrews won the contract for Crail station (£492 18s. 10d.) and Newhall cottage (£226 5s. 11d.), while Robert Scott of Boarhills was awarded the contract for Kingsbarns station (£367 4s. 9d.) and the cottage there (£297 2s. 9d.) - in all the buildings on this section of the line were to cost a total of £2,630 18s. 11½d., a mere fraction of what they would have cost a century later! An order was placed with H. & R. Miller of Edinburgh for 'ordinary station clocks' at £8 each and 'cabin clocks' at £5 each while there was keen tendering for the signalling required for the Anstruther to Kingsbarns section. In the end the signalling contract was won by the Railway Signalling Co of Fazakerley, Liverpool whose tender of £783 comfortably beat those of the London firms of Stevens & Son (£865 1s.) and Saxby & Farmer (£915) and the Worcester firm of McKenzie & Holland (£1,210). A contract was also entered into with the Postmaster General for the conveyance of Her Majesty's Mail between Anstruther and Crail, at an agreed annual payment by the Postmaster of £25.

## Oliphant to the Rescue

Work on the line continued until the early summer, when it became clear that all was not well with the principal contractor, Coghill. At first the work was delayed and some of the men appeared to have been laid off for no particular reason. Then, ominously, some of the contractors' suppliers began clamouring for money. It became clear that Coghill was approaching the point of being insolvent in relation to the several contracting works being carried on here and elsewhere in Scotland. Things had reached a sorry state when, on 8th July 1882, charity had to ensue as the A&StAR Directors minuted that they 'considered that the workmen employed on the railway are in a state of starvation or nearly so, and authorise the treasurer to make an interim payment of five shillings each on account of their wages to be retained out of money due'. A month later their worst fears were realised and at a Director's Meeting held on 9th August, 1882 Philip Oliphant gave them the doleful news that William Orr Coghill had been declared bankrupt. At his sequestration hearing in Inverness it was said that he was greatly in debt, having incurred losses throughout Scotland in current projects including the building of new army barracks at Inverness, municipal buildings in Greenock and the construction of the Anstruther & St Andrews Railway - on the latter project alone Coghill had already expended some £13,740 but had received so far only £9,112 from the company.

The Board now had no alternative but to press on with the work themselves. The *East of Fife Record* of 29th September takes up the story:

As our readers are aware, the works for the construction of this railway, the completion of which is looked forward to as being certain to develop the prospects of one of the best agricultural districts in the country, were at first delayed and then ultimately stopped in consequence of the failure of Messrs Coghill & Co, the contractors. Indeed it may safely be said that, for all that was done, the summer was practically lost. Immediately after the bankruptcy of the contractors, the Directors of the company took energetic steps to get the construction of the undertaking into their own hands, and after some little delay these were successful, and a start was at once made to carry out these works with vigour. The plant of the former contractors, which has been utilised as much as possible, was left in a greatly worn and dilapidated condition. Notwithstanding the very confused state in which the line had been left, considerable progress has been made, and it is now confidently anticipated that, unless bad weather or other unforeseen obstacles come in the way, the section from Anstruther to Kingsbarns will be completed and ready for traffic by the middle of January next. As so many of our readers are interested in the new railway, we proceed to state the present state of the works.

Commencing at Anstruther, the permanent way is laid from the junction with the East of Fife branch of the North British Railway up to near the new station. Here there is a cutting fully 300 yards long, the earth from which is to be utilised in forming the embankment at Kilrenny Common. From a point a little beyond the bridge over the St Andrews Road on to Rennyhill, the permanent way is all laid, making all together about three miles completed. Between Kilrenny and Crail there is at present nothing doing, but the 6,000 yards of banking required between these points will probably be executed by the end of October. Near Crail a gang of about 50 men are working at the cutting occasionally at night and day shifts at Damside. Here the work is exceedingly difficult, the late contractors having taken off the soft surface, leaving below hard rock lying the contrary way. This portion, however, will probably be ready for the laying of the permanent way in about a month. Near Cambo the masons are engaged in building the viaduct, while further on, about seven miles from Anstruther, the bridge there is in an advanced state. The platform and loading bank at Kingsbarns are also in course of being completed. At Kilduncan Burn a large bridge, with a span of 25 feet, has to be erected, but workmen are already engaged upon the structure. The company have the use of Craighead quarry, and a squad of men are employed in getting out the stones required for the bridges. From Bonnington to St Andrews, a distance of five miles, little or nothing has been done. As regards the wire fencing, it is entirely completed all the way from Anstruther to Bonnington, a distance of ten miles, so that only a third of this portion of the work remains to be done. At Anstruther the station buildings are being rapidly pushed on by Mr Wallace, the contractor, and the mason work is far advanced. As soon as it is completed, Mr Wallace will commence to the cottages being erected at the level crossings at Thirdpart and Kirkmay.

The men are now in proper working order, and as it is in contemplation to take on more hands it may be expected that the progress made will be even more rapid than it has been during the short time which has elapsed since the works were recommenced, and which reflects great credit on the gentlemen under whose superintendence they are being carried on - viz. Mr Thorburn, the resident engineer, and Mr Barrett, the Company's inspector. It will thus be seen that the shareholders and the general public in the district have every reason to be satisfied with the arrangements made by the Directors and Mr Oliphant, secretary, in their interests.

### Troubled Progress

On 3rd October, 1882 the *East of Fife Record* reported that good progress was being made on the works, that the weather was generally favourable and that within the next fortnight the permanent way would be completed between Anstruther and Crail. The article continued by stating:

An important alteration, which will facilitate the laying down of ballast stones, has been made at Caiplie. Instead of simply working in a hole and having to use a steam crane to fill the waggons, the latter are pulled up the hill and they come to a face of rock of about 20 feet, and the stones fall themselves into the waggons, which on being started run down to the railway. Another quarry has also been opened at Cambo. The locomotive at present in use is in very bad condition but another is expected shortly from Leeds, and will be employed in removing the earth from the cuttings, the old one being reserved for ballast stones. The number of men employed this week is 170.

The locomotive referred to was obviously a source of further trouble for on 2nd December the Engineer was authorized to hire another locomotive and 'to purchase a dozen waggons or thereby' for ballast purposes.

At the half-yearly Meeting on 29th October, 1882 the shareholders ratified the Directors' decision to use direct labour to carry on the works after the financial failure of the contractor. The Chairman then advised them that he expected the line to be open as far as Kingsbarns for general traffic 'about the beginning of next year and probably to Boarhills for goods traffic soon afterwards'. He then went on to comment that:

With reference to the remaining portion of the line, from Cairnsmill to St Andrews, the cost of a station at Argyle is stated by the engineer to be £3,000. In the event of the North British Railway Company not bringing their line of railway up to Argyle, the engineer estimates that the cost to the Company of taking the line themselves to the present station at the Links, St Andrews, with a siding or platform for collecting tickets at St Andrews, where passengers could get in or out, would be £6,000 exclusive of the land, but in that case the sum of £3,000 for the terminal station at Argyle, as well as the land required for that station, would be saved. The sum of £6,000 must be raised by additional shares.

In November 1882 notice was given of a Bill to extend the line from the proposed terminus at Argyle to join up with the St Andrews Railway line at the Links station and within weeks an agreement had been drawn up between the A&StAR and the NBR. In terms, the former company was to construct the linking line together with separate passenger and goods stations to serve the town and the latter company was to subscribe the sum of £5,000 towards this cost in return for which it would be entitled to joint use of the new stations and the line from its junction with the existing St Andrews branch, free of any toll or other charge for traffic - a situation which, given the unsuitability of the existing branch terminus, was highly advantageous to the North British as well as relieving the Anstruther & St Andrews company of part of the capital costs of what could only be an otherwise expensive project. The Bill was passed on 16th July, 1883 and the Anstruther & St Andrews Railway Act ( 46 & 47 Vict., cap. c ) came into being.

On 22nd December the company's minute book records that:

The Secretary laid before the meeting correspondence with Messrs Innes & Mackay and Messrs Butters Bros as to the locomotive engine on the works and which is at present in disrepair and had not been in use for several weeks. The Meeting required the Secretary to write to the trustees on Messrs Coghill's estate and Messrs Butters Bros for their consent to put the locomotive engine into proper repair upon the condition that whoever is found to be the owner should ultimately repay the amount which may be expended by the Company in the meantime reserving all questions of ownership in the meantime.

This offer was rejected and the locomotive was repaired at the company's expense.

In order to speed the works up the company now resolved to pay the navvies employed on the construction works an enhanced rate of pay and, although it was said in March 1883 that 'shovel and chisel are likewise being plied with new energy', this caused some concern locally for the already endemic drunkenness of the navvies, particularly on their twice-monthly pay-days, was notorious. These navvies, mostly of Irish extraction and from wretchedly poor backgrounds, were accommodated in the Caiplie Hut, a wooden bothy situated roughly halfway between Anstruther and Crail. Conditions there were far from adequate and, given the nature of the physical work upon which they were engaged and the fact that they were largely country-bred and unused to the sort of money which they received, it was, perhaps, hardly surprising that drink was consumed with such abandon. On 12th April the *Fifeshire Journal* reported that one of their number, Peter Farrell, had been fined for being drunk and disorderly in Pittenweem High Street, having received, in one lump sum, 11 days' pay from Coghill, his previous employer. On 5th May, 1883 matters came to a head when, after an all-day bout of drinking, a group of navvies was allowed to spend the night sleeping it off in the bar of the Freemasons Hotel in Shore Street, Anstruther. One of their number, Joseph Robins, managed to fall over and catch his shirt collar on a brass knob and his friends, being so incapacitated by drink as to fail to notice this, allowed him to strangle himself as a result. The sequel saw another death when the following day his grief-stricken friends set out from the Caiplie Bothy to drink yet more and, in St Monance, one of them died from alcohol poisoning.

On 8th March it was decided that the Boarhills station building would be similar to that at Kingsbarns but that no cottages were to be built there. The Engineer expressed the view that the railway would be opened as far as Boarhills by the first of June 'at the latest' and it was said that the works were so advanced that the installation of the telegraph wires and signalling equipment could now go ahead.

### Harnessing the Iron Horse

By the beginning of May the line was substantially complete and although the company had not been intending to open any section of the line until all the works had been finished, lobbying from local farmers made it change its mind and, notwithstanding the absence of a Board of Trade certificate, the Directors decided to open the line for a 'limited goods service' to be operated between Anstruther and Crail with their own locomotive - this being either that taken over from Coghill or the new engine from Leeds. According to the *Fifeshire Journal* of 3rd May, 1883:

> The Wednesday of this week is not the least eventful day in the story of the East Neuk, witnessing as it did, the first public service on the new railway line to Crail. It was brought about thus. In order to have their fed oxen trucked at the door (so as to save the weary and tedious journey to Anstruther) the farmers of the district communicated with the North British authorities, who, in the most praiseworthy way, consented to open the junction to Crail for special service, so far as it shall be required or necessary for the convenience of local trade. Accordingly, on the morning in question, some twenty one prime oxen from the famous byres of Cambo and Balcomie were trucked at the new station. There was a fourth wagon with malt from Mr Keys brewery attached to the train which steamed away amidst ringing cheers over the event, which cannot fail to herald a new and brighter era for royal old Crail. The train was run by the traction engine* to the Anstruther junction, where it was attached to the ordinary special for transit across the Forth.

This *ad hoc* service was apparently a success for on 31st May the *Journal* reported that:

> A powerful six-wheeled North British locomotive was steamed to Anstruther on Monday in order to accelerate the operations in view of the opening of the line to Kingsbarns at the end of June, and also to assist in the goods traffic, which has already been developing in a very encouraging extent as far as Crail. So well, in fact does the convenience recommend itself, the truckage of cattle, corn, manure and general merchandise is computed at 30 tons per day, though the traffic has only been in the morning or in the evening, so as to not interfere with the regular duties of the useful little engine belonging to the Directors. A new impulse, however, will now be given to the work: our readers will best judge of this when we say that the big iron horse now in harness is about to draw over 80 tons or about three times more than the 'little pug', the service of which in particular situations, as in the short curves at the quarry, has a value all their own.

The same report also commented that arrangements were being made to expedite the works still to be finished:

> The squads are now on 'five-quarter time' under the energetic superintendence of Mr Barrett, while in view of the improved service, the ballasting, already finished a mile on the further side of Crail, will make headway at the rate of about 300 cubic yards a day. Messrs Birrell have now completed the neat wire fence, and suspended the gates on at least ten miles of the line; and from the characteristic energy shown by Mr Morgan of Crieff in putting up the rails or pallisades at the various roads, there is reason to expect that the fulfilling of his contract will be far advanced about the middle of June.

July passed and the works were still in progress. Then at the end of that month the Directors resolved that, subject to the inspection of the Board of Trade and on receipt of a satisfactory report, the line to Boarhills would be

---

* Presumably the reporter was referring to the contractor's locomotive rather than to a traction engine as such.

opened to all traffic on or about Friday 17th August. The *Fifeshire Journal* of 2nd August commented that this resolution 'would be naturally hailed with the liveliest interest in Crail, which is crowded with visitors as it seldom was before'. The paper went on to report that:

> It was expected that the line from Anstruther to Boarhills would have been completed this week but Saturday being pay day a large number of the navvies did not resume work until Wednesday and yesterday, so that a few days delay will take place. A number of the North British Railway officials are expected to go on to the line next week and the Board of Trade are then to be asked to inspect the line. Immediately after their report is received the line will be opened to passenger traffic. A considerable quantity of goods is being carried between Anstruther and Crail.

A meeting was arranged between representatives of the North British and the Anstruther & St Andrews and an agreement reached whereby the latter company undertook to maintain the line until 1st March, 1884 and would employ three surfacemen who were to occupy the houses provided at the level crossings on the new line. In addition the proposed timetable was laid before the meeting and it was resolved that the line would be worked by a tank engine; the timetable was later amended by the NBR so as to provide better connections with the Leven & East of Fife section trains. On 16th August the company came to an agreement with William Kirkaldy, coach hirer, Anstruther, that he would run an omnibus between Boarhills and St Andrews 'two or more times per day as the Company may require at ten shillings per double run for six months'. The few remaining construction works were apparently carried out with alacrity and three days later the line was in such a condition that it was intimated that it was now ready for inspection by Major Marindin of the Railway Department of the Board of Trade.

### The Visit of Major Marindin

On 28th August, 1883 the Major submitted the following report:

> Sir, I have the honour to report for the information of the Board of Trade that, in compliance with the instructions contained in your minute of the 20th instant, I have inspected the completed portion of the Anstruther & St Andrews Railway from Anstruther to Boarhills.
>
> This single-line commences at a junction with the North British single line from Thornton Junction to Anstruther, and terminates at present at Boarhills, about 4½ miles from St Andrews, but will then, when completed, form a junction at St Andrews with the North British Railway from Leuchars. The portion submitted for inspection is 9 miles, 3 chains in length and it is single throughout, with a passing loop at Kingsbarns station. Land has not been purchased and the bridges have not been constructed for a double line. It is to be worked by the North British Railway Company, and the old North British terminal station at Anstruther will become a goods station.
>
> The permanent way is of the North British pattern, and consists of double-headed steel rails in 24 feet lengths, and weighing 75lbs per yard, fixed by outside oak keys on 34lb cast iron chairs and fished at the joints with plates weighing 20lbs per pair. The sleepers are of Scotch larch, 9 feet in length and 10 inches by 4½ inches in section, and there are 8

sleepers to each rail length. The ballast is principally of broken stone and partly of gravel, and it is stated to be laid to a depth of 10 inches below the sleepers. The fencing consists of stone walls, post and rail fencing, hedges and wire fencing.

There are stations at: Anstruther, Crail: 4 miles, 22 chains to 4 miles 48 chains; Kingsbarns: 7 miles, 22.8 chains to 7 miles, 41.5 chains; Boarhills: 8 miles, 73 chains to 8 miles, 79.5 chains. There is no engine turntable on the new line but provision has been made for one at St Andrews.

The steepest gradient has an inclination of 1 in 60, and the sharpest curve has a radius of 17½ chains. The works are very light. There is one embankment, 20 feet in height and one cutting, 18 feet in depth, but all the others are of small dimensions.

There are 8 bridges under the line, 4 of which are across small streams. All of these have masonry abutments, 4 of 12 feet and 9 feet span have wrought iron girders, 3 have masonry arches and 1 has a brick arch. There is also one viaduct with 5 spans of 40 feet and 60 feet in height, which has masonry piers and brick arches. There are 7 overbridges, all of which are constructed with masonry abutments and arches, except one, which has a brick arch. There are also 7 culverts of 4 feet and 3 feet in diameter. There are no tunnels. There is one authorised public road crossing, and three occupational road crossings, all provided with lodges and gates. The masonry throughout is of a high class and all the works are of substantial construction and are standing well. The second arch from the north end of the viaduct at 8 miles 70 chains shows signs of settlement, and it should be carefully watched. The girders are of sufficient theoretical strength and gave small deflections under test ...

The station platforms and buildings afford good accommodation ...

The report went on to suggest a number of improvements and rectifications which required to be made, all of a fairly minor nature including those drainage, fencing and other matters such as the placing of additional name boards at Kingsbarns and Boarhills stations. Some concerns were raised in relation to the Kenly Burn viaduct, whose arch was showing signs of settlement and in consequence required tying and a careful watch being kept on it and in addition it was felt that a parapet rail was needed for the deck of that structure. In relation to the new Anstruther station:

As the North British Railway considers it necessary that some of the carriages coming from Thornton Junction should be detached at Anstruther, it will be necessary to provide means for doing so by the addition of a loop siding, which will eventually probably be required as a passing loop, as the accommodation of the new Anstruther station is barely sufficient. Orders were given to have all these matters attended to at once, and are subject to a report being sent in after the necessary work is completed and to a re-inspection being made, if thought necessary, I can recommend that when a satisfactory undertaking as to the working of the line by one engine in steam has been received, sanction may be given for it to be opened for passenger traffic.

The newly-built passing loop at Crail.
*Reproduced from the 25", 1894 Ordnance Survey Map*

NBR Holmes class 'N' 4-4-0 No. 598 heads a Leven-bound train through Crail *c.*1910 - the poster on the gable end advertises the timings of the Forth Steamers.
*NBRSG Hennigan Collection*

Crail in the late 1920s with the original footbridge, the new booking office and the LNER posterboards - note the presence of electric lighting and the gables which have now been shorn of their ball finials. *Jim Page Collection*

The main station building at Crail looking towards Anstruther -note the NBR drinking fountain on the left and the 'British Rail' poster, 4th September, 1965. *Norman Turnbull*

*Above:* A panorama of the up platform at Crail with a group of passengers discussing the likely arrival of the next train; to the right a poster gives details of the 1962 Summer Travel Arrangements.
*Jim Hay*

*Left:* Contrasting signs at Crail - the date '1881' appears to relate to the date of the station building's design rather than the date upon which it was built.
*J.L. Stevenson*

*Above right:* The small NBR waiting room on the down platform at Crail in 1962.
*Jim Hay*

*Right:* The same building after closure - note the 'shadow' of the vanished totem! 15th August, 1967.          *Brian Malaws*

The 1898 general waiting room on the up platform at Crail after closure, 15th August, 1967.
*Brian Malaws*

Crail - a view of the station buildings showing the less than impressive 1920 booking office and the jumble of old coaches at the entrance to the goods yard, 4th December, 1966.
*Hamish Stevenson*

Crail signal box, 1962.

*Jim Hay*

Crail from the north end as 'B1' class No. 61344 prepares to run round is train for the last time on Saturday 4th September, 1965.

*Norman Turnbull*

The 2.15 pm Dundee to Edinburgh service waits at the up platform at Crail alongside the newly-arrived 1.20 pm Saturdays-only service from Edinburgh, 3rd October, 1959.          *Roy Hamilton*

An unusual scene at Crail where 'B1' class No. 61244 *Strang Steel* with an Edinburgh-bound special on the 'wrong line' overtakes No. 61133 on a Crail to Thornton local, 22nd August, 1964.
*C.C. Thornburn*

# Chapter Four

## East Neuk Encircled:
## The Anstruther & St Andrews Railway 1883-1887

*'There need ... be little fear but that the railway will prove a remunerative*
*undertaking like the two others that it will be connected at each end.'*
Fifeshire Journal, 1884

### All Stations to Boarhills

On Saturday 1st September, 1883 public services commenced over the
Anstruther to Boarhills section of the line, and the first train was witnessed by
a large crowd of wellwishers. The *Fifeshire Journal* reported that:

> Much public interest was manifested in the opening on Saturday, of the Anstruther & St
> Andrews Railway. The inaugural service, as we may call the arrival of the first train at
> the station at 6 am, led to a considerable number of spectators on the bridge and the
> platform. Unfortunately the lowering clouds began to break in the course of the
> afternoon, and shower after shower fell with pelting violence. Notwithstanding that,
> however, as many as 108 passengers left the town for the several stations on the new
> line. By a curious coincidence, the train service from the west to Anstruther was
> inaugurated exactly 20 years before - namely on Tuesday 1st September, 1863 - when 80
> tickets were issued for the first train and 150 for the others of the day. Not a few family
> parties have been passing along the route, and on all sides one hears the same
> unqualified expressions of delight over the experience of the journey.

An initial shuttle service of five trains per day operating between Boarhills
and Pittenweem, calling *en route* at Kingsbarns, Crail and the new station at
Anstruther was provided - the choice of Pittenweem as a temporary terminus
was curious but inevitable, given the fact that the line through Anstruther's new
passenger station was, at that time, single with no passing loop or siding and no
means of turning the locomotive and thus trains on the new line were continued
through to Pittenweem, where the locomotive could then run round its train.
The NBR Leven & East of Fife Section trains from Leven continued to use the
old station at Anstruther but passengers from the Boarhills line were not
obliged to change carriages at Pittenweem as the Anstruther train collected their
carriages while the locomotive ran round their train via the goods loop and
waited in a siding. After the train from Anstruther picked up the carriages and
took them on to Thornton, the Boarhills locomotive then waited for the through
carriages conveyed by the next train from Thornton to Anstruther. An
additional Pittenweem to Boarhills service was provided on Saturday evenings
and, in common with the Leven & East of Fife line there were no Sunday
services. From Boarhills the railway-sponsored coach service was in operation
to St Andrews and provided a thrice daily connection, the last bus being
retimed on Saturdays so as to connect with the later railway service.

During the first week the new trains daily carried between 50 and 60
passengers - a not inconsiderable feat. However, the absence of a common station
at Anstruther and the need for trains to run on to Pittenweem was a definite

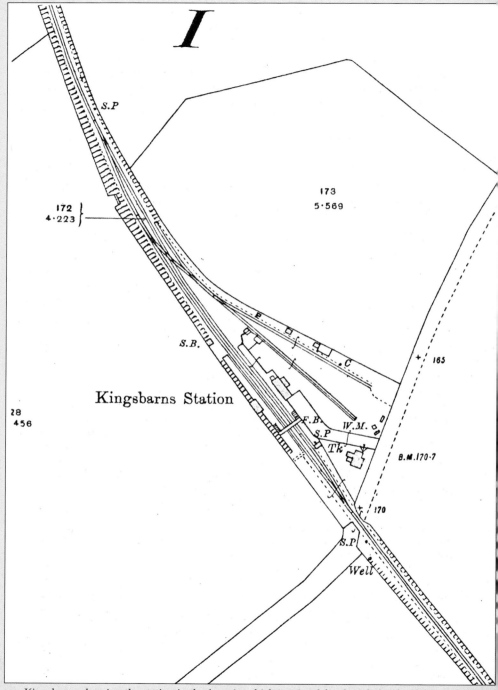

I

S.P

172
4·223

173
5·569

S.B.

165

Kingsbarns Station

28
456

F.B

W.M.

S.P

Tk

B.M.170·7

170

S.P

Well

Kingsbarns showing the station in the form in which it existed for the whole of its life.
*Reproduced from the 25″, 1894 Ordnance Survey Map*

drawback, albeit a temporary one, and was a complicated, time-wasting and cumbersome procedure to say the least. On 4th October, 1883 the company, following the requirement imposed by the Board of Trade, approved the building of a passing loop at Anstruther, although the North British refused to contribute to the cost. Within a week the loop at Anstruther was under construction and, according to the Minutes of 17th December, was to be completed by the end of that month. On 28th December the *Journal* commented that:

> Yesterday the passenger traffic was discontinued at the station of the North British Railway, and henceforth it will be conducted at the new station of the Anstruther & St Andrews Railway. The trains on the latter line have hitherto been running between Boarhills and Pittenweem but they are now only to run between Anstruther and Boarhills. The goods traffic will as usual be carried out at the old station.

and the NBR decreed to its staff, in Circular A 135-83 dated 21st December, that:

> The Leven & East of Fife branch trains now run to and from the New (Anstruther & St Andrews Railway) station at Anstruther at the same times as they were formerly booked to run to and fro the old (North British) station being used now only for Fish, Goods and Minerals trains. The Anstruther & St Andrews branch passenger trains have continued to run to and from the New (Anstruther & St Andrews ) station at Anstruther at the same times as which they were formerly appointed to run except that the 3.40 train from Boarhills to Anstruther will commencing from 1st January leave at 3.30 pm and run as shewn. Note: the passenger vehicles from and to Boarhills run through and from Thornton attached to the first and last Thornton trains.

The service of five passenger trains to Boarhills, the first being mixed and the others conveying all three classes of passengers, continued and on 8th January, 1884 the loop and various signalling alterations at Anstruther (New) were inspected by Major Marindin, who found them to be satisfactory.

The new line made an end-on junction at Anstruther with the North British and then ran eastwards, crossing the Dreel Burn, to reach the new passenger station. From here it struck out in a north-easterly direction over the fields until paralleling the coast road for a short distance and then turning to the north of Crail town, the station being situated on the edge of the built-up area. After Crail the line turned inland to take a north-westerly course to Kingsbarns station, situated on a minor road to Dunino a good mile to the west of the village. The siting of this station had been a controversial decision and, in the words of the Chairman of the company 'no one more strongly urged that the station of Kingsbarns should be contiguous to the village ... than our engineer, Mr Buchanan'; it appears that a combination of pressure from local landowners, including Cleghorn of Stravithie, and a desire to serve as many agricultural customers as possible had led to the routeing of the line away from the village. Leaving Kingsbarns the line proceeded over farmland for a mile and a half to Boarhills, crossing *en route* the Kilduncan Burn and, at Boarhills, meeting with the Kenly Burn - this stream effectively drained the northern part of the East Neuk, passing the village in its den or ravine before entering the sea a mile to the east. The line then crossed over it on the only substantial structure on the whole line, the Kenly Burn or Boarhills viaduct. Once across the viaduct the station at Boarhills was reached, again inconveniently situated since it lay a third of a mile from the village. Since Boarhills was destined to be the terminus of the line for the next four years a temporary engine shed, made of wood, with a pit was provided 'on the passing siding' at that station - the Board of Trade, however, objected that the shed was too close to the running line and required that it be removed to a more suitable position. There were three gated level crossings in all, namely at Thirdpart and Kirkmay (between Anstruther and Crail) and Newhall (between Crail and Boarhills), the houses there being occupied by surfacemen working on the line, their wives attending to the gates in lieu of rent.

### End in Sight

At the beginning of September 1883 the Anstruther & St Andrews Board met and agreed that at present they would not proceed with the extension from Boarhills to St Andrews, notwithstanding the fact that some of the work had already been carried out, the principal of which was the 'fine girder bridge that is to carry the line over the Bonnyton Road, about a half mile from Boarhills station'. The Board, recognising that the line already built had cost something like £5,000 per mile, faced up to the fact that if it were to proceed further 'whether by contract or otherwise, a large sum will have to be borrowed to perfect the scheme' and noted that an arrangement had already been made with Coghill's trustee in bankruptcy for the transfer of their former contractor's plant to the company. However, they were determined to press on as rapidly as they could for, without the completion of the line to St Andrews, the whole scheme might well be doomed. There were, indeed, further problems that were to bedevil the company, most of which were financial. What was becoming increasingly apparent was that the original estimates of Coghill and indeed the company's own engineers, were unrealistic and that the final cost of the line was likely to be in the order of £125,000, or more than double that which the company had budgeted for. The 1883 Act had given the company powers to raise additional capital up to the value of £30,000 and this, along with the contribution of £5,000 from the North British, was for the time being all that the beleaguered Directors could rely upon. It was clear that economies would have to be practised and at an early stage the Engineer was told to modify the cost of the station plans already submitted and the Board, in considering plans for a new goods shed at Crail which had been requested by the North British, delayed consideration *sine die* 'in view of the present state of the funds'.

There were changes in the management of the company with John Edward Dovey, Chartered Accountant, of Hanover Street, Edinburgh succeeding Philip Oliphant upon his retirement due to failing eyesight in November 1883. Dovey's salary as Secretary and Treasurer was agreed with him at £150 pa. In the same month an increase in the number of Directors to five was authorized with the additional appointment of Lieutenant Colonel Erskine and James Bain (the representative of the Bank of Scotland, the company's bankers) to the Board. On a somewhat lighter note the Minutes record under the heading of 'Footwarmers at Boarhills station' that a suggestion that the passenger carriages on the line be heated with footwarmers ( in effect metal hot water bottles) had been agreed to by the NBR and that:

Colonel Moneypenny reported that in terms of the remit to him he had written to Mr McLaren, Passenger Superintendent of the North British Railway, proposing to obtain hot water from the boiler of the locomotive for the footwarmers and Mr McLaren had accepted the suggestion and would give effect to it as a temporary measure.

However, all was not well with the finances of the Anstruther & St Andrews Railway and by December the company's creditors were again pressing for settlements of the debts owed to them. The company, aware of the need to raise further capital, now considered asking those to whom they owed money to allow a three month period of delay in paying in return for a settlement of all accounts with 5 per cent interest added at the end of this period.

In January 1884 a concern was raised that the revenue from the line would be minimal until through trains were running to St Andrews. This was borne out by the fact that the gross traffic revenue in the first three months after opening amounted to £480 11s. 0d. whereas the working expenses amounted to £547 18s. 3d., some of which was due to the 'dead' mileage between Anstruther and Pittenweem pending the completion of the loop at the former station. The northern extension was, however, in abeyance and on 11th February, 1884 it was minuted that 'in view of the undesirability of increasing the company's indebtedness, the engineer has been told to stop the works and to make temporary arrangements in the meantime for the storage of plant and the keeping of horses for their works' - indeed 14 of these horses had already been sold by public roup (auction) at Cupar market in September 1883. The company was anxious not to incur the further expense of feeding horses for which there was no work.

It was also resolved that the coach from Boarhills to St Andrews be kept running in the meantime. Then, in March, it was announced that concessions had been obtained from the North British and that there was every possibility that the construction of the new line would be undertaken shortly, completion being financed by the issue of 5 per cent preference stock as permitted by the 1883 Act. At the same time the Chairman reassured the shareholders that there was a steady increase in the goods traffic carried over the portion of line already opened - in December 1883 the total of forwarded and received wagons loaded with goods and minerals had been 445, while in January and February 1884 the total had been 546 and 692 respectively.

### Two Sides of a Penny

In April 1884 the *Journal* attempted to assuage the unease of the potential investors in the line by stating that:

> One who invests his money in a new concern can be pardoned for asking, and endeavouring to ascertain, whether there is a likelihood of it paying and yielding him some return. This view may be looked upon as rather ulterior by those persons who affect to think themselves above considering monetary matters. Such persons, however, who attempt this affectation outwardly, generally follow the usual course in looking at the two sides of a penny when called upon to subscribe to any project. But that the Directors have thoroughly considered the present and future prospects of the line is clearly evident from a carefully compiled statement which is inserted in the Prospectus.

In making up the estimate the plan followed was to take the coaching traffic, passengers and parcels by omnibuses, post conveyances and hiring &c, through the district covered by the railway and it was found that this could not be put down to less than £7 per day, or £2,191 per year of 313 working days. In this no account is taken of the large number of passengers who are conveyed to St Andrews, Anstruther &c, in private vehicles which are numerous, and who will in future travel by rail. The Directors assume that the railway when finished will increase the traffic to three times the amount of the coaching and hiring, and put down the sum of £6,573. To this is added the traffic in goods, which they estimate at £6,753, which makes a total estimated traffic of £13,326 for the year. From this there falls to be deducted £6,913 for passenger tax, cartages and working expenses, £1,530 for debenture interest and feu duties, and £920 for taxes and local burdens and general expenses of management and direction. This would make an expenditure of £9,363, and leave an estimated net revenue of £3,963. Of this there would be taken to meet the dividend of 5 per cent on £45,000 of preference stock £2,250, which would leave a margin available for dividend on the ordinary share capital stock of the company (equal to 3 per cent on £57,000) the sum of £1,713.

The Directors declare that the above is a reliable approximation of the probable results of the line, and that in that case there is everything to induce the shareholders to take up the preference shares, so that the railway may be finished in two years. There need, therefore, be little fear but that the railway will prove a remunerative undertaking like the two others that it will be connected at each end. We earnestly trust that the Directors will have a favourable result to report at the meeting on the 28th inst and be able to state that all the preference shares have been taken up. The North British company have given a marked proof of confidence in the undertaking, by agreeing to work the traffic from 31st January 1884 to 31st January 1891 at 50 per cent of the gross receipts, irrespective of the amount of the traffic on the understanding that the junction at St Andrews will be effected and the whole line completed within two years. The shareholders then can safely invest more of their money when they have the assurance that this is undoubtedly the case, for Mr Walker [NBR General Manager], we may be sure, would never have given such an agreement unless he was confident of the new railway being a financial success.

In June the Board tried to persuade the NBR to contribute further capital of £10,000, pointing out that the cost of the proposed junction line at St Andrews was now estimated at £22,000, as against the original estimate of £12,700. The North British eventually agreed to subscribe the £10,000 promised eight days after the junction line was opened to traffic.* In August the bus contract with Kirkaldy was extended although there was subsequent mention of an improved bus service running in the summer months and being provided by a Mr Rusack of St Andrews.† By November 1884 all the remaining land required between Boarhills and Kinness Burn# had been purchased and by May 1885 the Directors were seeking the agreement of the shareholders to put the work in the hands of the contractors even though £5,000 of capital had still to be raised. In the same month the North British agreed to extend the 1880 working agreement

* This agreement followed on the NBR obtaining statutory powers to contribute to the Anstruther company 'such further sums of money as they think fit not exceeding in the whole £10,000 by virtue of section 33 of the North British Railway Act 1887 (50 & 51 Vict. cap. lxxxi) passed on 5th July, 1887.
† John Wilhelm Christof Rusack, a native of Lower Saxony and of Huguenot extraction, became a notable local entrepreneur and, in addition to later running the refreshment room at St Andrews station, was also responsible for building Rusack's Marine Hotel.
# The Kinness Burn rises to the west of St Andrews near to Clatto Hill and flows to the sea through the southern suburbs of St Andrews and into the harbour.

for a further five years, (i.e. from 1891 to 1896) and to extend the time for completion of the line to 31st December, 1886. On 18th November, 1885 a further agreement was reached with the NBR whereby the company was released from the obligation in the 1883 Act to construct a new goods station at St Andrews subject to the Anstruther & St Andrews company paying for a new signal box at St Andrews Links station.

### Clay and Stone

At the half-yearly Meeting held in the same month the Chairman was able to tell the shareholders that they were now convening in very different circumstances, that great progress had been made on the line and that the Directors had secured a first rate main contractor, James Young & Company, to complete the works, their contract being confirmed as being effective as from 16th June, 1884 - in the Chairman's words: 'the right man in the right place at last!' The contract was to be divided into two parts, both of which had been let to Young, namely No. 1 (Boarhills to Mount Melville) and No. 2 (Mount Melville to St Andrews Links). John Buchanan & Company were reappointed as consulting engineers, after which John Buchanan exhibited to the meeting new plans for the station at St Andrews. Both Young and Buchanan then received applause from the shareholders. In the same month as the meeting work on the line recommenced and although the winter of 1885-6 was a severe one in East Fife, and the weather encountered in the following August was described as 'unseasonal', the work continued on so that, by the autumn of that year, the shareholders were told that all was satisfactory. At the next Half-yearly Meeting, chaired by Dr Cleghorn in the absence of Mr Purvis, who had been detained in Hawaii 'by private affairs',* it was said that the existing part of the railway had already served many purposes and that 2,000 tons of freestone from Kenly Quarry had been transported to Elie to build a new church there; in addition 12 or 14 boys were travelling daily over the line to the Waid Academy in Anstruther.

Work progressed again from March 1886, the worst of the winter weather now being over and the 'heavy and tenacious clay' that formed the lower stratum of the ground at the Doubledykes Road in St Andrews was finally cut through. In that month, however, the only fatal accident to befall the contractors on the extension from Boarhills took place when Evandra Ross 'a native of Inverness-shire, aged 56' was killed when a box full of stone and earth was being lifted by crane in the quarry at Stravithie and the chains broke, causing the box to fall on to him from a height of 12 feet. On a happier note John Buchanan was, on 14th April, able to report to the Directors in the following terms:

> The severity of the weather during the past winter has greatly retarded the works, but making allowance for the detention from this cause, considerable progress has been made by the contractors since the date of the last report. On Contract No. 1 work to the

---

* Mr Purvis was visiting his plantation and sugar mill at Kukuihaele. He subsequently introduced the Macadamia nut to Hawaii, now one of the islands' principal exports. The Purvis family continued to be a presence in Hawaii until 1928 and, as a result of their friendship with the Hawaiian royal family, the king and princess of that country visited various places in Scotland including Anstruther and Kinaldy.

extent of 66%, and on Contract No. 2, 26% of the total value has now been executed, and of the station buildings and cottages at level crossings on that part of the line embraced in Contract No. 1 22% has been executed ... Of the permanent way, 8,400 lineal yards - upwards of 5 miles - has been laid.

*Earthworks* - 51,000 cubic yards of earthworks have been removed on Contract No. 1 and 27,000 cubic yards on Contract No. 2, equivalent to 89% and 35% of the respective contract quantities.

*Road Alterations* - On Contract No. 1 15,000 cubic yards, or 70% of the earthworks required to form road embankments have been put in position and 55,000 cubic yards or 15% of the excavations required to form roads on Contract No. 2 have been removed and put to bank.

*Bridges* - 64% of the bridges and large culverts on Contract No. 1 have been erected, namely at Easter Balrymonth, Prior Mill, Alanhill and Cairns Mill, and in Contract No. 2, 15% has been built at Cairnsmill Den, Canongate Road and Double Dykes Road.

*Culverts and Drainage* - All the small culverts on Contract No. 1 have been built and of the intercepting field drains required 3,200 linear yards have been laid on Contract No. 1 and 2,500 linear yards on Contract No. 2, being 75% of the total required in each case.

*Fencing* - 8,800 linear yards of fencing have been erected on Contract No. 1 and 6,600 linear yards on Contract No. 2, being respectively 64% and 81% of the total.

*Permanent Way* - On Contract No.1, 6,800 linear yards of the permanent way have been laid down equal to 82% of the whole, and on Contract No. 2 1,600 linear yards, equal to 40% of the whole.

*Station Buildings* - The station buildings at Stravithie, and the cottage for the level crossing at Easter Balrymonth are roofed in, and are in course of completion, and the erection of the station buildings at Mount Melville has been commenced. The contractors have got a stock at the quarry [of] rock ready for removal and being removed to the site of the several works to be erected, and considerable progress will now be made with the masonry of the bridges and the station buildings.

In June Colonel Moneypenny died, his place on the Board being taken by George Fortune of Barnsmuir, Crail and a Joint Committee with the North British Railway was formed to deal with all questions arising in connection with the proposed joint station at St Andrews, the plans for which had already been approved 'in principle'. In the same month the company raised with the NBR the question of accommodation for railway employees at Stravithie and Mount Melville stations, in the vicinity of which there were no cottages or other houses in which staff could reside. Eventually the North British agreed to contribute to the building of cottages there, the cost of which was £309 each. The only major civil engineering task left now was the excavation of 50 yards or so of cutting near to the Kinness Burn. Several weeks later it was said that the railway works were being pushed forward with much vigour and that night and day shifts were being employed with naptha lamps being used to give illumination when necessary.

By September 1886 it was being reported that the works were now substantially complete and that many of the navvies had been paid off. Much of the track had been laid up to the outskirts of St Andrews and that the foundations for the new station there were under construction. In the same month the company carried out an inspection of the finished parts of the line with a special train being run for the Directors, the Engineer and the contractor. A few days later a party of distinguished guests, including both Princess Victoria and Princess Louise of Schleswig-Holstein, visited the construction site.

## Pushing Ahead

The Minutes of 1st February 1887 record that,

...a letter having been read from Mr Purvis (the Chairman) raising the question as to whether this station should not be called *Strathvithie* as being probably the original name of the locality, the Directors after full consideration decided that the shorter name of Stravithie should be adopted.

This was probably a wise decision for Stravithie is not situated in a Strath-like wide valley and in actual fact its name was more probably derived from a long-lost 'rath', i.e. a garden or enclosure. As with many Scottish place names, however, controversy reigns and an alternative of *Strath Beithean*, 'strath of the birch trees', has also been suggested even though this does not seem to reflect the topography of the area.

The plans for St Andrews New station were also being prepared and it was proposed that there would be a single island platform with the usual offices thereon, situated in a cutting and reached by a footbridge. Some thought was being given to the approach roads thereto, the necessity for a luggage lift to deal with the exceptional quantities of luggage which were handled there and the provision of refreshment facilities. In connection with the latter, an offer from Mr Rusack of £50 at a commencing annual rent for a refreshment room on the station was agreed. A tender from the Railway Signal Company of Fazakerley of £701 for the provision of signals between Boarhills and St Andrews was accepted by the Board 'on the condition that the work is completed to the satisfaction of the engineer on or before 1st March, 1887'.

On 3rd February, 1887 the *Fifeshire Journal* reported that since the advent of better weather,

...railway matters have been pushed forward with great speed. The completion of the St Andrews station is within sight, and should favourable weather continue, the work will be done in fairly good time. The first girder across the bridge at the St Andrews-Cupar road has been placed in position. It is of malleable iron, and turns the scale somewhat about 8 tons 14 cwt. The placing of so huge a piece of workmanship has attracted much attention and excited comment. The portion of retaining wall at the south side of the station threatens to give way, so it has been decided to rebuild it. It is expected that the new railway will be open on 1st April, and the contractor is pushing the work ahead with energy.

A month later it proved necessary to give the contractor a further extension of time 'in consequence of the interruption to work caused by the frost of December and January' and it was said that the new railway would, accordingly, not be opened until the beginning of May.

## Obstacles Removed

By Easter of 1887 the work was substantially complete and on 28th May Major General C.S. Hutchinson of the Royal Engineers, in the presence of the company's Engineer, Secretary, Chairman and other Board members, inspected the line on behalf of the Railway Inspectorate:

Sir, I have the honour to report that ... in compliance with the instructions of 16th inst. I have inspected a portion of the A & St Andrews Railway:

This portion, which is a single line 6 miles 69 chains long, commencing at Boarhills station (so far as which the line was authorised to be opened in August 1883) and extends to a point close to the old St Andrews station on the line between St Andrews and Leuchars, with which line it forms an end on junction.

The gauge is 4 foot 8½ inches, the width at formation level is 15 feet in cuttings, and 16 feet in embankments and there is not less than a 6 foot space between the lines or rails when there is more than one, viz. at the stations. The permanent way is similar to that on the opened portion of the line. The steepest gradient is about 1 in 49½ and the sharpest curve (except at St Andrews station) has a radius of 13½ chains. No land has been purchased for the future doubling of the line, except for the level 22 chains, where the formation has been made and an under bridge constructed for a double line.

The works on the line consist of: (1) Eight over bridges: 6, widest span 18 feet, are constructed with stone abutments and stone or brick arches, 1 of 14ft span has stone abutments and a top composed of wrought iron girders and jackarches, and 1 of 27ft span is entirely of timber. (2) Six under bridges: span 12ft is constructed with stone abutments and a brick-arched top, and 5, longest span 44ft 9inches are built with stone abutments and various iron girder tops, steel flooring being used in the widest bridge. (3) Two viaducts or stream bridges, one of 3 arches of 30ft each, is built with stone piers or abutments and with brick arches, and one, span 26ft has stone abutments and a wrought iron girder top. (4) Four large culverts, these, widest 10ft, have stone or concrete walls with brick or stone arches, and one, 5ft wide, concrete walls carrying rolled joists with brick arches turned between them. (5) Several retaining walls built with stone or concrete, with the exception of the under-bridge at 14 miles 28 chains and of the viaduct at 15 miles 28 chains, where there are slight settlements which should be carefully watched. These works appear to have been substantially constructed and to be standing well. The girders have sufficient strength by calculations and those under the line gave moderate deflections under test.

There are no tunnels or public road level crossings. In the case of two semi-public road level crossings, over which several parties have a right of way, proper gates and cottages have been provided. The fencing is partly stone walls, partly post and rail, and partly (and principally) post and wire. The new stations are Stravithy,* Mount Melville and St Andrews New Station, where proper accommodation has been provided. St Andrews New Station is arranged as a passing place with an island platform. There are sidings at all 3 stations.

The signal arrangements have been provided for by the erection of new cabins at the 3 stations, of a new cabin at St Andrews Old Station and by some alteration in the existing cabin at Boarhills - these cabins contain the following number of levers:

Boarhills - 12 working levers/0 spare levers
Stravithy - 8 working levers/0 spare levers
Mount Melville - 8 working levers/0 spare levers
St Andrews (New) - 9 working levers/0 spare levers
St Andrews (Old) - 13 working levers/7 spare levers

I observed the following requirements:
The starting signals should precede the distant signals.
At Stravithy station, the siding points should be reversed, brought close to the end of the platforms and lengthened. The quarry siding points (locked with Annets key) should also be reversed and brought nearer to the cabin and the up home signal placed at the fouling point of this siding with the main line.
The hand railing of the river bridge at 13 miles 44 chains (close to Mount Melville Station) should be heightened.

---

* It is not clear why the Board of Trade consistently used this alternative spelling which seems to have been an anachronism by then.

An additional siding should be put in at Mount Melville Station, and the distance between the rails and the platform slightly increased.

The rail joints are tight and should be opened on the inside of the curve at 13 miles 70 chains.

Double tie rods should be put in at all double safety points, and the distances between these points and the main line should not exceed 6 feet,

At old St Andrews station , No. 4 and No. 5 levers should be interlocked with No. 8, the back of the platform should be fenced, a crossover road and an old tank on the platform have to be removed.

Some of the block instruments have not been fixed.

At St Andrews New Station, in consequence of the signalman being unable to see a down train standing at the home signals, an additional lifting bar should be provided near the down home signal, this bar to be worked with the up starting signal lever.

The line requires slewing over at the over-bridge at 11 miles 42 chains.

The line is to be worked with the train staff and ticket and with the block telegraph and an understanding to this effect should be given by the Anstruther & St Andrews Company and concurred by the North British who are to work the line. This undertaking should also apply to the line between Anstruther Junction and Boarhills, which is to be similarly worked, instead of with only one engine, according to the original undertaking. It would also be desirable that the line between Leuchars Junction and St Andrews Old Station should be provided with the block telegraph, so that the working between Anstruther and Leuchars Junction may be similar throughout.

In consequence of there being no engine turntable on the Anstruther & St Andrews line, the Companies must also undertake to stop all passenger trains at all stations unless they are running between terminal stations provided with engine turntables.*

Owing to the steepness of the gradients on the new line the greatest possible care will have to be exercised in working the traffic, and especially the goods traffic, and the companies should give an undertaking to take trains off the main line and to perform no shunting operations on it:

At Stravithy Station with trains proceeding from Anstruther and

At Mount Melville with trains proceeding to Anstruther.

It is desired to open the new line on 1st June and the above requirements can all be completed by that time, except perhaps the additional siding accommodation at Stravithy and Mount Melville. Subject then (1) to the receipt of satisfactory undertakings as to mode of working, stopping of trains at two of the stations, (2) to the above mentioned requirements being reported complete, or in the event of the additional siding accommodation at Stravithy and Mount Melville not being provided in time to the goods traffic being worked meantime only by trains proceeding *to* Anstruther at Stravithy and *from* Anstruther at Mount Melville, and (3) to re-inspection on the first convenient opportunity, the Board of Trade might I suspect sanction the line between Boarhills and St Andrews being opened for passenger traffic. It would be a great advantage (on account of the steep gradient) to double the line between the two St Andrews stations, and I trust that this will be done as soon as possible.

On the evening of 30th June a telegram from Dr Cleghorn was received by the Secretary of the company informing him that he had obtained the consent of the Board of Trade to the immediate opening of the line to all traffic.

* This specific requirement was subsequently relaxed when a new order was issued on 6th July, 1887 where an exception was made to the general rule 'in cases where tank engines are used in all respects so constructed as to be fit for running at high speed in either direction and provided with sand pipes and continuous brake pipes at each end; (2) proper arrangements for the protection of the men on the footboard when running bunker first and (3) bunkers so constructed that the view of the drivers shall not be obstructed by the coal'.

'B1' class No. 61398 passes through Kingsbarns with the 4.08 pm St Andrews to Glasgow Buchanan Street service, 27th July, 1963.                                                                         *Roy Hamilton*

Kingsbarns in the 1930s with a down goods train waiting in the up platform - note the water tower in its original form.                                                                         *NRBSG Hennigan Collection*

Kingsbarns in the 1950s seen from the south - note the presence of the photographer's bicycle!

*Rex Conway Collection*

Kingsbarns on 21st August, 1952 looking south with the token platforms and, in the distance, the level crossing gates are closed against the line.

*A.G. Ellis*

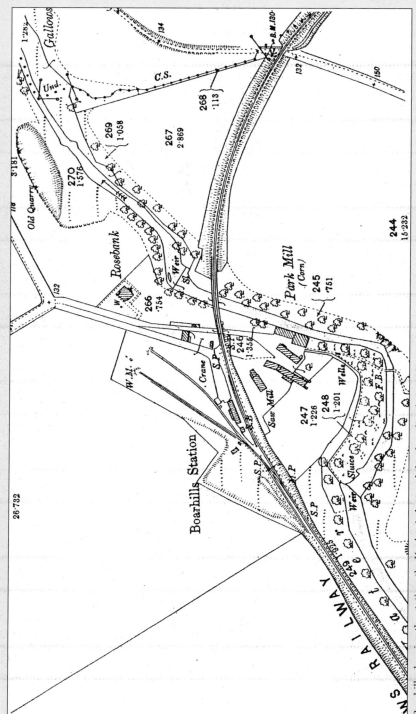

Boarhills showing the station, the Kenly viaduct and the short-lived signal box.

*Reproduced from the 25", 1894 Ordnance Survey Map*

The Kenly Green or Boarhills viaduct, the largest engineering feature on the Anstruther & St Andrews line, in July 2006.

*Bill Roberton*

A three-coach Metro-Cammell unit crosses the Boarhills viaduct on a Thornton to Dundee working, 25th July 1964 - the only photograph that the authors have ever seen of a train at this location.                                                                                                      *C.C. Thornburn*

Boarhills in the era when it was still open to passengers, looking towards St Andrews. Note the headshunt and track leading to the sidings situated behind the building.        *Jim Page Collection*

The 2.17 Dundee to Edinburgh service hauled by 'B1' class No. 61118 passes through Boarhills in the late 1950s. *Jim Page Collection*

The 9.08 am Saturdays-only Glasgow Queen Street to Dundee service, formed of two Derby class '108' dmus, passes through Boarhills on 25th July, 1964. *C.C. Thornburn*

*Above:*  Boarhills in 1962 - the fact that the station was last painted 11 years before is beginning to show!          *Jim Hay*

*Right:*  The lamp from the pump house at Boarhills - this small structure provided a supply of fresh water for locomotives on this section of the line.          *Jim Hay*

# Chapter Five

# Home Run:
# The Anstruther & St Andrews Railway 1887-1897

*'They would have had a great deal more traffic if the stations had been made closer to the villages.'*

George Fortune, Shareholder and Director, 1894

### A Good Many Passengers

On the morning of 1st July, 1887, with apparently a minimum of ceremony, the line between Boarhills and St Andrews, together with the stations at Stravithie, Mount Melville and St Andrews (New), were opened to all traffic and, according to the *Fifeshire Journal*, 'a good many passengers took advantage to patronise the new line'. The fact that the line was opened on the 35th anniversary to the day of the inauguration of services on the St Andrews Railway seems largely to have gone unnoticed but one assumes that the Directors of the Anstruther & St Andrews were so relieved finally to have the whole of the line opened that they eschewed such publicity. The first passenger tickets issued between St Andrews and Boarhills were issued to the Walker sisters who lived at Dauphins East in St Andrews on account of the fact that the engineer in charge of constructing the line had lodged with their parents; after their early start and first train journey the sisters walked back to St Andrews.* The existing horse omnibus service between Anstruther and St Andrews ceased to operate on 16th June, 1887, in anticipation of the opening of the railway, but the St Andrews to Crail service was reported to be 'holding out' for the time being. In his final report, dated 13th July, 1887, Major General Hutchinson reported that all of the requirements which he had insisted upon in his first report had been complied with by the company, except for the removal of the tank at St Andrews (Old) station, and that he was giving his sanction to the line being opened to passengers with retrospective effect.

On 24th March, 1888 the company Minutes recorded that the temporary locomotive shed at Boarhills had been demolished and that the Secretary had been instructed to advertise the wood with which it had been constructed to be offered for sale by private tender.

### Up the Hill

The line left Boarhills and headed in a generally westerly direction on an uphill gradient varying between 1 in 50 and 1 in 59 towards the next station at Stravithie, 2¼ miles away. The route between these two points lay across country far away from roads apart from a minor road between Boarhills and

---

* These tickets, numbered 0000 and 0001, were presented to the Museum of British Transport in the 1950s by J.M. Bennett, the then St Andrews station master.

# North British Railway Company.

**M**
### No. 1852.

*Notice to Engine Drivers, Guards, Signalmen, Station Masters, and others.*

## Opening of that portion of the Anstruther and St Andrews Railway which extends from Boarhills to St Andrews for General Traffic,

ON

# TUESDAY, 31st MAY 1887.

That portion of the Anstruther and St Andrews Railway which extends from Boarhills to St Andrews, including the Stations on it, viz.:— Stravithie, Mount Melville, and St Andrews (the present St Andrews Station at the termination of the New Railway will, in future, be called **St Andrews Links Station**) will be opened for Traffic purposes at 12 o'clock noon on the date above mentioned.

This portion of the Anstruther and St Andrews Railway will be worked under the combined systems of **Block Telegraph** and Train Staff and Train Ticket.

The Block Telegraph and Train Staff Sections, and the number and colour of the Train Staffs and Train Tickets, will be as under :—

| Name of Section. | Colour and Number of Train Staffs and Train Tickets. | |
|---|---|---|
| Kingsbarns and St Andrews    -    - | White | 2 |
| St Andrews and St Andrews Links    - | Green | 5 |
| St Andrews Links and Guardbridge    - | Red | 0 |

## Absolute Block Telegraph and Train Staff Working.

Trains or Engines worked over either of the above-named Sections must be Signalled in strict accordance with the Revised Regulations for Working by Tyers' Telegraph Signal, dated 23rd November 1880 ; and also in strict accordance with the Train Staff Regulations, as contained in Rules 355-374 inclusive of the Company's Book of Rules and Regulations.

It must be distinctly understood that Clause 11 of Tyer's Telegraph Signal Regulations will not be acted upon on the above Sections, and therefore a second Train or Engine must not be allowed to follow another Train or Engine into either of the Sections until the first Train or Engine has been Signalled clear.

Before giving the Driver of a Train or Engine the Train Staff or Train Ticket, the Station Master or Signalman at the Train Staff Station from which the Train or Engine is about to be despatched, must be careful to Signal on the Train or Engine by Tyers' Telegraph to the Station in advance, and until such Signal has been given, and properly acknowledged by the needle being turned to "Train on Line." the Station Master or Signalman must not deliver to the Driver either the Train Staff or Train Ticket.

---

The Contractor must have all his Engines, Wagons, Bogies, &c., cleared off the New Line above mentioned not later then 10 a.m. on 31st May 1887, so as to admit of the free and safe passage of the Company's Trains and Engines.

---

Inspector Hogg will attend and see the foregoing brought into force.

**J. WALKER,**
General Manager.

EDINBURGH, 25th May 1887.    (4½C)

Dunino. The station at Stravithie, which lay immediately east of the Anstruther to St Andrews road (the present B9131) and about 2½ miles from St Andrews by road, did not serve any village but instead was provided to serve farms and landed estates in the vicinity, such as Kinaldy, Gilmerton, Stravithie House as well as the small village of Dunino, a good mile to the south. Two of the Directors of the company, John Purvis and Dr Hugh Cleghorn, were landowners at, respectively, Kinaldy and Stravithie and it is likely that the siting of a station at Stravithie was, at least in part, attributed to this fact; the decision was roundly condemned by John Buchanan, the company's Engineer. The summit of the line, some 300 feet or so above sea level, was reached after which the descent towards St Andrews began on a gradient of 1 in 50 across Prior Muir, where a short-lived quarry siding was provided, continuing on an easier gradient in an north-westerly direction until Mount Melville was reached. Due to the steepness of the gradients, special precautions were needed in relation to shunting both at Stravithie and at Mount Melville. These amounted (in the words of the NBR 1894 Working Timetable) to:

(1) Owing to the steepness of the gradients, the greatest possible care must be exercised in the working at Stravithie Station with down trains - that is to say - with trains from the direction of Anstruther going in the direction of St Andrews, and also at Mount Melville with all up trains - that is to say - trains from the direction of St Andrews going in the direction of Anstruther.

(2) Before any shunting operations are to be commenced at either of these stations respectively with the trains specially referred to, the entire train, including of course the guard's van, must be shunted off the main line into the siding provided for that purpose so as to admit of the shunting operations being performed safely and in such a way as will ensure against the possibility of a portion of the train or any other vehicle running away on the main line down the steep incline.

(3) The siding provided for the purpose of putting a down train into at Stravithie and an up train at Mount Melville are each only 100 yards long. It therefore follows that guards of down trains having shunting to do at Mount Melville must not have more wagons on their trains than the sidings above mentioned can properly accommodate.

(4) The following notice has been printed on a board placed at the points leading from the main line to the sidings at Stravithie.

'Before shunting operations are commenced on any down train at Stravithie Station, the whole train must be shunted into the siding provided for that purpose, so as to admit of the shunting operations being performed with perfect safety and in such a way as will ensure against the possibility of any portion of the train and any other vehicle running away on the main line down the steep incline.'

A similar notice, relating to up trains, was placed at Mount Melville, both of which remained in place until the eventual closure of the line.

Mount Melville was a lonely place, lying 1½ miles south-west of St Andrews, serving a number of farms and estates including the eponymous Mount Melville House and estate, ¾ mile to the north-west, which was the seat of the Melville family.* After Mount Melville the line ran under the A915 St Andrews to Largo road (since realigned) and ran to the west of Cairnsmill Farm before entering the deep valley known as the Cairns Den, continuing at a downhill

---

* In 1900 the Mount Melville estate was sold to James Younger of Alloa, a scion of the famed brewing family; Younger then built Mount Melville House. The estate was sold in 1947 to Fife County Council and now forms part of Craigtoun Country Park. for an account of the miniature railway that operated and still operates in the country park, see *The St Andrews Railway.*

*Right:* The celebrated 'Notice to Staff' at Mount Melville - whatever happened to it and its counterpart at Stravithie after closure?
*Nigel Dyckhoff*

*Below:* A clear view of the notice at Stravithie, 17th August, 1963. *C.C. Thornburn*

## NOTICE TO STAFF.

BEFORE SHUNTINC OPERATIONS ARE COMMENCED BY ANY DOWN TRAIN AT STRAVITHIE STATION THE WHOLE TRAIN MUST BE SHUNTED INTO THE SIDINC. PROVIDED FOR THAT PURPOSE SO AS TO ADMIT OF THE SHUNTINC OPERATIONS BEINC PERFORMED WITH PERFECT SAFETY, AND IN SUCH A WAY AS WILL ENSURE AGAINST THE POSSIBILITY OF ANY PORTION OF THE TRAIN OR ANY OTHER VEHICLE, RUNNINC AWAY ON THE MAIN LINE DOWN THE TEEP INCLINE.

JULY 12 1887.                                          BY ORDER.

gradient of 1 in 49 for nearly 1½ miles and sweeping in a curve to the east before heading north east into St Andrews on an easier gradient of 1 in 60 and 1 in 63. The only structure of any importance on this section of the line was then reached, namely the Kinness Burn viaduct, consisting of three semi-circular brick and masonry arches carrying the railway across the Kinness Burn after which the line then entered the built-up area of St Andrews and passed through a cutting before entering St Andrews New station.

This was a joint station for passenger traffic only and was somewhat restricted having a single island platform situated in a cutting. Both the North British and the Anstruther & St Andrews companies used the station there being, from the outset, some through services between Leuchars and Thornton via Anstruther. There was, however, no room for any goods facilities and all goods trains continued to use the original station, now dubbed St Andrews Links or St Andrews Old while the new station was officially named, somewhat unoriginally, St Andrews (New). After leaving the new station the line ran on an embankment and crossed over the main road from Guardbridge to the town (the A91) by means of a single-span girder bridge called the Petheram bridge. The company minutes of 18th April, 1888 give the reason for the bridge being so named:

> On the motion of the Chairman, it was agreed to name the railway bridge over the Deviation Road, St Andrews 'The Petheram Bridge' in honour of Mr Petheram in respect that the proposal (ultimately adopted by the Board) to effect the railway junction at St Andrews by diverting the Leuchars Road (in lieu of carrying it over the railway by a high embankment, as originally proposed by Mr Buchanan) eminated from Mr Petheram. It was also agreed that the Company should defray the expense of cutting the name of the bridge upon it.

Buchanan, it will be remembered, was the consulting civil engineer to the company while Henry Petheram was the County Road Surveyor for the St Andrews district of Fife. The line then continued along an embankment until it came to the St Andrews Links, 28 chains or 616 yards from the New station.

From the outset traffic seems to have been encouraging and at the half-yearly meeting of the company held in October 1887 the Chairman told the shareholders that:

> Traffic on the line had been greater than they anticipated. It had taken the North British Railway Company by surprise, and that Company found that they had made one of the best bargains on taking the railway over. The railway had been largely taken advantage of by visitors to the East of Fife, and that by another summer he had no doubt that it would be much more patronised.

## Cuttings from the Minute Books

Although the majority of the entries in the company's Minute Books deal with the perilous financial situation of the Anstruther & St Andrews Railway and continuing settlement of claims made against them, there is also some light thrown upon the everyday activities and concerns of this small rural line. Within a month of the opening there was correspondence with the North British regarding the great delays which were anticipated if the tablet system was not brought into immediate use. Complaints were being made that the new station at St Andrews was 'situated in a hole' and that a luggage hoist was needed to reach the platform. They reveal that the Board were considering the distribution of the profits from the bookstall and from the display of advertisements on the platform of the New station. The latter matter was resolved when the Minutes recorded that there was a suggestion that these sums 'in equity' should be equally divided between the two companies 'inasmuch as a greater proportion of the traffic coming into St Andrews does not arise on the local line'. Another early concern was the lack of any protection for passengers against the Siberian winds which haunted the western end of the island platform and a proposal, not followed up, was made for a draught screen to be erected. A lamp to light the Boarhills station approach road at a cost of 'about 23s. 0d.' was authorized, as was the lengthening of the Crail station potato loading ramp but proposals for reducing the ordinary fares on the line in order to develop the local passenger traffic and, separately, to issue cheap fares for students residing in the East Neuk but who required to travel to St Andrews to attend University classes came to naught. A claim brought by a local farmer for the loss of cattle caused by ingestion of white lead paint which the contractor had negligently left uncovered next to a field was settled for £75.

Traffic in the first few months was encouraging from the passenger point of view and disappointing for goods: 'The new line has seen great numbers using the train during the summer months to visit the east of Fife and the company were in no doubt that future summers would prove the same'. On the whole line there was only ever mention of one private siding, namely the Stravithie Quarry Siding, immediately to the west of Stravithie station, and which was built to serve a stone quarry. The Minutes for 1st February, 1887 record a resolution to proceed with the construction of a siding to serve this quarry and to defer for subsequent consideration the question of the allocation of the cost as between the proprietor and the company. In the Minutes of 8th October, 1889 it was recorded that the Company Secretary had made a settlement with Dr Cleghorn, one of the Directors who was also the owner of the quarry, in the sum of £187 0s. 9d. for the cost of the siding, and also of £180 payable to him for the value of the stone in the land acquired by the company. The siding was altered and extended in 1896 but went out of use some time before 1902, after which there is no further mention of it in the NBR register of sidings. There were two other applications for private sidings, including one for the Argyle Brewery, St Andrews, near to the St Andrews New station. This was proposed in 1886 and was costed out at £1,300. Mr Ireland, the proprietor of the brewery, proposed that the siding be constructed at the expense of the railway company although the Board made a counter-proposal that it should be constructed partly at his expense. Neither offer was accepted and on 17th September, 1886 the Minutes record that 'the proposed siding has been allowed to drop'.

Given the largely rural nature of the terrain served by the line it is perhaps not surprising that the only other private siding proposal was that mentioned in the Minutes of 6th April, 1896 under the heading 'Freestone Quarry at Nether Kenly - Application for a Siding':

Mr Dovey submitted an application on behalf of the University Court of St Andrews, mentioning that this quarry was about to be opened up and asking the Company to provide a siding westwards from Boarhills station contiguous to the farm road from the bridge over the Kenly to the highway leading from St Andrews to Crail by Bonnyton to the Anstruther & St Andrews Railway. The meeting instructed the Secretary to reply that the Company cannot undertake the construction of the proposed siding, facilities will be given for the proprietor of the quarry, subject to the Board of Trade and the approval of the North British Railway.

The siding was never built.

Other matters dealt with included the desire of the North British to have the water tank at Kingsbarns (where the supply was unreliable) moved to Boarhills, where a steam pump was to be installed to ensure that a correct volume of water was always maintained. In March 1888 authorization was sought of the NBR to erect cattle pens and loading banks at Crail, Kingsbarns and Stravithie stations, and this work was sanctioned. A curious touch was added by the affair of the Kingsbarns station master's house for in October 1892 it was reported that the company were seriously concerned by the state of it and that the Chairman had examined the same:

> ... and had found it quite inadequate for the requirements of the station-master. He had a large family, and they were inefficiently housed. There was a horrible cesspool lying about three feet off his bedroom window. Two station-masters had already died in the place, and the health of the present occupant was by no means good. They had a duty to perform in this respect, and he could assure them that it was done by proper economy.

The duty was duly complied with and in February 1894 the alterations to the station house were approved in the sum of £12 4s. 7d. One can only hope that the Kingsbarns station master, his wife and his nine children lived to a ripe old age. Seven months later the local sanitary inspectors condemned the water and sanitary arrangements at Mount Melville and Stravithie stations and, although the North British found the water supply at Stravithie 'thoroughly wholesome', it cost a further £5 1s. to assuage those troublesome officials.

### Crail Complains

A long standing grievance, expressed throughout the period of independence and afterwards, was the justified feeling of the inhabitants of Crail that they were being unfairly treated by the North British in that the summer express trains from the west terminated at Anstruther and that, in consequence, the town was being denied their fair share of the visitors which the other settlements further along the coast enjoyed. As far back as March 1889 Dovey, as Company Secretary, had been instructed to keep the North British under notice of the desirability of continuing on to Crail the present fast summer train from Edinburgh to Anstruther. The latter company replied, however, that alterations would be required at Crail to enable this to happen, namely the provision of a loop at an estimated cost of £1,100, a sum which the Anstruther & St Andrews company was not prepared to entertain. The *East of Fife Record* concluded, in an editorial of May 1889, that in relation to the Crail summer express trains:

The Assistant Secretary,
(Railway Department)

J. E. DOVEY.
CHARTERED ACCOUNTANT.    Board of Trade,

London, SW.

Edinburgh 2, Hill Street.
17 April 1890.

Sir

**4289**

ANSTRUTHER & ST ANDREWS RAILWAY COMPANY.

R. 844.

Referring to the favor of your circular letter of 5. Feb? enclosing Draft of proposed Order to be issued on this Line under the power conferred upon the Board of Trade by the Regulation of Railways Act 1889, I beg in regard to requirements marked (a.) and (b.) to state that my Directors understand that the Government Inspectors on the occasion of the Inspection of this Line ( from Anstruther to Boarhills in August 1883. and from Boarhills to St. Andrews in May 1887. ) reported to the Department that this Railway was fully equipped in the particulars specified, and with regard to requirements under (c.) I have to add that the Rolling Stock on this Company's Line is entirely provided by the North British Railway Company under a Working agreement scheduled to this Company's Act of 1880.

My Directors will be glad to hear that this letter is satisfactory to the Board, and I remain,

Sir,

Your obedient Servant,

John E. Dovey

Secretary & Treasurer.

---

*Above & right:* Correspondence between John Dovey and the Board of Trade relating to the operation of the line.

J. E. DOVEY.
CHARTERED ACCOUNTANT.

The Assistant Secretary.
(Railway Department).
Board of Trade
7. Whitehall Gardens, London S.W.
Edinburgh 2. Hill Street.
17. Nov. 1893.

ANSTRUTHER & St ANDREWS RAILWAY COMPANY.

I beg to acknowledge the receipt this morning of the Board's letter of 16. inst. (R.6426.).

In reply I have to state that this Company is worked by the North British Railway and that the require: :ments in the Order of date 14 November 1890 were duly submitted by me to the North British Company in order that any requirements under that Order which had not already been implemented might be given effect to. I had previously ascer: :tained from the Engineer of this Company that to the best of his belief the requirements of the Board of Trade had all been complied with so far as the structure of the Line is concerned.

I am forwarding your present communication to the General Manager of the North British Railway Company with a request that he will be so good as to communicate direct with you as regards the question of continuous Brakes and also that he will inform you that he has found our Line fully equipped in the other particulars covered by the Order.

I am, sir,
Your obedient Servant,
John Dovey.

Somehow or other we have not much faith that they will be successful. One reason for this is that they are proceeding in far too mealy-mouthed a manner for the North British officials to pay much attention to them ... The North British officials appear to have treated all the wishes of the Directors of the new railway in the past with contempt, and they know that they can afford to do this in the future as long as there is no opposition against them by land or sea.

The newspaper went on to allege that the only reason why the express had been extended to Elie and Anstruther in the previous season was that Galloway's steamer services had provided a rival to the railway and that the absence of a steamer to Crail meant no express train either, the want of which was responsible for there being no 'handsome marine hotel' in the burgh. The North British blamed the inadequate station facilities at Crail, the *Record* commenting that it was a wonder that the Board of Trade had passed them as suitable in the first place.

In December 1889 Provost Peattie of Crail attended an A&StAR Board meeting to discuss the matter of certain alterations being carried out at that station with a view to allowing the 5 pm express train from Edinburgh to Anstruther to be extended to Crail. The Directors proposed to send a plan of these alterations to the Board of Trade if they could find a way of surmounting the financial difficulty involved, the company's capital account 'being exhausted' – something of an understatement since, at that time, the company was some £4,500 in debt! Dovey then proposed:

That if the Provost of Crail and others who are specially interested in securing for Crail the traffic facilities which these alterations would allow are prepared to give their personal security to a special Bank Credit for the amount required [estimated at £5,000] he would be happy to reduce his salary by an amount sufficient to cover the interest on the said Bank Credit so as to secure that any increased traffic resulting from the improved facilities would be a clear gain to the Company's Revenue Account.

The Provost attempted to raise the necessary funds but by 12th April, 1890 had reported to the Board that he had not been able to do so. At the same meeting Dovey stated that he had corresponded with the North British regarding the extension of the summer train to Crail but that they had not seen their way to do it. Two weeks later Provost Peattie was again urging upon the Directors the great need for a fast train service to and from Crail and the introduction of cheap Saturday fares between the company's stations and Dundee and other centres of population in the summer months. The local press kept up the agitation and in June 1893 John Conacher, NBR General Manager, visited Crail; in the following season a Saturday afternoon express train to and from Crail *was* run, namely a 1.30 pm from Waverley which returned from Crail at 6.28 pm although local opinion was divided as to its use - from the operational point of view the train had to run beyond Crail to Kingsbarns so that the loop there could be used to enable the engine to run-round the carriages; this brought a small amount of summer holiday traffic to Kingsbarns. It was clear, however, that if there was to be any significant improvement in services to Crail then alterations would require to be carried out on the line and that the Anstruther & St Andrews Railway was not in a position to finance these without a substantial injection of capital, something which it clearly neither had nor could find a way of raising.

## So Near and Yet So Far

A complaint which was often repeated related to the apparent discouragement by the North British of through traffic over the Anstruther & St Andrews line both by an absence of trains and by perverse ticketing arrangements and poor connections at St Andrews. This caused one commentator to remark that 'To be so near and yet so far from St Andrews is tantalising'. John Purvis wrote to the local press that in relation to the refusal of the North British to allow passengers to re-book at St Andrews by the same train they were travelling by:

> The NBR Co., are, (in common with all other railways) entitled to refuse to do so - see para. vi, page 114 of their official timetables. The rule was not, however, generally acted on till quite recently, and till it was found that large number of passengers habitually travelled first class with third-class tickets, so much so, that one day, on the tickets being checked at Mount Melville station, upwards of 6s. was recovered from persons doing so, and consequently very stringent orders have since been sent out to the several stationmasters to try and check this nefarious practice, and your correspondent has consequently in common with many, to suffer for the misdoings of others.

A shareholder put the matter succinctly by allocating the blame to 'many persons of knavish proclivities from the East Neuk direction' who defrauded the company in this way and 'thus making the withdrawal of re-booking inevitable to the great disappointment and annoyance of honest folk – the innocent suffering for the guilty'.

Despite these misgivings a summer timetable of five trains each way between St Andrews and Anstruther was provided with the majority of these running on to Thornton and providing onward connections to Edinburgh and Glasgow with the usual running time over the section between St Andrews and Anstruther taking 40 minutes or so, an average start to stop speed of 25 mph with five intermediate stops. The winter timetable was sparser and one recurrent complaint was the absence of any southbound service in the evenings.

If that were not enough it was said that the third-class carriages on the line were draughty, decrepit and a disgrace although the Edinburgh *Evening News* claimed that those East Fifers who criticised their stock had obviously never travelled on the North Leith branch where the carriages were even worse! On 28th April 1890 the Board:

> …unanimously resolved to address a strong remonstrance to the North British against the further use of partially-partitioned draughty third-class carriages and to lodge a complaint of the frequent want of cleanliness in the condition of these carriages.

Attempts to encourage passenger traffic were seen by the Board to be hampered by the intransigence of the North British or by their refusal to provide a full range of cheap fares which might encourage day-trippers and other previously untapped sources of revenue. But the state of the line itself, and in particular of the absence of crossing loops on the long single-line sections, and the fact that revenue had to be shared between the North British and the Anstruther & St Andrews companies gave little incentive to the former to seriously address many of the issues raised.

Some attempts to provide additional services were not successful - an example being a Tuesdays-only Cupar to Leuchars connection put on to allow farmers from the East Neuk to attend Cupar market. This service, although 'much appreciated', managed to attract in the six weeks leading up to 27th July, 1889 a total of three, two, nine, four, one and eight passengers respectively joining at stations between Crail to Mount Melville. However, with the exception of Crail, the siting of the other stations on the Anstruther & St Andrews line might well have contributed to the lack of traffic. Indeed at the half-yearly meeting of the company held in April 1892 one of the shareholders, George Fortune, actually complained that:

> It was one of the biggest mistakes of the line from the first not to follow the sea line all the way from Anstruther to St Andrews. That had been one of the greatest blunders of the line. They would have had a great deal more traffic if the stations had been made closer to the villages.

### Fare and Unfair

George Fortune was not, however, the only critic of the line, for in the previous year the *Dundee Advertiser* had published the following letter from an anonymous writer:

A SUGGESTION TO THE ANSTRUTHER & ST ANDREWS RAILWAY COMPANY
This is one of the railway undertakings that came into existence a good few years ago with many captivating promises, but towards which the ordinary shareholders have ever since been looking in vain for any dividends. No doubt the preference shares have fared better. They have come in for some small attention, and are favoured with a dividend about equal to the moderate rate of interest which the Scotch Banks are at present paying to their happy depositors. But that is all. Now, why should this be? Here is a line of railway leading to some of the most picturesque and salubrious places in Scotland, yet very meagerly patronised by the travelling public generally or by the occasional holiday-seeker in particular. There are thousands in Dundee, for instance, who are unaware of the beauties both of land and sea which a trip on this line of railway affords, simply because there are no means taken to open up the line in a popular way to the working classes. The Company makes no concessions, but charge the statutory fare, and altogether seems regardless whether that line is patronised or not by the public. I would suggest, therefore, in view of the approaching season, when everyone is anxious to know of some new place to have a run to, that the Directors of the Anstruther & St Andrews Railway Company should bestir themselves to the extent of at least putting on a cheap train every Saturday afternoon, leaving Dundee at say 2.30, with a return fare of 1s. to all stations as far as Anstruther. The North British, of course, has to be consulted, but that Company ought to be prepared to make some sacrifice on behalf of the smaller line, which is indeed part of its own system and one of its own feeders. If such a suggestion as this were carried out it would have the effect of making this line popular. It would bring a good deal of trade to several of the small towns along the route, which in turn would add to the railway traffic, and in course of time the ordinary shareholders would be brought within measurable distance of some little return for their money. What is wanted is to have the line popularised, and that can only be done by inviting the great masses of the people to travel over it at a very low return fare. [However 'A.N.' was able to conclude on a more optimistic note] I was glad to observe while passing Mount Melville station the other morning that there seemed to be a considerable improvement in goods traffic at that station. Coal, lime, nitrate, moss litter, potatoes, turnips and sundry other goods were being laden or disladen, and altogether the aspect seemed a little cheery in that out-of-the-way station.

A contemporary report, published in the *East of Fife Record*, suggested that the shareholders of the company were very much in favour of the introduction of cheaper fares to all destinations on the line and that 'on the occasion of the half-yearly meetings, free passes should be granted to shareholders, male and female, so that they may appear at these meetings and let their views be known'.

### An Independent Decade

The Anstruther & St Andrews Railway remained independent of the North British until almost the end of the century, notwithstanding the fact that its services were operated by the North British and at both ends of the line it connected with that company. In the six months ending with 31st January, 1887 the traffic receipts (less passenger tax) for the section from Anstruther to Boarhills amounted to £1,115 4s. 6d. - the figures for the corresponding period in the following year, when the Boarhills to St Andrews section was opened, amounted to £2,668 15s. 10d. - in annual terms a rise of receipts from just under £250 per mile to £333 per mile. A dividend of 1½ per cent was declared, a return on capital which even the Chairman of the company admitted was small 'but yet it was a beginning'. Concerns were expressed that goods traffic was not as buoyant as had been hoped but that the passenger traffic was encouraging, and could be increased by the distribution of additional handbills and 'he noted that they had got a good deal of twopences from Mount Melville from people in the rural district coming to that station and going into St Andrews to make their purchases'.

In 1889 Dovey is recorded as having discussions with Mr Johnstone of Allanhill on the question of securing for the company more of the potato traffic in the district. Johnstone was of the view that if the railway could compete against the shipping rates to London by sea from local harbours, it ought to be possible to secure a place in the London markets as the potatoes from East Fife were 'better (more mealy) than the West of Scotland potatoes'. The Directors resolved that they would ascertain the views of local merchants and try to secure more traffic for the railway but in June of that year were informed by the North British that, in the words of John Walker, 'I am afraid it is hopeless to expect that we should prevent that being largely shipped at St Andrews and Crail, as the water freight is so low that the railway cannot successfully compete against it'. Notwithstanding this, the loading bank at Crail was extended in 1891 at a cost of £10, the company feeling that this expenditure was justified by an expected growth in the potato traffic.

The financial position of the company, however, never improved greatly and traffic receipts remained at the £4,500 to £5,000 per annum level, with dividends of 1 and 1½ per cent being declared for most of the time, with a dip caused by the effects of the 1891 railway strike. From 1893 onwards, however, receipts showed a slight increase and a 2 per cent dividend was given. In October 1892 the shareholders of the Anstruther & St Andrews passed a motion that the North British should be approached to ascertain what they might be prepared to offer for the purchase of their company, but the Directors on 12th December resolved to take no action, stating that the proposal was 'inimical to their interests'. At the same Board Meeting the matter of the junction at Allanhill,

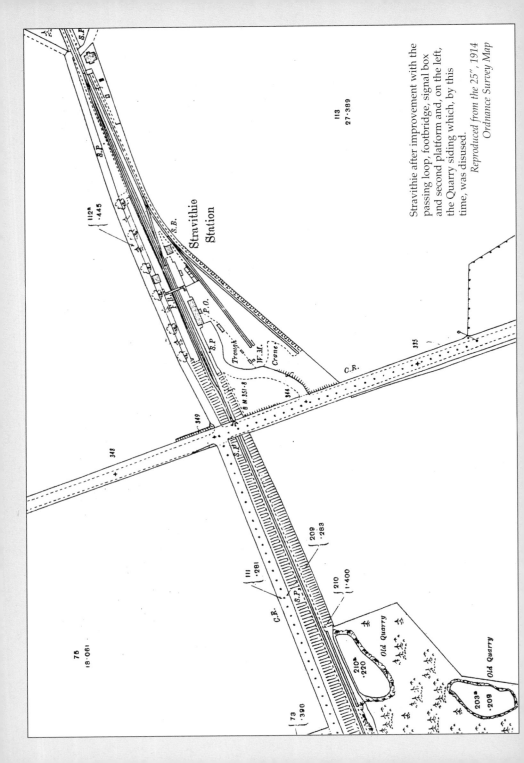

Stravithie after improvement with the passing loop, footbridge, signal box and second platform and, on the left, the Quarry siding which, by this time, was disused.

*Reproduced from the 25", 1914 Ordnance Survey Map*

close to Stravithie station, with the proposed East Fife Central Railway (EFCR) was considered. This independent company which in 1893 had acquired powers to build a network of standard gauge goods lines within the area bounded by the NBR main line and the East Fife coastal railway was a cause of some alarm to the Anstruther & St Andrews Board. The EFCR*, was to have a 'main line' starting from a junction close to Cameron Bridge on the Leven & East of Fife section and running for some 12 miles, 2 furlongs in length through Kennoway and Ceres to join the North British main line at Dairsie, between Cupar and Leuchars. A subsidiary line also 12 miles and 2 furlongs in length was to leave the main line at Montrave and run via Largoward and Lochty to join up with the Anstruther & St Andrews close to Stravithie. Two other connecting spur lines were also provided for. The main purpose of the East Fife Central was to tap the rich agricultural traffic of the area as well as to develop the potential of the coal deposits in the area but the promoters could not resist mischievously pointing out that the distance by rail from Leven and Dundee would be shortened by 10 miles and from Leven to St Andrews by eight. In the event the only part of the line to be constructed was the section from Cameron Bridge to Lochty, a remote farmstead some five miles north-west of Anstruther and four miles south of Stravithie - by no stretch of the imagination could Lochty be described as being near to St Andrews, let alone near to anywhere at all. By February 1893 a decision had been taken to petition against these proposals. On 2nd June the Anstruther & St Andrews company resolved to drop the opposition to the East Fife Central Bill subject to the North British granting the Anstruther & St Andrews an extension of the 1880 working agreement 'in perpetuity' in view of the possibility that the new line to Stravithie might prove detrimental to their interests. The potential threat of the East Fife Central faded into insignificance so far as the Anstruther & St Andrews company was concerned, and the opposition was later dropped but the question of the continuation of the working agreement with the Norh British became ever more pressing.

### A Signalman's Mistake

Almost exactly five months after the disaster at St Andrews Links,† a similar accident occurred at Anstruther (New), by far the busiest station between Leven and St Andrews. For many years the layout at the station had been a cause for concern, having still only a single platform and the passing loop insisted upon by the Board of Trade back at the opening of the line. Then, on 12th December, 1896, matters came to a head when an up passenger train from Thornton to Dundee, due to enter the loop, was inadvertently signalled to enter the platform line where it collided with an up train from Dundee which was waiting there. The considerable impact caused the destruction of the buffers on both locomotives with only slight damage to the stock but 10 passengers and the Anstruther station master were injured, resulting in successful claims against

---

* The full history of the company will appear in the last volume in this series, *The East of Fife Central Railway (The Lochty Branch)*.

† This accident involved the 8.05 pm Leuchars Junction to St Andrews train on Saturday 11th July, 1896 and is dealt with in *The St Andrews Railway*.

the NBR amounting to over £1,139 6s. 8d.* Ten days later Major Marindin visited the scene by special train, calling *en route* at Burntisland to inspect another accident site. In his report, submitted to the NBR in the following month, the Major found that the cause of the collision was due to the mistake of signalman William Fairbairn, who had been on duty for nine hours 'and frankly admitted that he alone was responsible for what had occurred'. However, the Major went on to remark that the accident, although due to Fairbairn's mistake, was the result of the improper use for passing trains at a station not laid out or signalled for that purpose, the loop being merely a goods siding with no facing point, no point locking appliances, no fixed signals for entering the loop and no second platform as is required at passing stations 'and if it be necessary to continue to cross trains at Anstruther, the station should be laid out properly'.

The *East of Fife Record* of 22nd January, 1897 commented that:

> The Railway Company have been aware of these grievous defaults for long. They have been pointed out to them over and over again, but nothing has been done to remedy them. Now, however, it will be expected that the improvement of the station should be at once taken up and carried through to prevent all possibility of an accident or collision in the future. If the Railway Company declines to do anything and allows things to go on as at present, a question in the House of Commons to the President of the Board of Trade, would have a good effect in having the improvements effected. For their own sake, the North British Company should see to it and provide the double platform accommodation required. They can get plenty of ground for the purpose on the north side of the line, and the summer traffic would be all the more easily managed in this way than by the methods employed for years.

It was, however, another three years before the matter was finally resolved.


### Towards an East Fife Monopoly

What, perhaps, was becoming increasingly obvious to all was that the Anstruther & St Andrews was a small local company which had a limited capital and no effective voice against the North British and that however much the company made efforts to increase its traffic it would continue to pay its shareholders a fairly miserable return on their capital. The 1880 working agreement between the Anstruther & St Andrews and the North British companies was extended to 1896 but the latter company was not inclined to extend the agreement further and by the end of 1893 the NBR Directors were investigating the possibilities of acquiring shares in the former at a cost of about £2 or so per share. In this they were frustrated because none were available at less than £7 each (the par value of these shares being £10). George Bruce, a solicitor in Leven with whom Conacher had been dealing, wrote to him on 5th March, 1894 in respect of acquiring the Railway Signalling Company's 45 Preference shares at £7 10s. each, but

> ...they won't sell them for less, and they give the reason that they believe the Company will eventually be absorbed by the North British Railway Coy and these shares will then be worth par. I fear several shareholders have got this notion into their heads, and I

---

* In a subsequent accident at Anstruther station on 3rd June, 1901 a 'slight collision' resulted in the NBR having to pay out £82 6s. by way of compensation.

understand that the rumour that your Company is in some way assisting the East Fife
Central Railway strengthens this notion.

The shares were never purchased but the era of independence was coming to
an end and although the North British agreed to two further extensions of the
working agreement, the first to 31st March, 1897 and the last to 31st May, 1897,
these were regarded as final and it was made clear that they would not extend
it beyond this time.

The reasons were clear in that the North British saw that it could benefit from
the increasing trade of the area if it had full control of the line and could make it
fit for the traffic which it envisaged would follow upon a general upgrading of its
facilities. In a letter dated 12th August, 1896 John Conacher stated to the
Anstruther & St Andrews Board that his Directors were of the view that it would
be better to enter into an agreement for the amalgamation of the companies rather
than accept the stock transfer arrangements which the smaller company had
already suggested to them. This met with a negative response and the request
that the working agreement be extended by a further five years. It was clear,
however, that the only real issue now remaining was the question of what the
shareholders would be receiving in return for the company surrendering its
independence. Negotiations continued throughout 1896 but the Directors of the
Anstruther & St Andrews, sensing the inevitable, eventually agreed terms with
the North British for the amalgamation of the two companies and on 22nd
February, 1897 a special meeting of the local company's shareholders was held to
ratify the proposed agreement which had been reached.

The shareholders gave their consent and on 15th July, 1897 the North British
Railway (General Powers) Act (60 & 61 Vict., cap. cxxvii ) passed into law. This
provided for the absorption of the Anstruther & St Andrews company by the
North British with effect from 1st August, 1897. The terms struck were that the
deferred ordinary shares held by the North British, amounting to £5,000 and
which had arisen from the building of St Andrews New station were cancelled
- in other words no value was to be attributed to them. The ordinary
shareholders of the Anstruther & St Andrews, who between them held £57,000
worth of shares, each of £10 par value, were given cash to the value of £3 10s.
0d. per share, that is to say that they received a total of £19,950 in cash
(excluding the call in arrears of £114 4s. 5d.) or a mere 35 per cent of the par
value of their original capital investment. The holders of the £55,000 worth of 5
per cent preference shares also fared badly, for they received in exchange for
each £10 nominal value 5 per cent preference share one £10 nominal value 3 per
cent NBR consolidated lien stock, which effectively meant a 40 per cent
reduction in the dividend returns which they could expect. Secretary Dovey
was given £500 compensation for loss of office and the free passes for himself
and the other Directors of the company were agreed to. The final meeting of the
Anstruther & St Andrews company was held in October 1897. One can only
imagine that the Directors and shareholders were left to contemplate the
mistakes which they had made when the route of the line was being chosen and
the fact that much of the money which they had so enthusiastically put up for
the venture was now, to all intents and purposes, lost.

Stravithie looking towards Crail at about the time of its closure to passengers in 1930. The loop and footbridge have already been removed  but the small waiting room and nameboard on the up platform have been left in place and the post office on the down platform is open for business.                                                           *D. Yuill Collection*

Stravithie looking south, 21st August, 1956. In evidence is the crossing keeper's house and white painted crossing hut erected when the signal box was closed in 1926 The line of trees in the background forms the distinctive windbreak at Easter Balrymonth.                    *A.G. Ellis*

Stravithie station and goods yard in 1963, looking towards St Andrews. *C.C. Thornburn*

Stravithie station buildings, 1962 - a typical Anstruther & St Andrews structure which survives to the present day. *Jim Hay*

Metro-Cammell dmus passing: Stravithie (*above*) a Dundee service on 5th September, 1964 - note the remains of the running-in board next to the bicycle. *Below:* the 2.42 pm Dundee to Edinburgh service (displaying 'Anstruther' on its rear blind) on 2nd September, 1965 - two days before the closure of the line.

*(Both) C.C. Thornburn*

The 2.42 pm Dundee to Edinburgh service breasts the summit at Stravithie and passes the site of the quarry siding, 2nd September, 1965.                *C.C. Thornburn*

Mount Melville station.                *Reproduced from the 25", 1914 Ordnance Survey Map*

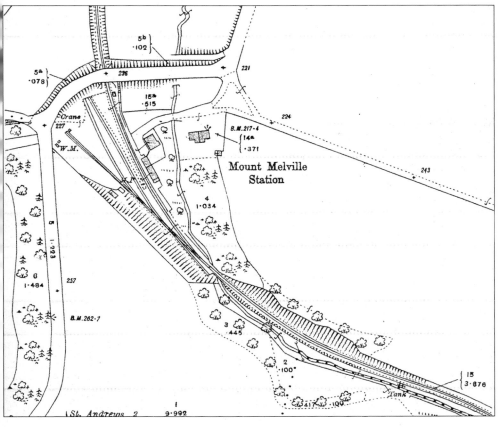

Mount Melville, 1904 - this George Fleming postcard was postmarked '15 Nov 1945' and appears not to have been sent by a railway enthusiast, thus demonstrating either the long-lasting appeal of the local postcard or, more probably, the shortages of the immediate post-war period!
*Alan Brotchie Collection*

The station master's house and main station buildings at Mount Melville in 1954, some 24 years after its closure to passengers.          *Nigel Dyckhoff*

View of Mount Melville from the goods yard, 16th May, 1949. *J.L.Stevenson*

Passing Mount Melville in 1954 - 'B1' class No. 61118 drifts through with a Leuchars to Thornton working. *Nigel Dyckhoff*

Mount Melville with the St Andrews University special of 25th October, 1960 showing (*above*) the view looking towards Crail and (*below*) looking toward St Andrews - note the mix of Gresley and Mark I stock on the train.

(*Both*) *Stations UK*

# Chapter Six

# Brave New World:
# The North British Railway 1897-1922

*'There is not in the whole of the North British system a more unsatisfactory service of trains than that which pertains to stations between Anstruther and St Andrews'*
Coastal Burgh Observer

## Divide and conquer

In April 1897 the North British, anticipating its imminent acquisition of the Anstruther & St Andrews Railway, had already turned its thoughts to the difficulties in working the line between those points. In particular the NBR realised that it was severely hampered by the constraints imposed by the fact that there was a sole passing loop on the whole 15-mile section, namely that provided at Kingsbarns station. In the words of David Deuchars, superintendent of the line:

> The increasing number of people who are resorting to Crail from the west during the summer months has led to numerous applications for an improved train service to and from Glasgow, which is absolutely necessary to afford if we are to cultivate the traffic.

At the same time it was recommended that tablet working be established over the whole line and, with this in mind, by the autumn the decision had been taken to provide a passing loop and second platform at Crail at an estimated cost of £2,292, this sum was later increased to £2,500 to include a short siding to hold four wagons at the south end of the up platform to allow vehicles to be attached to an up train 'without the present difficulties'. These works were approved by the Directors on 17th December, 1897. In October of the same year Deuchars also suggested that the line be divided at Stravithie and this resulted in the provision of a passing loop and second platform together with a new shelter and footbridge, a signal box and the lengthening of the existing platform at an estimated cost of £2,292 with a short siding to enable a local landowner, Major Sprott, to offload horses and carriages there. The proposal for this siding was later dropped and the estimate for the remaining works reduced to £2,036.

On 13th January, 1898 the Directors approved the amended plans and the land needed was acquired from its owner, The University of St Andrews, by the beginning of March. At Crail the passing loop, second platform with its small wooden waiting room and footbridge were all brought into use at 4 am on Saturday 7th May, 1898 as was the signal box, the latter being the work of James Forrester, a joiner from Anstruther Wester. A fortnight before the *East of Fife Record* had commented that 'dissatisfaction has generally been expressed at the small waiting room put up' but nevertheless on 19th May the company wrote to the Board of Trade requesting an inspection of both the Crail and Stravithie works to be carried out. The new loop, platform and signal box at Stravithie were opened with the passage of the 1.05 pm goods train from St Andrews

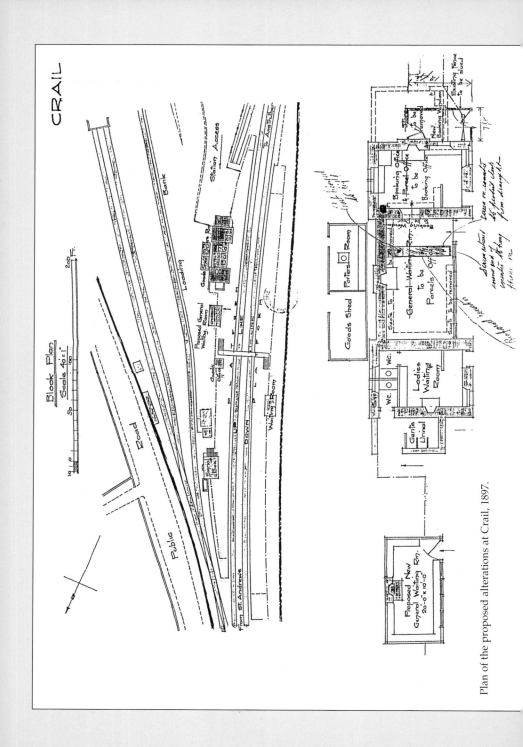

Plan of the proposed alterations at Crail, 1897.

Links to Thornton on Tuesday 31st May, 1898. Major Marindin carried out his inspection and on 2nd June retrospectively approved the alterations at Crail and Strathvithie, subject to certain minor rectifications which were then carried out.

In a detailed article which one suspects may have been little more than a press release from the NBR, the *Record* told its readers that,

> With the dividing of the long section between Anstruther and Kingsbarns - a distance of over seven miles - which took place on Saturday, the present method of working by train staff and ticket, combined with block telegraph, between these stations was abolished, and working by tablet substituted between Anstruther Junction and Anstruther Station, Anstruther Station and Crail and Crail and Kingsbarns. To railway people and the general public this will be a great boon, as it sometimes happens that, through accident, trains running out of course or other unforeseen circumstances, the staff is at the 'wrong' end, and as no driver is allowed to proceed without seeing it or having it in his possession, the distance between the staff sections has to be traversed on foot by an official, designated a 'redcap', with a staff to bring on the train. The tablet does away with all this, and provided that the line is clear there is always a tablet available at either station, kept in an electrically locked instrument, which it is impossible for the signalman to remove at the one end without the permission of the signalman at the other end. Crail having become a block telegraph station, it follows that trains can now cross at this rapidly-growing summer resort, which should enable the Railway Company to considerably add to their services of trains between Dundee, Edinburgh, Glasgow &c., particularly on Saturdays and holidays, as also in the early morning.

The effectiveness of this 'great boon', at least in its early days, was questionable as barely two months later the same paper was complaining that the train service to Anstruther and Crail had become 'completely disorganised' at the end of July with some specials running three to four hours late 'and there was a great deal of grumbling among the summer visitors especially at the long delay'.

Two further projects that would have benefited the Anstruther & St Andrews line were, however, put into abeyance, namely the NBR Board's 1898 proposals to double both the section of the Leven & East of Fife line from Thornton to Leven and the former St Andrews Railway branch from Leuchars; the former works were eventually carried out in 1909-1910 but the latter was not proceeded with at all.

### Anstruther Improved

What was, however, surprising was that the 'New' station at Anstruther, scene of the 1896 accident and the subsequent Board of Trade report, was left in its original unsafe state for so long. In January 1900 a Commons question put by Mr Dalziel, the Member for the Kirkcaldy Burghs, to the President of the Board of Trade as to whether the NBR were going to make the necessary alterations to the station layout. His reply was that the Directors had not, as yet, come to any decision. The *East of Fife Record* commented, in its issue of 2nd February, that:

# North British Railway Company.

M
No. 3178.

*Notice to Engine-drivers, Guards, Signalmen,*
*and others.*

## Altered Mode of Working between Kingsbarns and Anstruther, and division of the Section at Stravithie,

TO COME INTO FORCE ON

## TUESDAY, 31st MAY 1898.

Commencing with the 1-5 p.m. Goods Train from St Andrews' Links Station to Thornton on the date above-mentioned, the present mode of working by Train Staff and Ticket, combined with Block Telegraph System, will be discontinued, and working by Train Tablet No. 6 substituted, and thereafter all Trains (Up and Down) must be signalled in strict accordance with the Regulations for Working Trains over Single Lines by means of Train Tablet System (No. 6), as contained in the General Appendix (No. 27), pages 16-24 inclusive.

The Tablet Stations will be—

Kingsbarns and Stravithie.
Stravithie and St Andrews Station.

NOTE.—The Siding points at Boarhills on the Kingsbarns and Stravithie Section, the Quarry Siding and Mount Melville Station on the Stravithie and St Andrews Section will be secured by Tablet Locks (No. 6), and must be worked in accordance with the instructions contained in the Northern portion of the Appendix (27), page 9. Simultaneously with the foregoing the fixed Signals at these places will be removed.

Inspector Hogg will attend and see the foregoing brought into use.

## Alteration of Hours of Switching at the undernoted Signal-box.

### (Amended Notice.)

Commencing on SUNDAY, 5TH JUNE 1898, and until further notice, the undernoted Block Telegraph Signal-box will be switched "Out of Circuit" at the times given below.

The Regulations for Switching, as contained in the current Appendix (No. 27) to the Working Time Tables, page 14, must be strictly adhered to.

| NAME OF SIGNAL-BOX. | WEEK-DAYS. | | SUNDAYS. | |
|---|---|---|---|---|
| | From | To | From | To |
| London Road Junction | 1-0 a.m. | 5-0 a.m. | 1-0 a.m. <br> 8-15 a.m. <br> 2-5 p.m. <br> 9-20 p.m. | 7-0 a.m. <br> 12-45 p.m. <br> 4-30 p.m. <br> 5-0 a.m. Mon. |

EDINBURGH, 27*th May* 1898.     (5-C)

J. CONACHER,
**General Manager.**

The North British Railway Company will now have to give consideration to the question of improving Anstruther Station … The President of the Board of Trade expressed regret that the Company had not even considered the recommendations [of January 1897] and while he admitted that he had no power to compel the alterations to be made, he stated that he was in communication with the Company on the subject. It is to be earnestly hoped that the president will publish the correspondence when completed, and let the public in the East of Fife know what reasons the Company have given for their refusal to provide a safe station and proper accommodation at Anstruther. They apparently can afford to build a passing station at Stravithie where we question if there is an average of 12 passengers a week, and so far as the public can see, the splendid accommodation there, which is seldom if ever required, might, with a great deal more advantage to the Company and the public, have been made at Anstruther. The Company have made, and are still making a very heavy profit out of Anstruther at present by the winter herring fishing, and the community deserves some consideration at their hands.

The North British reacted to this criticism and by June their Works Committee had authorized schemes for both the station alterations at a cost of some £4,071 and the construction of an access road between the Old and New stations at a cost of £2,150 - the latter having been requested by local traders and farmers. The station alteration plans consisted of the doubling of the line between Anstruther Junction and the east end of the New station, the provision of a second platform to the north of the present platform (which was to be lengthened by 100 feet) together with a footbridge linking the two platforms and an extensive resignalling scheme between the Junction and New station. This did not, apparently, satisfy local feelings and the *Record* opined that the NBR should replace the original Anstruther & St Andrews station with a completely new station with an island platform and direct road access.

The convenience and comfort of the public and the officials are not factors which weigh much with the Railway Company in providing stations in the east of Fife, at least apart from Elie, and it is now rumoured that a small shed* is to be erected on the new platform at Anstruther to do duty as a shelter for a very few passengers. The passengers are to reach the platform by an overhead bridge, and heavy luggage and goods are to be lugged from one platform to the other as occasion may demand. Why should the Railway Company grudge a little extra expense to make improvements and alterations which would be a credit to them as well as of great advantage to the public.

The company was not moved and, after some deliberation, provided a bracket footbridge on the Dreel Burn viaduct to enable people to access the passenger station better but the cart road was never constructed. The waiting room building on the new down passenger platform was a substantial structure (as opposed to the 'small sheds' at St Monance and Stravithie) and attracted no further adverse comment. Other improvements, including the installation of a new locomotive turntable, were made at the Old (goods) station in order to improve its efficacy.†

---

\* This was a reference to the pretty, but somewhat basic, waiting rooms provided by the NBR on the new platforms at St Monance and Stravithie.

† The Old station improvements are dealt with in *The Leven & East of Fife Railway*.

*New for Old*

As the result of the apparent activities of an anonymous wilful fire raiser in the St Andrews area, the city found itself without either a passenger or a goods station in the summer of 1901.* The first to go was the original St Andrews Railway Links goods station, when, at about 7 pm on the evening of Saturday 29th June, smoke was detected coming from the north end of the former trainshed. By 10 pm the fire was out, but the shed and offices and the entire records of the goods depot had all been destroyed and damage estimated at £300 sustained. Train services were severely disrupted and eventually a new brick-built structure appeared in place of the burnt-out trainshed. But, within a week of the fire at St Andrews Links, much worse was to follow. On the night of Wednesday 3rd July the wooden buildings of the Anstruther & St Andrews station at St Andrews (New), which had only been in existence for some 14 years, were ablaze and damage estimated at £2,000 was caused by the time that the town's fire brigade could extinguish the fire. Of the original buildings only the footbridge, bookstall, gentlemen's lavatory and signal box could be saved and the entire remainder of the island platform's buildings were lost. The Town Council were quick to petition the North British not merely to rebuild the gutted structures but instead to provide a more lavish and fitting station for a place of such importance. The NBR, however, having costed the Council's proposals was quick to point out that the cost of such provision would be some £16,382, part of which was due to the heavy and expensive civil engineering works which would have to be undertaken including the widening of the cutting and the building of new retaining walls. Instead the company proposed that there should be a like for like replacement of the lost buildings. Not only would this only cost some £3,800 but that this sum would in any case be met by the fire insurers and thus would cost the company nothing. The Council persisted in their demands but the North British got its own way and informed the Board of Trade, to whom the Town Council had reported the matter, that a temporary structure had been provided and that it had accepted a tender for a straightforward rebuilding. The new 'new' station was eventually completed in May 1903 and the only concession to improvement was the fact that a mechanical luggage hoist had now been provided in order that staff could better cope with the sometimes heavy demands for passengers trunks and cases, particularly at the beginning and end of school and university terms. In 1906 a second staircase to the platform was provided but, despite further proposals to replace what was still seen locally as an inadequate station, the 1903 rebuilt structure soldiered on until its eventual complete closure in 1969.

*Guests and Gripes*

The combined Anstruther & St Andrews and Leven & East of Fife line was entirely single track and, especially during the holiday season, the 40 mile-long route was unable to cope with the demands that traffic was increasingly placing upon it. A start to improving the facilities had already been made at Crail and similar works were carried out at Elie and St Monance while the line from

---

* For a fuller account of the destruction and rebuilding of the New station see *The St Andrews Railway*.

Thornton to Leven was doubled throughout in 1910 and a new passing loop at what was to be known as Kilconquhar West was put in two years later.

At Crail traffic had increased to such a level that the *East Fife Record* commented that:

> before the railway was introduced, Crail was just as quiet as Peebles or the Grave, but it was now just like Edinburgh. Arrivals and departures of trains at the beginning of July and August each year with passengers and luggage are the despair of omnibus drivers, while obliging shop-keepers carry on a roaring trade as compared with coaching days.

These words were echoed by Stewart Dick in *The Pageant of the Forth* when he remarked that 'Before the railway came to Crail, a few years ago, it was very much out of the world' before commenting on the present. An updated edition of Jackson's *Guide to Crail*, while making similar remarks as to Crail in pre-railway days, went on to remark that:

> All that has been changed, however, since the railway has superseded the immemorial mode of conveyance. Formerly, our largest contingent of visitors came from Edinburgh and neighbourhood; now large numbers of our friends who bring summer with them are from Glasgow and the west of Scotland, preferring as they do the drier and more bracing climate of the East Neuk to the humid and relaxing climate of the West Coast. But it would be idle to specify where our visitors mostly hail from ... as they now come from all parts of Scotland, while England too is well represented every summer, increasingly so in recent years.

Although there were still complaints as to the inadequacies of the train service a more immediate matter at the station was the absence of a place in which the holidaymaker's not inconsiderable amounts of luggage could be stored and the inconvenience caused thereby. Accordingly the North British resolved in 1904 to build a new luggage room at the entrance to Crail station; this was completed in June of that year.

One possible innovation on the Anstruther & St Andrews line that was considered by the NBR, but ultimately not proceeded with, was the introduction of either push-pull 'motor' trains or even self-contained steam railmotors, providing local shuttle services between Leven and Anstruther and Anstruther and St Andrews. The idea may well have come from criticism expressed locally that services over the coast line were slow and irregular and that they failed to serve local communities properly. By way of example, a series of reports in the summer of 1906 suggested that improvements to local roads and the emergence of the motor bus could benefit locals and visitors alike and that 'a motor car service around the Fife coast, say from Kirkcaldy to St Andrews ... would be a great success and convenience'. Other railway companies flirted with cheap to run short trains or railmotors which would stop at additional 'haltes' which could consist of little more than a nameboard or short platform. Another item reported in the *Record* in the same year contained the information that 'the NBR are building some steam cars which are to be tried experimentally on the East of Fife Railway'. The NBR immediately denied the rumour and seems ultimately to have rejected such ideas for the East Neuk - a more frequent passenger service between Crail and St Andrews might well have been of use to the public but the fact that the small handful of trains that did run were hardly filled to capacity did not suggest that there was an untapped market. The sparse and widely dispersed rural population of the district and the fact that all of the local villages with one exception were already served by stations did not suggest that there was much scope for any 'haltes' in the district. The one exception was Kilrenny, a mile from Anstruther but close to the line, but with a tiny and still declining population this small inland village would be unlikely to contribute much by way of revenue and, situated as it was amidst undulating gradients, might well have added to the operating difficulties on that section of the line.

Although the North British might have liked to continue on its path of improvements to local train services, its often perilous finances sometimes dictated otherwise and in 1908, as part of an economy drive throughout the system, several services in the area were retimed or withdrawn. This had a knock-on effect when connections at Anstruther between trains over the Leven & East of Fife and those which had come over the Anstruther & St Andrews sections deteriorated to the extent that Sir Ralph Anstruther of Balcaskie wrote to the North British stating that:

> I am sorry to see that the already dilatory service to the East of Fife is to be more tardy. To those who know the circumstances it must appear unnecessary to prolong the journey to Anstruther by more than quarter of an hour both at 1.50 and 4.25. Even if it is necessary to reduce the number of trains, it seems bad policy to allow the efficiency of the service to deteriorate.

### The Great Blizzard

The closing days of 1906 were well remembered in East Fife for the great storm that swept across the land with such force on Boxing Day that by the evening the whole area was six inches deep in snow and the last trains of the day were severely disrupted. That night it continued to snow heavily and by morning the telegraph wires were down, a goods shed at Anstruther station had collapsed and the roads were blocked. Trains struggled through the worsening conditions but the 5 pm from Edinburgh could travel no further than St Monance while the 5.40 pm from Dundee became embedded in a snow drift at Stravithie, with its hapless 20 or so passengers 'housed in the booking office of the station, and with a roaring fire, made as comfortable as circumstances permitted'. Since the station master there had not been expecting guests, there was a shortage of food although the division of such food and tobacco as there was did take place. The passengers included a newly-married couple and their friends who were expecting to attend a supper in their honour at Cellardyke Town Hall 'but though the feast was spread it had to be partaken of and the rejoicings carried through without the principals'. The gale reached its climax between midnight and 1 am, completely cutting Stravithie off from the outside world, the station house disappearing beneath a mound of snow in the cutting. A snow plough and gang of men were sent out to rescue the passengers and dig out the train; they managed the first task but only succeeded in derailing the train.* An attempt was made to get the passengers to Crail but in the afternoon they were taken by horse brake back to St Andrews to resume their broken journey home, arriving at Cellardyke some 24 hours late after travelling via Leuchars, Thornton and Leven. It was three days before trains were running again throughout the area and still several days later when all local roads were open again. A similar, but lesser, blizzard occurred almost exactly two years later when the early train from Dundee was snowed up at Stravithie and another train was stuck in drifts between Guardbridge and St Andrews; once again the line ended up by being closed for another couple of days.

## A Death in Kilrenny

Fatal accidents on the Anstruther & St Andrews line were, fortunately, rare but on the morning of 28th April, 1910 an accident occurred at the overbridge which carried the Kilrenny Common to Muiredge footpath across the section of the line between Anstruther and Crail near to Innergellie Wood. On that day Henry Moyes, aged 29, was the driver of the 7.55 am passenger train from Anstruther to Dundee. A few minutes after the train had left Anstruther, driver Moyes climbed on to the top of the tender for reasons which were not entirely clear and was struck by the bridge with such force that he was killed. The Board of Trade accident report concludes that:

> The accident was due to a breach of a special instruction which warns drivers and firemen against leaving the footplate of an engine in motion. Moyes must have been aware of the instruction, for his signature was produced at the inquiry to show that he had read the circular in which the order was issued.

Henry Moyes has, apparently, not been forgotten for even now on, or close to, the anniversary of his death a bunch of cut flowers has regularly been placed on the parapet of the bridge.

## The Coast Expressed

In 1911, as part of a programme of introducing fast (in a relative sense) named express trains, the North British introduced a through train from Glasgow to Crail via Anstruther, leaving the city on a Friday evening with the return working leaving Crail on a Monday morning. This train, bearing a headboard which proclaimed it to be 'The Fifeshire Coast Express' ran for the summer season only but was revived again with effect from 1st July, 1912 as a daily train leaving Glasgow Queen Street on Mondays to Fridays at 4 pm and, running via Winchburgh and Kirkcaldy, called at all principal stations on the Fife coast line, before reaching Crail at 6.30 pm.† There was no equivalent Saturday service, the train being designed largely to cater for the need of businessmen travelling daily to and from their places of work in Glasgow while their families were enjoying the delights of the East Fife coast. The train ran during each summer season until 1914 when it was withdrawn as a wartime economy measure.

---

* Several hours later, the same snow contributed to the appalling collision at Elliot Junction, in which 22 persons died.
† A similar named train, 'The Lothian Coast Express', operated on the southern shore of the Forth - see *The North Berwick and Gullane Branch Lines* (Oakwood Press).

# NORTH BRITISH RAILWAY.

## NEW EXPRESS
## MORNING AND EVENING TRAINS

BETWEEN

# DUNDEE
### (TAY BRIDGE)

AND

# EAST OF FIFE RESORTS.

| | | a.m. | | | | p.m. |
|---|---|---|---|---|---|---|
| ANSTRUTHER ... leave | | 8 22 | DUNDEE (Tay Bridge) leave | | 5 | 0 |
| CRAIL ... ... „ | | 8 33 | LEUCHARS ... arrive | | 5 | 15 |
| KINGSBARNS ... „ | | 8 41 | ST ANDREWS... „ | | 5 | 28 |
| STRAVITHIE ... „ | | 8 49 | STRAVITHIE .. „ | | 5 | 38 |
| ST ANDREWS... „ | | 9 0 | KINGSBARNS ... „ | | 5 | 46 |
| GUARDBRIDGE „ | | 9 9 | CRAIL ... ... „ | | 5 | 55 |
| LEUCHARS ... „ | | 9 15 | ANSTRUTHER ... „ | | 6 | 5 |
| DUNDEE (Tay Bridge) arrive | | 9 30 | | | | |

## REDUCED FORTNIGHTLY SEASON TICKET RATES.

**REDUCED FORTNIGHTLY SEASON TICKET RATES** will come into operation from DUNDEE (Tay Bridge and Esplanade Stations) on 1st JULY, as under :—

| | 1st Class. | 3rd Class. | | | 1st Class. | 3rd Class. |
|---|---|---|---|---|---|---|
| | s. D. | s. D. | | | s. D. | s. D. |
| LEVEN ... ... | 23 6 | 16 9 | | ANSTRUTHER ... ... | 20 9 | 14 6 |
| LUNDIN LINKS ... | 23 6 | 16 9 | Via Crail or via Thornton. | CRAIL ... ... | 18 9 | 12 6 |
| LARGO ... ... | 23 6 | 16 9 | | ABERDOUR ... ... | 24 6 | 18 3 |
| ELIE ... ... | 23 6 | 16 9 | | BURNTISLAND ... ... | 23 0 | 17 0 |
| | | | | KINGHORN ... ... | 23 0 | 17 0 |

Five per cent. additional is charged on the First Class Rates for Government Duty.

*For full particulars of Train Service see pages 16-23 and 88-91.*

*North British Curiosities*

The everyday activities on the line between Anstruther and Leuchars were reported, on a somewhat hit and miss basis, by the local press but they combine to give the flavour of what it was like to be a traveller on this far-flung part of the North British system. One such report, which appeared in the *East of Fife Record* of 5th October, 1906:

On Monday night the passengers in a first-class compartment of a train leaving Dundee at 5.45pm for Anstruther had a rather alarming experience. Just after Boarhills the oil-lamp exploded breaking the glass into fragments and scattering the contents all over the carriage. The passengers were naturally much alarmed, but fortunately none were in the least hurt.

Although there were no major catastrophes on the line at this time, one all-too-common accident of its time was reported in the *Record* of 22nd December, 1910:

An unfortunate accident occurred at St Andrews on Friday. A cart laden with potatoes, and drawn by two horses, belonging to Mr Andrew Clark, farmer, Auld Barns, was being driven across the railway line at the south toll between Mount Melville and St Andrews, the two men in charge owing to the mist failed to observe the approach of a train. The train dashed into the horses, one of which was dragged for 12 yards along the line, and was killed on the spot. The other horse was so badly inured that it died within a few minutes. No damage was done to the engine, and the men in charge of the horses escaped unhurt. The horses were valued at £30.

Another item which catches the flavour of its time appeared in the *Fifeshire Journal* of 9th March, 1871 under the heading of 'Narrow escape of the Fife Fox Hounds'.

On Friday, while the pack were out hunting and running on the scent on that portion of the line of rails between Seafield and Guardbridge, the train came dashing up and had it not been for the promptitude with which the engine-driver pulled up, the probability is that a large number of the pack would have been run over and killed.

Passengers famous and infamous, ordinary and special, have all travelled on the trains that once served St Andrews and although many paid their fares, albeit with reluctance, others did not. In the *East Fife Record* of 19th October, 1916 the following appeared:

A sequel to St Andrews market was evidenced at Cupar Sheriff Court last week when John Bell, farmer Randerston, Kingsbarns, was charged with having on 2nd October, at Kingsbarns Railway Station, refused to produce his passenger ticket on demand. He admitted the offence, stating that he had meant it as a joke. The prosecutor (J.L. Anderson) stated that this occurred after the market at St Andrews and that some liquor had been going. The accused afterwards expressed his regret at what had occurred, but the N.B. railway company wished it to be brought to court as a warning. Sheriff Armour-Hannay said that 'the Company, being short-handed, are not disposed to take a joke of that sort'. A fine of 10s., with 20s. of expenses, was imposed.

*A War to End all Wars*

On 4th August, 1914 war was declared against Germany and the North British immediately came under government control. Holiday traffic was curtailed but Crail became something of a military centre for officers on leave and its hotels and boarding-houses prospered, although in 1915 the Balcomie Golf Club was in severe financial difficulties apparently as a consequence of so many of its members being away on active service. In the same year the Links Hotel was closed down, due to the unfortunate fact that the German proprietor of the latter had been interned as an enemy alien. In the March 1916 timetable certain passenger train services were curtailed, and these included the first train of the day from Dundee to Crail, and the afternoon Edinburgh to Crail service, which was cut short at Anstruther. After some lobbying by the inhabitants of Crail and on behalf of the pupils of the Waid Academy* who lived in Crail and who used the service to return home, a reply from the General Manager of the North British was received to the effect that the service was the best which the company could provide with the resources presently at their command. But the North British relented and in May announced that:

> With a view to meet so far as possible the requirements of summer visitors to Crail, the Directors, unless some unforeseen circumstance should arise in the interval that would render this impractical, will adopt an increased service during the summer months, when it is anticipated that the demand for goods and mineral traffic will not be so heavy as these are at present.

This restoration took place from 1st June and it was said that the avoidance of 'the pleasure [*sic*] of a four-mile tramp' was 'greatly appreciated by some of the Waid Academy pupils, especially when the weather is in one of its uncongenial moods, as it is so often in these parts'. By October these concessions had been largely withdrawn and the *Coastal Burghs Observer* commented that, once again,

> …with the exception of a few isolated places in the West Highlands, it is only fair to say that there is not in the whole of the North British system a more unsatisfactory service of trains than that which pertains to stations between Anstruther and St Andrews.

The Whitsuntide public holiday of 1916 was cancelled by the Government so that it would not detract from the great offensive on the Western Front and this was followed by cancellation of the August bank holiday. The *Observer* commented that 'the time for holidays will come later' but that 'Crail is full of expectation that, notwithstanding the embargo as to holidays, August will prove to be a record month for visitors'. It was later recorded that all of the coast towns appeared to have enjoyed a late surge in numbers of visitors arriving by train despite the absence of any official holiday. But the autumn holiday was disappointing 'in striking contrast to what it used to be on such occasions previous to the war'.

---

* The secondary school for the district conveniently situated next to Anstruther station, the Waid Academy drew (and continues to draw) pupils from over a wide area due to its excellent reputation.

## Closed for the Duration

On 1st January, 1917 the most stringent measures yet were put into effect by the Railway Executive Committee. Passenger fares throughout Britain were raised by a uniform 50 per cent in order to combat galloping inflation with striking downturns in the number of tickets issued at local stations during that year, especially as tourist and other discounted fares had already been abolished in 1915 - one only has to look at the 25 per cent fall in passenger numbers at Crail in 1917 to realise how this increase dampened down demand. In order to prepare for a massive push on the Western Front and to release men, coal and locomotives for France, other measures were also put into effect. These included the closure for the duration, under the auspices of the Board of Trade, of some 400 stations throughout the country, including some 51 on the North British system. Five Fife closures were announced in the national press on 22nd December, 1916 and these including, on the coastal line, Mount Melville, Boarhills and, somewhat surprisingly, Pittenweem.*

The closure of Mount Melville and Boarhills to all traffic was effective from New Year's Day 1917 and although the two stations between them handled less than 25 passengers per week and were little more than wayside halts they were nevertheless busier than the intermediate station at Stravithie. However Stravithie was a crossing point and block post and, since staff would still be required there in any event, it remained open - to have closed it would have left too long a stretch of line to be operated as one section. Potential passengers for Mount Melville and Boarhills were now faced with a long walk along unlit country roads to and from St Andrews or Stravithie unless they could rely on the kindness of others to give them a lift in passing vans, horse-traps or even motor cars, although this latter form of transport was still rare and its fuel difficult to obtain in wartime conditions. Goods traffic was, however, another matter and, given the German U-boat campaign on the high seas, the Government were anxious to encourage local farmers to grow as much food as they could. Accordingly Mount Melville and Boarhills were partially re-opened to goods traffic on 21st March, 1917; the nature of this re-opening being that on three days a week only full wagon load traffic was dealt with on the condition that the loading and unloading of the wagons had to be carried out by the consignees and consignors themselves with no assistance from railway staff. The paperwork and supervision of this traffic was dealt with by the Stravithie staff in the case of Mount Melville station and by the Kingsbarns staff in the case of Boarhills.

All of the local stations between St Andrews and Anstruther handled an increased amount of agricultural traffic, largely as a result of the Government's intention to overcome the German U-boat blockade of allied shipping which, largely successfully, prevented Britain from receiving its accustomed import of foodstuffs from the Empire and elsewhere. Another item in short supply was timber given that the usual supply of pit props and softwood from Scandinavia was not getting through due to submarine raiders. Many local woodlands were cut down to help the war effort - one example was that of the Airdrie Woods, three miles west of Crail, timber from which was brought to the station goods yard there by horse-drawn lorries, on which the tree trunks were suspended from an inverted U-frame mounted on the back of the lorry.

* The closure of Pittenweem (dealt with in the companion volume *The Leven & East of Fife Railway*) was met with loud and continued local protests but the closure of Mount Melville and Boarhills seems to have attracted little interest; the two other Fife stations temporarily closed on that day were Halbeath and Sinclairtown.

# North British Railway Company.

CHIEF GOODS MANAGER'S OFFICE,

*GLASGOW, 8th January, 1917.*

CIRCULAR No. L. 332/2,104.

To Agents and others concerned.

## Closing of certain Goods Stations and Sidings on the North British, Caledonian, and Glasgow and South Western Railways, as from 1st January, 1917.

With reference to General Manager's Circular M. 5252, dated 28th December, 1916 ; until further notice, the undermentioned Goods Stations and Sidings, except as otherwise indicated, will be closed for Goods, Mineral, and Live Stock traffic.

For your guidance, the names of the Stations to which traffic may be forwarded in lieu of the places closed are given herein, but, of course, where one or more Stations are named, it will be for the Traders to decide at which Station delivery is to be taken, and to consign the traffic accordingly.

### 1. NORTH BRITISH GOODS STATIONS AND SIDINGS.

| (1)<br>Stations or Sidings closed except as otherwise indicated. | (2)<br>Alternative Stations to or from which traffic may be consigned. | (3)<br>Stations to deal with traffic in full loads as indicated by Note (b), also traffic with Private Sidings hitherto under Stations closed. |
| --- | --- | --- |
| *Bargeddie, ... ... | Easterhouse, ... ... ... ... | Easterhouse. |
| †Boarhills, ... ... ... | Kingsbarns or Stravithie. | |
| *Campsie Glen, ... ... | Lennoxtown or Strathblane, ... ... | Lennoxtown. |
| ‡Carntyne Sidings,... ... | Parkhead or Shettleston, ... ... | Parkhead. |
| †Clackmannan Road, ... | Clackmannan and Kennet, ... ... | Alloa. |
| *Gilmerton, ... ... | Millerhill, Dalkeith, or Loanhead, ... | Millerhill. |
| *Halbeath, ... ... | Dunfermline (Upper) or Crossgates, ... | Townhill Junction. |
| †Kingskettle, ... ... | Ladybank or Falkland Road, ... | Ladybank. |
| †Mount Melville, ... ... | St. Andrews or Stravithie. | |
| †Mount Vernon, ... ... | Shettleston, Broomhouse, or Mount Vernon (Cal.), | Shettleston. |
| †Pittenweem, ... ... | Anstruther or St. Monans. | |
| †Port Carlisle, ... ... | Drumburgh or Bowness (Cal.). | |
| *Possilpark, ... ... | ... ... ... ... ... | Saracen. |
| *Rosslynlee, ... ... | Rosslyn Castle, ... ... ... ... | Rosslyn Castle. |
| †Sauchie, ... ... ... | Alloa or Alva, ... ... ... ... | Alloa. |
| †Saughton, ... ... ... | Corstorphine or Gogar. | |
| †Trinity and Newhaven, ... | Granton. | |
| †West Wemyss, ... ... | Thornton or Wemyss Castle. | |

NOTES :—

    (a) The Stations indicated thus † are entirely closed for Goods Train traffic.

    (b) The Stations indicated thus * are to be treated as Sidings under charge of the Stations mentioned in column 3 so far as traffic in full wagon loads is concerned, provided Traders undertake all labour, &c., services on the traffic at their own risk and expense.

    (c) The Sidings indicated thus ‡ remain open for Mineral and Station to Station traffic only in full wagon loads.

## Wings Over Crail

By the second year of the war great strides had been made in the development of what was described in *The Fringes of Fife* as the 'most portentious of all man's recent inventions, the aeroplane' and although it was seen principally as an adjunct of the Royal Navy it was already beginning to come into its own as a war machine. Locally two level sites close to the sea were chosen as suitable places upon which aerodromes with grass runways and other facilities could be constructed, namely Leuchars where there was already in existence a somewhat primitive facilities for flying machines and Crail, where in 1916 a naval air station for the Royal Naval Air Service was proposed on open farmland a little to the south of Balcomie and lying roughly half-way between the village and Fife Ness.

The contractor chosen, on this contract, for the works was the large civil engineering firm of John Laing & Sons, who employed some 300 skilled workmen and a much greater number of labourers, with over 100 horse-drawn carts being used to haul the lighter materials. The station at Crail was used as the delivery point for bulk raw materials such as cement, bricks, timber, steel girders and plant and although there was no temporary contractor's line laid (the Balcomie road being already made up) heavy materials were conveyed between the station and construction site by two large steam lorries, augmented by petrol-driven vehicles where necessary. A special workmen's train (with a bus connection) was run for the conveyance of Laing's workmen during the construction period, leaving Thornton Junction at 5.15 am, calling at all stations with the exception of the closed Pittenweem, before arriving at Crail at 6.20 am. The return journey left Crail at 6.30 pm, again calling to set down at all stations excepting Pittenweem and arrived back at Thornton at 7.33 pm - a clear indication that during wartime, a 12-hour shift for working men was both necessary and patriotic. This additional service seems to have been well-used while it lasted and in particular Anstruther was a favoured town for the workers to reside in, giving it a lively air which, given the absence of holidaymakers, was greatly appreciated. The effect on passenger figures at Crail was marked - from a pre-war average of some 21,000 booked passengers the numbers leapt up to 99,500 in 1918 and 36,700 in 1919, with passenger revenue reaching a peak in the former year. Merchandise and mineral traffic in 1918 showed a three-fold increase and both the tonnage of coal and number of livestock handled at Crail almost doubled in that year. Even though the boost was short-lived the total revenue at Crail for 1918 was almost £9,500 compared to a pre-war average of a little over £2,000. The aerodrome was opened by the newly-formed Royal Air Force (the successor to the Flying Corps) in July 1918 as a training depot station using a variety of aircraft principally for fighter reconnaissance. In the following month the American 120th Aero Squadron was stationed there - the aircraft were brought to Crail on low-loader wagons and then towed by a powerful tractor unit from the goods yard to the airfield. When the war ended on 11th November both the airfield and the workmen's train serving it were still in operation and from March to June 1919, 104 Squadron of the RAF was based here.

### Normal Service Resumed

In the immediate aftermath of war the railways of East Fife attempted to return to normal. As from 1st February, 1919 the stations at Pittenweem, Mount Melville and Boarhills were re-opened to passenger and goods traffic and, although the additional wartime traffic on the line had disappeared (with the exception of Leuchars Junction, mentioned above), ordinary passengers returned in great numbers. Indeed the first two or three years of peace saw almost all local stations enjoy record numbers of passengers as holidaymakers and locals returned to the trains with a vengeance. In March 1919 the North British announced that for the summer season the 'Fife Coast Express' (the 'shire' having been dropped as being by then an anachronism), suspended for the war, would be reinstated and would now consist of two separate trains, namely a 7.15 am Crail to Glasgow service arriving at Queen Street at 9.40 am with intermediate calls at all stations to Leven with the exception of St Monance and Kilconquhar, and another train bound for Edinburgh which left Crail 10 minutes later and which called at the same intermediate stations with an arrival at Waverley at 9.14 am. The return workings left Glasgow at 4.05 pm arriving at Crail at 6.27 and from Edinburgh at 4.50 pm arriving at 6.38 with the same intermediate stops as on the outward journeys. According to the *East Fife Observer,*

> …this service is specially designed to facilitate those who desire to reside at the Fifeshire coast with its splendid golf courses and other attractions while attending to their business in the city during the day.

These trains operated on Mondays to Fridays only but there was an additional Saturday working from Edinburgh to Crail which left at 1.06 pm in the path of the previous golfers' train. The Glasgow express service conveyed a dining car serving breakfast on the outward run and tea on the return service.

For the 1920 season the Glasgow expresses were extended to St Andrews which they left at 6.50 am and returned from Glasgow at 4.10 pm, arriving at St Andrews at 6.55; they ran 'fast' between Crail and St Andrews stations. From 1923 the Express was extended to run beyond St Andrews to terminate and start from Dundee (Tay Bridge) although this was in reality to assist its operation rather than provide a necessary service to passengers. Other less exalted services from Crail to Glasgow left, in some cases, much to be desired and the North British General Manager's files contain correspondence on the subject.

At Crail alterations were carried out at the station in 1920 in order to cope with the increase in traffic and on the agricultural front business was such that record levels of goods were carried; additional traffic included potatoes from the Boarhills and Kingsbarns area bound for the devastated towns of France and Belgium. In contrast, Crail airfield was closed down in 1919 and lay dormant until work commenced on rebuilding it as a Royal Naval Air Station in September 1939. However, the boom in the local economy was to be relatively short-lived and a national railwaymen's strike for higher wages (brought about by rampant inflation) and an eight-hour working day caused a curtailment of all services for a few days from 26th September, 1919. Emergency food distribution centres were established at both St Andrews and Anstruther and essential supplies, newspapers and mails were carried by road. The strike ended on 5th October, when wages were raised and, as a concomitant, passenger fares were, once again, raised to new levels. A national coal strike called in April 1921 had a severe effect on local railway services; coal for household use was rationed and the Crail gasworks temporarily closed.

Ostensibly as a result of both the war and the strikes, the Government were now inclined to continue with their supervision of the railways by setting up a Ministry of Transport and by putting into effect a scheme of concentrating the haphazard and competing 121 or so pre-war railway companies into four major groupings formed on a geographical basis, by voluntary means or otherwise. But, notwithstanding the lengthening shadows, the last years of North British rule were, on the whole, relatively uneventful and traffic appeared to be buoyant with record levels of traffic being achieved at many of the stations on the line. However, the company was understandably cautious and in some ways was already taking minor economy measures in order to conserve its meagre resources. These had in a very real sense taken a prolonged battering in the war with a lack of maintenance combined with a heavy demand for its services taking their toll, especially as takeover from London was becoming a probability rather than a mere possibility. With economy in mind, certain refreshment and other facilities on NBR trains were curtailed and the tea car was withdrawn from the 'Fife Coast Express' with effect from 13th August, 1920.

When the Railways Act 1921 was eventually passed it was clear that an east coast Grouping was to include both the North British and Great North of Scotland Companies and William Whitelaw, the ebullient Chairman of the North British, was to become Chairman of the new London & North Eastern Railway.

The Kinnesburn viaduct, April 2006 - this fine structure can be walked over long after the last train has departed.                                                              *Alan Simpson*

The Scottish Region television train, double-headed by 'B1s' Nos. 61292 and 61293 crosses the Kinnessburn viaduct on 1st June, 1962.                    *C.C. Thornburn*

An unidentified 'J37' class about to pass under the Lade Braes humpback bridge in March 1954.
                                                                *Dr E.M. Patterson*

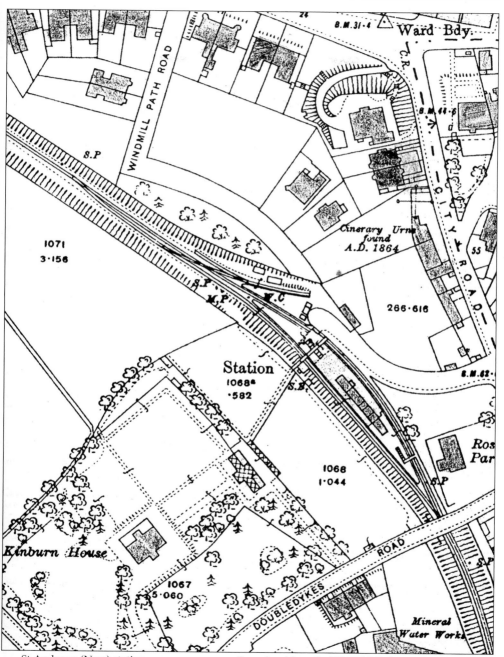

St Andrews (New) station.                    *Reproduced from the 25", 1914 Ordnance Survey Map*

The down platform face at St Andrews in 1954 showing (*above*) the view looking towards Leuchars and (*below*) the view looking towards Crail showing, *top right*, the main entrance to the station.                                                                          (*Both*) *Nigel Dyckhoff*

A view looking north from the Doubledykes Road bridge with a train arrived from Anstruther in the down platform and a train awaited at the up.
*Rex Conway Collection*

The Anstruther & St Andrews Railway water tank at the north end of St Andrews, seen in 1954.
*Nigel Dyckhoff*

An animated scene at St Andrews as the 1.54 pm from Glasgow via Leuchars headed by 'B1' class No. 61178 stands at the south end of the station; note the anachronistic advertisement for the Victoria Café and the leading coach - No. GE1905E was built as part of the 1945-46 'Junior Scotsman' East Coast Main Line sets and was later allocated to the Great Eastern Division of BR Eastern Region.

*C.C. Thornburn*

# Chapter Seven

## London Calling, Figures Falling:
## The London & North Eastern Railway 1923-1947

*'There is every reason to suspect a drastic reduction in the
East Fife Coast passenger service almost immediately.'*
*The East Fife Observer, 1930*

### London Calling

On 1st January, 1923 the railway Grouping arrangements came into effect and control of the entire North British system passed into the hands of the London & North Eastern Railway (LNER) whose headquarters were situated in that city. The local arrangements for train control and traffic management set up by the North British in the years immediately preceding the Grouping were kept on, at least initially, although the new initials 'L. & N.E.R.' (abbreviated in 1924 to LNER) began to appear throughout the area from an early date, both on locomotives and stock and on timetables, posters and other publicity. Yet what was probably one of the most significant features of the 25 years that the LNER existed was that there was little investment in the Anstruther & St Andrews line and only a slow retrenchment barely balanced by belated attempts by the new company to capture new business or, at least, to counteract the withering away of the existing traffic. On a more sanguine note, however, a trade unionist speaking at a local railwaymen's dinner at the Royal Hotel in Anstruther commented that although railwaymen would never give away their new-won right to an eight-hour working day, they might have to give 'a little in other respects' in view of the growing competition from motor traffic and its possible effect on their employment. Indeed, this competition was already causing problems in the area and passenger numbers at local stations were beginning to fall markedly. The 'Fife Coast Express', however, continued to run each summer season.

### Figures Falling

In June 1923 the grandly-named General Motor Carrying Company (GMC) of Kirkcaldy opened a new depot in St Andrews and commenced a bus service from St Andrews to Anstruther via Crail, paralleling the railway line and serving Boarhills by a far more direct route than that of the railway, Kingsbarns village as opposed to its distant station, Crail, Kilrenny, Cellardyke and Anstruther.* Other routes in the area followed and in December 1924 David Ramage of Lundin Links began a Leven to St Andrews service which used the Largoward road (A915); not only did this provide a much more direct route between these towns but in addition ran past Mount Melville station, giving the area served by it a shorter route into the centre of St Andrews; the service was extended westwards to Kirkcaldy in 1928 and

---

* Eventually the GMC was acquired by the Wemyss & District Tramways concern and, after the purchase by the LMS and LNER of various Scottish bus companies, became part of W. Alexander & Sons (Fife) Ltd, later part of the nationalised Scottish Bus Group.

The deadly rivals to the local train: (*upper*) Gardner's bus CK4166, a Leyland LT1 acquired from a Lancashire operator in 1929 and said to have been one of the first two diesel-engined buses to run in Fife, is seen at Shore Street, Anstruther on a St Andrews via Dunino service in 1930 and (*lower*) a Wemyss Tramways Albion on a GMC St Andrews to Leven via the coast service passing through Kingsbarns village in about 1930.          (*Both*) *Authors' Collection*

Parish Church, Kingsbarns, Fife

became a Buckhaven to St Andrews service in 1930. Another local entrepreneur Tom Gardner, who traded as Gardner's Motor Services, in 1925 commenced a regular bus service from Anstruther to St Andrews via the coast road and this route was later extended westwards to start at Leven and eastwards to terminate at Newport-on-Tay. He also operated (briefly) a St Andrews town service and in addition a route from St Andrews to Anstruther via the direct road through Dunino and Stravithie, thus halving the distance travelled by train between the two termini and ensuring that the scarce passenger traffic at Stravithie station would be lost for ever. A particular innovation of this service was the workmen's buses run in the morning and evening from Anstruther to St Andrews via Dunino at specialy reduced fares. Another local bus operator was G.W.S. Morris of Broadleys, Crail who operated both a daily Crail to Balcomie service and a Saturday-only Crail to St Andrews service; although the Balcomie service was a valuable feeder between the station, town and golfcourse, the Saturday service was in direct competition with the railway.

The net effect of this bus competition was that, although traffic to the North was scarcely affected, the absence of a road bridge across the Tay putting paid to any real bus competition, local traffic on the coastal line was badly affected, particularly that between St Andrews and Crail, where the decline in traffic became most marked; long-distance traffic, however, was little affected for the new buses were still barely comfortable and unable as yet to compete with the railway for the lucrative Dundee, Glasgow and Edinburgh trade. The response of the LNER to declining patronage was, however, slow. Although they reconsidered the idea of operating push-pull 'motor trains' or steam railcars on stretches of the coastal line (an idea that had been previously considered by the North British in 1921) they rejected the same, probably because of the fact that there was little room for new halts or even the re-siting of existing stations and there were few communities, with the exception of Kilrenny, that were not already served by rail, albeit that the existing stations were often far from the places that they were supposed to serve. A more practical alternative was a reduction in fares and in particular the introduction of a new range of special tickets that were designed to attract new traffic. On the goods front competition was also becoming apparent with the increasing number of motor lorries and vans that were beginning to supplant the horse throughout the county. A general reduction in goods rates was imposed throughout the system but, as time would prove, both these measures came too late.

## Industrial Unrest

In January 1924 local drivers and firemen joined in the national strike of footplatemen called to resist a cut in wage rates and this had some effect on East Fife trains, particularly on goods services. Members of the National Union of Railwaymen did not, however, join in the action although an interesting news item reported in the *East Fife Observer* of 24th January was that pupils at the Waid Academy who lived in Kingsbarns and Crail 'were forced to patronise the motors, believing that the train which they usually depended upon to convey them to Anstruther was "off". As a matter of fact, on Monday and Tuesday at least, a train did run from Crail'.

Two years later, however, railway services throughout Britain ground to a halt when railwaymen of all grades decided to join in a General Strike called to show solidarity with the miners and, since East Fife included a coal mining area that had been known for a certain degree of militancy, the response was a solid one.

No trains ran over the Anstruther & St Andrews section for several days after Tuesday 4th May, 1926, the beginning of the strike, and although gradually services were resumed, there was a noticeable dip in the number of annual bookings at local stations in that year. Ultimately the strike did irretrievable harm to the local railway economy for it reminded those living in the East Neuk that, whereas they could rely on the nascent bus services, they could not always rely on the railway.

### The Axeman Cometh

In August 1925 a plan was put forward to combine the stations at St Andrews and Mount Melville so far as management was concerned and thereby the LNER hoped to make an annual saving of £155, this sum representing the Mount Melville station master's salary. This was the second proposal that the company had made which involved a combination of local stations, the first, namely making the Stravithie station master responsible for Mount Melville in addition having foundered because that gentleman in addition to his duties in his normal capacity, also 'takes his regular turn in the signal box and also attends to the level crossing there' and it was adjudged that he would be unable to cope with managing Mount Melville as well. It was therefore unremarkable that now some doubts were expressed about the ability of the St Andrews station master to take on further duties given that 'he already has enough to do without taking another station under his charge'. However, despite these misgivings, financial considerations eventually prevailed and the posts of St Andrews and Mount Melville station masters were eventually combined in October of that year. Other economies then followed with the closure of Stravithie signal box on 22nd August, 1926 and abolition of its crossing loop which left Kingsbarns as the only intermediate block post and passing place between St Andrews and Crail, with eight mile sections on either side - a good indication of the fact that the LNER did not hold out any real hopes for an increase in traffic on the Anstruther & St Andrews section. Indeed, given that no regular passenger trains had ever been scheduled to pass each other at Stravithie, it seems doubtful if the second platform there had seen any regular use since its construction in 1898 and in retrospect the traffic projections of the North British seem to have been wildly optimistic. Further economies ensued when, on 12th September, 1926, the arrangements at Anstruther were much simplified by the closure of Anstruther Station signal box and the lengthening of the block section there to become Crail to Anstruther Junction. This was accompanied by the shortening at its eastern end of the former double-track section to become a crossing loop between Anstruther Junction and the Dreel Burn viaduct and the placing of buffer stops at the Crail end of the down platform so that the down road became a terminus with the up platform road remaining as the sole through route. These alterations were necessitated by the fact that the signalman at the Junction box did not have a view of the lines beyond the Dreel Burn viaduct because of the curvature of the route at that point and could therefore not monitor train movements through Anstruther station.

### Four stations lost

By the end of the 1920s The LNER was, in common with the other British railway companies, suffering from a financial downturn brought about by the continuing trade depression on an unprecedented scale. This downturn was replicated locally where although the total annual passenger revenue from all the stations between Guardbridge and Anstruther nominally rose from £21,219 to £34,316 and goods revenue rose from £12,637 to £27,562 between 1913 and 1929, these figures, in reality, represented a fairly substantial loss given that wages and operating costs had more than doubled and the actual number of annual passenger bookings had fallen from 276,570 to 241,627 in that period as competing bus services abstracted more and more local passengers. A measure of this continuing decline was that, by 1934, bookings had fallen yet further to 215,621.

The fall in passenger bookings was particularly notable at the badly-sited stations situated between St Andrews and Crail. Here bookings had fallen drastically since the war - in the case of Kingsbarns the number of passengers in 1929 was only 23 per cent of the pre-war figure, while at Boarhills it was 11 per cent, at Stravithie 22 per cent and at Mount Melville 20 per cent. In total the number of passengers using these four stations annually was just over 4,000 compared with the 20,000 or so that had used the stations in 1913. The revenue was negligible - just over £1,000 from all four stations representing, in real terms, a substantial fall and, almost certainly, a net loss when wages and the cost of fuel used in stopping trains there were taken into account. It was thus unsurprising that the LNER was no longer willing to shoulder this burden.

On 4th September, 1930 the *East Fife Observer* reported that:

> There is every reason to expect a drastic reduction in the East Fife Coast passenger service of the LNER almost immediately. The matter, it is believed, has been under the consideration of the management for some time, and although it has not been definitely settled, it is very probable that before the end of the month the passenger service at the stations between St Andrews and Crail will be entirely abolished. The stations to be affected are understood to be Kingsbarns, Boarhills, Stravithie and Mount Melville. This step would appear to be forcing itself on the management of the LNER as a result of the way that bus competition has grown in popularity for short local travelling. Although the idea afoot is to close the passenger side of the business at the stations mentioned, it is understood goods and merchandise will be handled as before, passenger train parcels being carried to Crail or St Andrews.

Matters were not helped by the absence of a good passenger service over the Anstruther & St Andrews line as the *East Fife Observer* of 31st October, 1929 commented upon:

Very often the remark has been passed that it is easy to get into Anstruther but difficult to get out of it. It is difficult to get to the towns north and south, and to Dundee especially the railway service leaves much to be desired. Travellers can now go by bus to St Andrews or Newport, and have the benefit of a fuller rail service than East Fife enjoys. The Railway Company are not keeping abreast of modern needs so far as the passenger traffic to Dundee is concerned, and the buses are reaping the benefits. Will East Fife always be handicapped by a meagre rail service?

The following week the same newspaper commented:

The report that the Railway Company are to close the stations between Crail and St Andrews on a question of expenditure is significant. Recently the bus traffic between East Fife and St Andrews has been considerable and to such an extent was this traffic developed that the Railway Company was bound to suffer. The closing of these stations would lead one to believe that the bus companies have scored a victory. Now, however, there should be a speedy run between East Fife and Dundee and this may induce travellers to go by rail again when these useless stops have been eliminated.

A few days later the LNER announced publicly that, with effect from Monday 22nd September, all passenger services calling at Kingsbarns, Boarhills, Stravithie and Mount Melville would be withdrawn* although, there being no Sunday trains, the last passenger trains called at those stations on Saturday the 20th. There were no public protests or closing ceremonies and it was clear that these stations had ceased to be of any real concern to the local population. Trains between Crail and St Andrews were, indeed, speeded up but in reality only a few minutes was saved as a combination of speed restrictions and the need to exchange the token at Kingsbarns precluded any real improvement in the schedules. For accountancy purposes Boarhills was placed in charge of Kingsbarns and Stravithie while St Andrews remained in charge of Mount Melville. According to the LNER General Manager's circular issued at the time of their closure, each station was required to send its now obsolete ticket stocks to the company's divisional accountant at Edinburgh and henceforth all parcels and miscellaneous (i.e. guard's van traffic) was to be conveyed by goods trains from those stations 'to and from Crail or St Andrews as the case may be'. Nevertheless the four stations remained remarkably complete even retaining their clocks and nameboards. The stations remained open for goods traffic, and provided a curious reminder of George Fortune's observation that, had they been closer to the villages, these stations would have attracted a much greater clientele.

---

* The *Railway Magazine* of November 1930 reported that 'Ninety railway stations - 27 on the LMSR and 63 on the LNER - were closed for passenger traffic on September 21, thus bringing the total number of stations closed this year on the four big railway systems to 176, the figures being: LNER 88, LMSR 60, GWR 24 and SR 4. In all cases the stations closed are of secondary importance and, as a rule, motor-omnibus facilities more than compensate for the trains withdrawn. Generally the closed stations will still be available for parcels, horses, milk and perishable goods, for which special trains will run. Passengers travelling by the associated omnibus services are able to send their luggage in advance under the usual conditions from any of the stations which are closed to passengers'. The day in question saw the greatest ever number of British stations closed in one day.

## A Time of Contrasts

The 1930s were a time of great contrasts. To counter-act the spread of local bus services and the competition from the motor coach, the LNER made great efforts to encourage rail traffic and issued colourful art deco posters of St Andrews to publicise its attractions; less ambitious schemes for local publicity were entered into and jointly funded by the LNER and town councils of Anstruther and Crail. The company also hired out a series of glass-plate lantern lectures, including one that enjoyed a certain amount of popularity among local audiences, 'Edinburgh to Aberdeen and the Coast of Fife'. In addition reduced fares were available and advertised and special excursions were encouraged, especially after the legislation which brought about the wider provision of paid holidays was put into effect. But financial strictures still dictated that little real capital expenditure could be undertaken and the main object of the LNER in relation to the area was largely one of maintaining the status quo. The holiday traffic to Crail and St Andrews continued almost unabated, although the pattern was beginning to change. Crail still managed to retain its largely middle-class spring and summer trade which tended to fill its guest houses and rented accommodation for a fortnight or month at a time. This may have been due to the enlightened policy of Crail's burgh council to avoid discordant development. In the words of George Scott Moncrieff in his *Lowlands of Scotland*, published in 1939,

> Crail has more in itself than almost any town in Scotland to attract the peaceful holidaymaker: for there has been a deliberate attempt to preserve the grand little houses in the streets - a thing practically unique in our country where toon councils beckon to visitors with one hand and with the other deny anything that may distinguish their burghs from Suburbia-sur-mere.

St Andrews, whose council may have been rather less enlightened, nevertheless attracted culture seekers and those simply wanting to enjoy its famous beaches with lengthy stays interspersed with day-trippers and weekend traffic - these last two sources of traffic being poached to some extent by buses, especially on Sundays when no trains ran.

Day excursions were also promoted and one example was reported in the *East Fife Reporter* of 24th May, 1934 under the headline 'Busy Scenes at Station. Guard's Van Thrown Open to Passengers':

> About 600 trippers took advantage of the cheap railway excursion from East Fife to Dundee on Saturday. Exceptional scenes were witnessed at the stations at Anstruther, Crail, Pittenweem and St Monance, where the excursion proved most popular. At Largo the train picked up only 7 passengers, but the seating accommodation was gradually filled to more than its normal capacity as the train wound its way eastwards. 14 trippers boarded the train at Kilconquhar, 15 at Elie, 39 at St Monance and 38 at Pittenweem. When the train arrived at Anstruther where 140 people were waiting on the platform it was found necessary to use the guard's van to find accommodation, while at Crail the train picked up an additional 88 excursionists.

**SPECIAL HALF-DAY EXCURSION**

**L·N·E·R**

# TUESDAY, 10th MAY

## TO

# Leven, Elie, Crail and St Andrews

### RETURN FARES—THIRD CLASS.

| FROM | TO | | | |
|---|---|---|---|---|
| | Leven. | Elie. | Crail. | St Andrews. |
| | s. d. | s. d. | s. d. | s. d. |
| GLASGOW (Queen Street) ... | 4 6 | 4 6 | 5 0 | 5 0 |
| FALKIRK (High) ... ... | 3 6 | 4 0 | 4 6 | 4 6 |

## SPECIAL TRAIN SERVICE

| OUTWARD JOURNEY | | RETURN JOURNEY | |
|---|---|---|---|
| | A.M. | | P.M. |
| Glasgow (Queen Street) depart | 11 0 | St Andrews ... ... depart | 8 14 |
| Falkirk (High) ... ... ,, | 11 33 | Crail ... ... ... ,, | 8 35 |
| Leven ... ... ... arrive | 12p51 | Elie ... ... ... ,, | 8 55 |
| Elie ... ... ... ,, | 1 15 | Leven ... ... ... ,, | 9 14 |
| Crail ... ... ... ,, | 1 35 | Falkirk (High) ... ... arrive | 10 25 |
| St Andrews ... ... ,, | 1 57 | Glasgow (Queen Street) ,, | 11 0 |

**RESERVATION OF SEATS.** Application should be made to Station-masters at Glasgow (Queen Street) and Falkirk (High).

*Tickets, Bills and all particulars can be obtained at the Stations shown and from :—*

Moses Buchanan, 22 Renfield Street ; Thos. Cook & Son, Ltd., 83 Buchanan Street; L.N.E.R. Town Office, 37 West George Street ; GLASGOW.

It will assist the Railway Company in making arrangements FOR YOUR COMFORT if you TAKE TICKETS IN ADVANCE.

NO LUGGAGE ALLOWED. CHILDREN over 3 and under 12 years, half-fares.

TICKETS are not transferable ;

are only available to and from Stations for which issued, and by excursion trains in both directions.

are not available for intermediate Stations ;

are issued subject to General Conditions and Regulations specified in the Company's current time tables.

*April 1927*      (10-M)      (S.C. 4159)

LNER handbill, 1927.

These total were impressive but did not set a record for northbound passengers from Anstruther or Crail - for example in July 1927 a five-shilling day excursion from Leven to Aberdeen via St Andrews attracted 204 passengers from Anstruther and 102 from Crail.

In a further bid to at least retain local passenger traffic at Anstruther, Crail and St Andrews, where on summer weekends trains were hopelessly overcrowded and on weekdays, summer and winter, they were often deserted, the LNER granted a certain amount of autonomy to local station masters, allowing them to regulate local fares so that they would compete better with bus fares on the parallel routes and in addition they were given carte blanche in the arrangement of excursions and special traffic at reduced rates, even from the four closed stations north of Crail; examples of the latter included a schoolboys' football excursion to Cowdenbeath from Boarhills in 1938 and a series of excursions from Boarhills and Kingsbarns to Glasgow to visit the Empire Exhibition in that same year.

Attempts were also made to retain purely local traffic which was being lost to local buses. In August 1929 the *East Fife Observer* contained a news item concerning a veritable St Andrews institution that had once provided much extra traffic on the railway:

> The annual Lammas Market was held on Monday and Tuesday of this week, and on both days large contingents from the east coast travelled to the popular fair. On Tuesday torrential rain somewhat damped the sprits of the holiday crowds, but nevertheless each motor bus carried a full compliment of passengers to and from the Auld Grey Toun.

The fact that there was no evening return service by rail south from St Andrews meant an inevitable loss of leisure traffic and it was therefore of little surprise that the bus would step in to fill the breach and a special bus return service was, from January 1931, operated to and from Anstruther 'in connection with the St Andrews Talkie Pictures'. The railway did fight back, however, and in October 1934 an additional 11.15 pm train service was provided on Saturday nights between Anstruther and Leven 'for patrons of the Regal cinema, Anstruther', while in August 1935 a special train was provided between Largo and all stations to St Andrews for the Lammas fair, with a late return service at 11.30 pm; the return fare from Crail and Anstruther to St Andrews being a mere 9*d*.!

Another welcome innovation was provided by the introduction of the railway camping coach and the LNER was the first British company to provide cheap rural holidays by providing these; as part of the second phase of their programme, a single camping coach was placed in the siding at Boarhills station ready for the 1937 season. The coach, which was painted in the same green and cream livery as the LNER tourist stock, had been converted out of a redundant Great Northern Railway six-wheeler, retained two of its original compartments as bedrooms which were connected by a new corridor, necessitating the ends of the beds being hinged so that they could be folded upwards when a through passage was needed. Complete with two primus stoves, a sink and draining board, the coach was available at a weekly summer rental of £2 10s., reduced to £2 in the off-season; for toilet facilities the campers had to use the nearby station buildings. The choice of Boarhills as a location was, perhaps, slightly odd given that there had been no passenger trains stopping there for five years and accordingly campers had to travel by rail to Crail or St Andrews and then take the bus - particularly bizarre given that to hire a camping coach in the first place it was necessary to book a minimum of four adult tickets to and from one's home station. However the beach at Boarhills was within walking distance and, as the LNER 'Camping Holidays' guide pointed out in its 'general remarks' about Boarhills the attractions included 'Coast and Country. Sea Bathing. Golf in near vicinity. Milk and provisions obtainable locally and from calling vans'. In 1938 the summer rental was increased to £3 3s. per week. In common with all other LNER camping coaches, the one at Boarhills was removed at the end of the 1939 season and never returned.

The basic problem associated with the Anstruther & St Andrews line, however, remained - beyond Crail there was little traffic of any sort and by 1937 this section appeared to be generating less than £100 per mile of receipts, let alone of profit! In common with a number of other lines in the Southern Scottish Area, the LNER instigated a review of the Crail to St Andrews section and although a serious proposal was put forward for the abandonment of this section and the complete closure of Kingsbarns, Boarhills, Stravithie and Mount Melville stations, this was not followed through and instead of St Andrews and Crail becoming terminus stations, the whole line survived. Others were less lucky - the Kincardine and Dunfermline line was breached to the east of Kincardine-on-Forth and operated as two separate branches and the Kirkcaldy & District line from Foulford Junction to Inverteil Junction was breached west of Auchtertool and treated the same way. One can only surmise that, with the worsening political situation in Europe, it was assumed that the whole of the East Fife coastal line would have some strategic importance in a coming war for, with the possible exception of keeping open a goods line between Crail and Kingsbarns, there seems to have been little economic justification for such an action. What is even more surprising is that not only did the line narrowly escape closure then, but that it managed to survive for almost another 30 years and still carried a full passenger service until the very end.

### Two Strange Mishaps

In the 1930s there were two strange mishaps on the Anstruther & St Andrews line which were reported in the *East Fife Reporter*. The first of these occurred at Kirkmay crossing in November 1932 under the heading 'Ploughman's Narrow Escape':

The level crossing about half-a-mile from Crail was the scene of an alarming accident yesterday, in which two runaway horses, belonging to John Duncan, Kirkmay Farm, Crail were pinned to death. Mr Duncan's land lies on either side of the railway, and Charles Watson, who was in charge of the horses, yolked to a plough, was making his way to the land known as Seafield, on the opposite side of the railway. The gate of the level crossing near him was open, the other being closed. The horses suddenly took fright when a special ballast train was just approaching from Crail and they bolted for the open gate. The train struck the nearest animal on the flank, and in turn knocked the other down. Both horses were killed instantaneously and were carried down the line for some distance. The ploughman had a narrow escape having stuck to his reins and had done his utmost to pull back the frightened animals.

On 3rd February, 1938 the following report appeared in the same paper:

Lt R.S. Laybourne, an officer attached to No. 1 Flying Training School, RAF Leuchars, was killed when a machine in which he was flying solo crashed on the railway line half-a-mile from Stravithie on Monday morning. Lt Laybourne was flying a Hawker Hart machine from the aerodrome in an easterly direction. A gang of eight railwaymen were engaged cutting the grass verge on the embankment. Among them were David Anderson (Anstruther), Kames Cormack (Pittenweem), James Stewart (Crail), David Anderson Jun., J. Seath, W. Woodcock and J. Woodcock (Kingsbarns).

James Stewart was the first of the men to arrive at the wrecked machine, and when intercepted by our reporter, related how he found the pilot in the cockpit, a gash under his chin and showing but a flicker of life. They tried to get the pilot free but found that one of his feet was jammed in the wreckage. They could not move him until the arrival of the police and by that time he was dead. Another workman recounted how they were working on the embankment when they heard the plane flying low overhead. They looked up for it was flying pretty low and then it suddenly went into a couple of spirals and crashed straight to the ground. The engine was still running at the time of the crash. Mr J. Duncan, Farmer, was walking across the field that adjoins the railway line when the crash occurred.

The propeller, which was smashed, and the undercarriage, which was flattened out, were buried in the north embankment of the line. The wing had struck a telegraph pole bending it over slightly. The tip of the wing had struck the wires and torn them down. The body of the machine lay straight across the line and the tail was resting on the grass verge on the opposite side, thus completely blocking the line.

The 8.39 train from St Andrews had just passed before the crash. The train coming towards St Andrews was due to have passed shortly afterwards. It was stopped at Kingsbarns and the line was cleared several hours later. An ambulance from the RAF base arrived on the scene and removed the body of Lt Laybourne to Leuchars. The deceased belongs to England.

### Defence of the Realm

In September 1939 all reduced rate ticket facilities were withdrawn by the Railway Executive Committee but life appears to have continued much as before on the former Anstruther & St Andrews Railway. Soon signs of war were seen, and the shaded lamps and splinter screens made the already decrepit passenger carriages seem even more seedy and pillboxes and other defence works began to appear alongside the line. As part of the war effort to defeat Nazi Germany 'through struggles to the stars', three airfields were constructed in the area served by the line and these were at Crail, Stravithie and Dunino; RAF Leuchars, immediately to the north, had been in continuous use since World War I. The most important of these new airfields was Crail, which arose from the reinstated and modernised World War I naval airfield at Balcomie, to the east of the town. Work commenced on the rebuilding of Crail airfield for the Royal Naval Air Services in September 1939 and the majority of the materials used in constructing the hard runways and associated buildings there came by rail from the west via Crail station - the reason why, in the winter of 1939-40, the viaduct at Largo was strengthened to accommodate heavier trains. Major work was needed for the original grass landing strips had long been ploughed up and the impressive concrete hangers dating from 1917 were demolished in the 1930s. Crail airfield opened, as HMS *Jackdaw*, on 1st October, 1940. The main use of the airfield in its early years was for torpedo bomber reconnaissance and torpedo training and Albacore and Swordfish, and later Barracuda and Avenger, aircraft were deployed from here. Part of the torpedo training exercises involved the placement of vessels out in the Firth which would then serve as targets against which dummy torpedoes could be deployed and a number of railway-owned cross-channel vessels which were temporarily unable to carry out their pre-war duties were so used including four Southern Railway ferries, *Isle of Thanet*, *Worthing* and *St Briac*, all of which had been built by Denny, Dumbarton in the 1920s and a South Eastern & Chatham Railway vessel, *Biarritz*, a 1914 product of the same yard. Other ships so used included the elderly Isle of Man Steam Packet Company vessels *Victoria*, *Viking* and *Manxmaid* - the latter having originally been launched in 1910 as the Channel Island ferry *Caeserea* of the London & South Western Railway. The Manx vessels and *Ceasarea* had all seen active service in the 1914-1918 hostilities and these and the Southern Railway ships were all returned to their original duties in 1945-6 with the exception of *St Briac* which was unfortunate enough to be sunk by a British mine in 1942.

In the summer of 1943 carrier trials were carried out at Crail and on occasions the airfield was used as an overflow facility for RAF Leuchars. At its height, HMS *Jackdaw* had some 2,000 personnel stationed there and this provided a welcome boost to the revenues of Crail station, particularly when the tourist trade had been severely curtailed. A flavour of what airmen arriving at Crail station during the blackout faced comes from the reminiscences of a member of the Canadian Fleet Air Arm:

> As the train pulled out we were left in complete darkness, scarcely daring to move lest we fell off the platform. Finally we were able to make out a dim light at the end of the station which turned out to be held by the Stationmaster. Being confronted by sailors in the middle of the night seemed to be a regular occurrence for him and he knew exactly what to do. After a short phone conversation he informed us that someone would be along shortly to pick us up. A small truck appeared. We loaded our gear aboard and off we went.

The goods yard was busy, too, for a considerable amount of supplies including food and domestic requisites, coal, fuel and aircraft parts, were all supplied by rail from the Royal Elizabeth Yard, a victualling yard situated in the shadow of the Forth Bridge. The airfield was closed at the end of 1946 and its buildings put to other uses although from 1953 to 1958 St Andrews University ATC cadets had Chipmunk aircraft stationed there.

RAF Stravithie was a different affair altogether. Situated half a mile or so south of Stravithie station on the road between St Andrews and Stravithie, this small site with grass runways came into use in May 1941 originally as a dispersal field for RAF Edzell and, both in its construction and later use, generated some additional goods traffic at Stravithie station. There is, however, no record of any special passenger trains having been worked to Stravithie, or of any ordinary passenger trains having made unscheduled stops there although given its proximity to a regular bus route the need for that would have been minimal. A noted feauture of the airfield was the large barrage balloon which was used in connection with the training of parachutists including many Poles who subsequently served in the Arnhem campaign. On one occasion a Hudson bomber, on an incoming flight to the airfield, narrowly missed the Purvis family home at Brigton and crashed on to the driveway, killing both of its crew. RAF Stravithie was decommissioned in 1946 and the land has returned to agricultural use.

The third of these airfields was RAF Dunino, somewhat misnamed in that it was situated two miles east of the village of that name and half-a-mile north west of Kingsbarns station. Opened in the summer of 1941, the airfield was something of a second-line installation and had undulating grass runways and its main buildings were placed close to the Kilduncan Burn. Originally the home of Lysanders, the airfield was transferred to the Navy in December 1942 and became HMS *Jackdaw* II, an annex of the Crail establishment. Between 1943 and 1946 the airfield was used for the storage of a large number of surplus naval aircraft. For a short period it appears to have been used as a temporary Prisoner of War camp. Accounts were given to the authors of servicemen having been picked up and deposited by passenger trains at the Kilduncan level crossing, presumably with the assistance of the Kingsbarns signalman. These stops were not officially sanctioned and there is no record of such stops or of any temporary platform, but given the somewhat isolated nature of the airfield and the distance from it to the Crail to St Andrews bus route, the practice of picking up and setting down personnel does not seem to have been an unreasonable one. Because of the undulating surface of the airfield it was deemed unsuitable for post-war use and was permanently closed in 1946, the land being retained by the navy until 1957 and then reverting to agricultural use, the buildings being used as a chicken farm.

In general each of the wartime airfields created additional traffic over the coastal line in the form of general stores, mail, aircrews and ground staff, the latter travelling by passenger train to Crail and St Andrews; some use was made of Stravithie and Kingsbarns for goods traffic but much of the stores were sent by road from St Andrews. Aircraft and major aircraft parts (such as replacement wings) were not, however, usually moved by rail but instead were transported by giant road tractors and trailers known, after the transatlantic liners, as 'Queen Marys'. Supplies of aviation fuel were not, so far as the authors are aware, delivered to Crail, Stravithie and Dunino airfields in tank wagons but were carried in metal oil drums to local stations, whence they were taken by road.

### Snow and Slow

With the advent of peace, the holiday traffic returned in force but the LNER was left in a poor state. Locomotives and stock and local stations had received little maintenance during the war and were now dirty and run-down but, despite a shortage of cash and materials, the company was still determined to make an effort. In January 1946 the *East Fife Observer* carried a story all too typical of those times under the heading 'Fast and Better Train Services Wanted - Complaint of Slowness on Crail Line':

We ourselves had an experience of dilatoriness at present prevailing on this particular branch line. Leaving Dundee by the afternoon train just before 5 o'clock, we expected to reach our destination in East Fife around half-past six. All went well until a point outside St Andrews was reached on the upgoing stretch, immediately to the north of Mount Melville station. It had been raining heavily, and owing to the slippery conditions of the rails, the engine wheels simply would not grip. Various attempts were made, backwards and forwards, until finally the driver had to give it up as a bad job. Part of the train was uncoupled while the remainder was pulled by the engine as far up as Mount Melville, and shunted to the siding there. The engine then returned and brought back the portion that had been left behind. The two parts were then linked up and the train proceeded on its way. The hold-up resulted in a loss of nearly an hour's time and there was a further delay, on the east coast part of the line, owing to the eastbound train, which was up to time, having to get the right of way. In our own case, the delay was not attended with undue hardship or inconvenience, except that it made us miss a most hearty supper at the St Monance Freemasons' Annual Dinner, which we very much regretted. At the same time, there are occasions when delays, such as this, may be attended with more serious consequences, and it is of all the more importance, therefore, that recurrences of this kind be made as few and far between as possible.

In the winter that followed the line between Crail and St Andrews was a number of times blocked by snow and the severe winter was followed by floods and fuel shortages. Not without a fight, the LNER attempted to thwart the Socialist Government's attempt to nationalise the railways of Britain - to no avail as from 1st January, 1948 the Anstruther & St Andrews Railway became the property of the Railway Executive of the British Transport Commission.

Five days after the inaugural post-war run of the 'Fife Coast Express', the train leaves St Andrews on 28th May, 1949 - note the plain grey livery of the streamlined stock (its first day of operation on this service) and the LNER-pattern headboard.     *J.L. Stevenson*

# Chapter Eight

# Excess Fare:
# From British Railways to the Present Day

*'Any remaining hardship would be insufficient to
justify the retention of the services'*

Tom Fraser, Minister of Transport

## Passengers Desert

Following the nationalisation of the railways, little changed in the East Neuk and although the trains changed liveries and British Railways (BR) totems appeared at Crail, St Andrews and Anstruther stations. Pre-war services were restored, including the 'Fife Coast Express' which had been suspended in 1939 but was reinstated on 23rd May, 1949 although now running only between St Andrews and Glasgow Queen Street via Crail. On 28th May of the same year articulated streamlined stock from the former 'Silver Jubilee'* of the LNER was allocated to the service (although no restaurant facilities were provided) and the 'Express' continued to run throughout the decade. However as the decade progressed it was becoming increasingly clear that, despite the buoyant summer holidays trains, the use of local trains by the general public was clearly on the wane - the exception to this decline seems to have been the Sunday trains from Crail to Thornton which, throughout the 1940s and 1950s, continued to be packed. Notwithstanding this exception, the railway was in trouble and, with rising incomes and the abolition of controls on petrol and on car production, this trouble grew with the passing years.

In the *Third Statistical Account of Scotland,†* the volume for Fife, published in 1952, contains the following entry for Crail:

> In the coaching days, the journey from Crail to St Andrews was a two-hour one, but now expresses make the journey to Glasgow and Edinburgh in two and one and a half hours respectively. Sunday trains are a well-patronised summer feature. Bus services are, however, much more popular than the trains, buses being more frequent, fares cheaper, and travelling comfortable because of the good road surfaces. Even the country roads in the most remote parts of the parish, not yet linked by buses, are well made and macadam-surfaced. No part of the parish is outwith easy walking distance of a bus route.

---

\* A short-lived LNER crack express train run between London and Newcastle and suspended on the outbreak of war.

† The *Statistical Account of Scotland* was first published in 1796-8 and was designed to reflect everyday life in each parish, including industries, transport and housing and 'the quantum of happiness enjoyed by its inhabitants and the means of its future improvement'. The second account was published in the 1830s and gives a good account of Scotland in the immediate pre-railway age while the third, published after World War II (the Fife volume appearing in 1951), tells of how Scotland's railways were faring in the motor age; it is selectively quoted in this chapter.

The great increase of passenger traffic at Crail station caused by the demands of HMS *Jackdaw* came to an end in 1946 but for three years afterwards a Royal Naval training establishment for boys, named HMS *Bruce*, was situated in the airfield's buildings. Intermittent use of the airfield by the Black Watch between 1953 and 1956 and by the Joint Services School for Linguistics from 1956 to 1960 helped to boost bookings to and from Crail which partially off-set the decline in local journeys. It also appeared, however, that the holiday trade was still holding up and even at that time of the Third Statistical Account it could be said that,

> House-letting, in the holiday season, may be said to be almost the keystone of Crail's economy. During the summer months, excellent business is done by letting rooms in private dwellings, and there are very few houses where accommodation is not available. There are seven hotels, three of them licensed, and four boarding-houses, which are all well patronised. A new venture - a Holiday Camp - began three years ago. The building, supplemented by the erection of caravans and chalets, can house 110 people at the . height of the season. The population during the summer months rises considerably, therefore, with no little benefit to the community.

However, much of this traffic was arriving by car and by buses from Glasgow and although the traditional pattern of holidays in places such as Crail seemed to be timeless and likely to continue for ever, the winds of change were already blowing.

The entries for St Andrews comments that bus services in the city are now popular while the Anstruther entry states that,

> Bus services to St Andrews and Leven are frequent and widely used. Railway travel has been less popular, for trains are less frequent and the station is a considerable distance from many parts of the town.

In the case of Kingsbarns parish the writer noted that the coming of bus services to the village in the 1920s meant a lot to the village and that since the regular, hourly, service was inaugurated 'many younger people have found work in neighbouring towns, girls as shop assistants and boys at the various trades, the bus service having encouraged many of them to leave Kingsbarns permanently'. In respect of the railway 'Freight trains, one each way daily, still uplift and deliver goods at the station'.

### Theft in Transit

On the goods front, things were in an even more serious decline. The local rural economy was facing serious difficulties caused by the disappearance of indigenous small-scale industries and from the railway's point of view, however, the downturn was even more serious. The motor lorry had been an ever present threat to short and medium length journeys since the end of World War I and in the 1930s such firms as M.B. Danskin of Strathkinness had begun to carry farm produce direct from the producers to warehouses, one example being sugar beet from local growers direct to the beet factory at Cupar - in many cases a markedly shorter distance was travelled than a train would have to take over the circuitous route by rail. As the size of vehicles increased, so did the threat with some firms expanding their staff to 20 or 30 drivers, augmented by an influx of army-trained lorry drivers at the end of World War II. As the *Third Statistical Account* related:

> The great benefit which the road haulage industry has to offer its customers is that of door-to-door delivery, which not only effects a saving of time, but also reduces the need for handling, which can be a most important matter when goods are heavy, awkward or liable to damage easily. Then, the firms' overheads are naturally less than those of the railway, so that, for many kinds of merchandise, advantageous rates can be quoted. Furthermore, at a time when standards of public morality have shown some decline, the fact that lorries and their loads remain in the charge of one man, or as few as possible, minimises the chance of theft in transit.

The fault did not lie entirely on the side of the railwaymen since a general run-down and lack of investment in innovations such as containerisation, modern goods depots and attractive rates could not be blamed on them and the fact that lorries could cream off the most attractive trade while leaving the railway with the residue did not help. A lack of co-ordination between the two modes of transport (despite the short period during which both were nationalised) led to the eventual dominance of the lorry and although local sidings and depots were still busy during the 1950s, the writing was clearly on the wall as evidenced by the fact that there was now only one regular daily goods service over the coastal line.

### The Changing Scene

By the 1950s the Anstruther & St Andrews line seemed to have sunk into a very real slumber and little out of the ordinary seems to have occurred. However, in 1954 the almost forgotten station at Kingsbarns was briefly in the news when, in December of that year, a travelling draper from Leven was going about his rounds in the district and inadvertently drove his car through the level crossing gates there and into the path of an incoming passenger train. The train hit the car and carried it a distance of 435 yards before coming to a stop; the unfortunate draper was killed instantly. Otherwise things were unchanged but it was becoming clear that, if the line was to remain open, then new stock and new methods of operation would be needed, particularly in the wake of the mounting losses being sustained by British Railways. In June 1959 twin-unit diesel multiple units (dmus) took over the Leuchars to St Andrews local services, as well as Dundee through services, and in addition certain of the Leven & East of Fife trains were dieselised leaving only the through St Andrews to Crail and Thornton, Glasgow and Edinburgh services as steam hauled, but not for long. In April 1960 dmu services were introduced on the great majority of East Coast local services between Edinburgh, Glasgow, Dundee and Aberdeen and these included services between the first two of these cities and Crail, as well as most of the Thornton to Anstruther, Crail and St Andrews services; the small sub-shed at Anstruther was closed as a result. Ironically the Fife Coast Express was a casualty

# CRAIL

## FIFESHIRE'S BRACING HEALTH RESORT

Photo by J. Valentine & Sons, Ltd., Dundee

SITUATED in the East Neuk of Fife, within two miles of Fifeness, Crail is famed for its pure and invigorating air, while the facilities it offers for outdoor recreation amidst healthful surroundings have made it a most popular seaside resort. Its best recommendation is to be found in the fact that many visitors return season after season, it being quite common to find families who have come to Crail for a score of summers.

A Royal Burgh of great antiquity, with buildings and records of much interest to the antiquary, its quaintness and old-world charm also appeal to those who wish a restful holiday. The season extends to the end of September, which is becoming an increasingly popular month, and can be highly recommended.

---

**BOWLING. GOLF – Balcomie, 18 holes. SUNDAY GOLF. PUTTING COURSE. SUNDAY PUTTING. SAFE BATHING for Children. BATHING, YACHTING and PADDLING POOL. SUNDAY TENNIS from 1 p.m. - Four Hard Courts.    : DANCING : DAILY SAILINGS FROM HARBOUR**

---

## CAMPING GROUNDS FOR TENTS AND CARAVANS
### Superb site (SAUCHOPE) overlooking Firth of Forth

*Excellent Accommodation in Hotels, Boarding Houses and Private Apartments*
**For List of Accommodation apply to Town Clerk (Dept. H.H.), Crail, Fife**

From the BR Scottish Region *Holiday Haunts*, 1960 edition.

of dieselisation, running for the last time on 5th September, 1959 - ironic because the summer through trains from Glasgow continued to be steam-hauled until closure. One local service that could not be operated by dmus was the 2.35 pm from Crail to Thornton, since dmus were not permitted to haul the sole fish van over the single-line from Crail, loaded with crabs and lobsters. Whether the dmus made much of a difference was debatable - undoubtedly they were more economical to operate and were popular with the public and may well have temporarily arrested the decline in passenger numbers but no serious attempt was made to reduce the running costs of the stations and line by, for instance, selling tickets on the train. Goods services continued to be steam-hauled and diesel locomotives were, so far as is known, rarely, if ever, seen on goods trains east of Crail.

Perhaps a graphic illustration of the struggle to keep the passenger service viable on the Anstruther & St Andrews line is the comparison between the rail and bus timetables between the two towns in the summer of 1962. There were four trains making the daily journey between Anstruther and St Andrews, namely the 8.48, 11.48 in the morning and the 7.01 and 9.32 in the evening with a journey time of between 32 and 38 minutes. There were a handful of additional Anstruther services via Leven that terminated at Crail and no Sunday trains on the line apart from the solitary Glasgow and Edinburgh services that terminated at Crail. In contrast buses ran hourly between 5.49 am and 9.49 pm, with a half-hourly service during most of the day; on Sundays there was an hourly service between 7.49 am and 9.49 pm. The journey time by bus was 38 minutes and unlike the train Cellardyke, Kilrenny, Kingsbarns and Boarhills were also served. In addition there were direct Anstruther to St Andrews services via Dunino, taking some 26 minutes while the journey by car on this route could be completed in less than 20 minutes. BR advertised cheap day returns from Anstruther to St Andrews for 3s. 9d., and also to a variety of destinations including Aberdour, Cowdenbeath, Kinghorn, Pittenweem and Sinclairtown as well as a wide variety of Holiday Roundabout Tickets offering a week's first and second class travel in a selected area for between 25s. and 37s. 6d. W. Alexander & Sons (Fife) Ltd offered a number of coach tours from Anstruther, varying from day tours to Aberdeen, Royal Deeside and the Trossachs, afternoon trips to Falkland Palace and Glamis Castle and evening excursions entitled 'Selected Mystery Tours' for a fare of 3s. 6d. So far as passengers were concerned, it seemed that the bus had well and truly won the battle!

### Closures Abound

An early casualty of the downturn in goods traffic was that of Mount Melville goods station. The St Andrews Local Committee of Fife County Council noted in November 1959 that British Railways proposed to convert the station to a public siding which would be unstaffed in the summer months, effecting an annual saving on wages of some £240. The Committee were told by their Chairman that the proposal was 'a reasonable one' and they unanimously agreed not to oppose it after it was pointed out that rail deliveries would be made from St Andrews by

Two Metro-Cammell 3-car sets, complete with 'whiskers' and bound for Dundee, enter Crail from the west on 13th July, 1963.                                                *C.C. Thornburn*

The new order? English Electric type '1' No. D8095 on an empty coaching stock special passes through Crail, 13th July, 1963.                                                *C.C. Thornburn*

lorry. This type of local delivery was an increasing trend as the railway tried to compete with road transport and by 1960 there was a widespread network of road deliveries from St Andrews and Anstruther goods yards which began to render the smaller goods stations and sidings largely redundant except for full wagon traffic of coal, potatoes and fertiliser. The effect of this on the revenues of the goods depots at Stravithie, Boarhills and Kingsbarns and the, by-now unstaffed, Mount Melville siding were profound for it was coupled with a decline in the use of household coal and a general shifting of goods traffic from rail to road. By the early 1960s these stations were seeing so little traffic other than wagonloads of household coal that it was clear that they could not survive for long. By the time Dr Beeching had reported that the major part of the coastal line was economically unviable and it was clear that the St Andrews to Leven line was likely to be closed in its entirety, the decision had probably already been taken to close these four intermediate goods stations and to concentrate such traffic as remained at St Andrews and Cupar, relying on direct road deliveries from those places to local customers. In truth, by then the complete loss of the minimal trade that would remain after this switch was probably of little concern to the British Railways Board who were, in any event, attempting to do away with such marginally viable traffic. Thus it was hardly surprising to see closure notices posted in the summer of 1964 and, there not appearing to have been any serious objections thereto, goods services at Kingsbarns, Boarhills, Stravithie and Mount Melville were discontinued with effect from 5th October, 1964. These four stations were, accordingly, closed to all traffic on this date almost 34 years after they had been closed to passengers; the only matter of note being that they had been able to survive this long, complete with their nameboards and original oil lamps!

### The Doctor Prescribes

Already rumours were being widely circulated in the area that the whole of the East Fife coastal line between St Andrews and Leven was doomed to closure and the local press urged those living in the area to fight any attempts to close the line. There was, however, no official confirmation of such a closure until, in March 1963, the British Railways Board published their infamous report named *The Reshaping of British Railways*, compiled under the chairmanship of Dr Richard Beeching. The report was a brave attempt to stop the horrendous mounting losses which the nationalised railway industry was making at the time, particularly in respect of little-used rural services which were draining away resources at an alarming rate. Listed in the report were the allegedly loss-making railway services which the Board proposed to discontinue as soon as possible. It was hardly surprising that the St Andrews to Crail line was included since by then its goods service had dwindled to virtually nothing and passenger loadings were light, even at the height of the summer season. What was less anticipated, however, was that the proposed closure was also to include the line between Crail and Leven, serving the important holiday resorts of Anstruther, Elie and Largo. Somewhat ominously, the Leuchars to St Andrews line and the Thornton to Leven lines were shown on the accompanying map coloured grey which signified 'not for development' but, at least for the present time, they were not scheduled for closure.

*MAKE THE MOST OF YOUR HOLIDAY*

# GO PLACES
# BY TRAIN

## HOLIDAY RUNABOUT TICKETS

provide unlimited rail travel at reduced cost over specified areas. Issued every day of the week and valid for seven consecutive days, including Sundays. The rates are 25/-, second class (37/6 first class) or 27/6 second class (41/3 first class) according to the area selected.

## CHEAP DAY TICKETS
## FROM ANSTRUTHER

|  | s. d. |  |  | s. d. |  |  | s. d. |
|---|---|---|---|---|---|---|---|
| Aberdour | 9 0 | Edinburgh | - 12 9 | Lochgelly - | - 8 3 |
| Burntisland | 8 3 | Falkirk - | - 13 9 | Pittenweem - | 0 7 |
| Cameron Bridge | 5 2 | Glasgow - | - 17 0 | St Andrews - | 3 9 |
| Cowdenbeath - | 9 0 | Kinghorn - | - 7 9 | St Monance - | 1 0 |
| Dundee - - | 8 6 | Kirkcaldy - | - 6 9 | Sinclairtown - | 6 6 |
| Dunfermline - | 10 0 | Leven - | - 4 0 | Thornton - - | 5 6 |

Tickets and full details can
be obtained at the station

BRITISH RAILWAYS

Anstruther cheap day tickets, 1963.

A committee was formed of the provosts of the five East Neuk burghs of Crail, Anstruther, Pittenweem, St Monance and Elie and Earlsferry to fight the closure* but St Andrews Town Council remained largely unaffected. In September 1963 the British Railways Board formally intimated to the local authorities their intention to withdraw the passenger service between Leven and St Andrews on a date to be announced. The response of the St Andrews Town Council was, somewhat surprisingly, muted and they merely 'resolved that they had no observations to make to the Board' about the proposed closure - a mark, perhaps, of the extremely poor patronage by this time of services between Crail and St Andrews and a great contrast to the Five Burghs Committee whose members exhorted that 'every possible protest should be lodged by the people living between St Andrews and Leven'.

The inhabitants of the East Neuk and their representatives, including Sir John Gilmour MP, fought on but in February 1965 the Labour Government, through their Transport Minister, Tom Fraser, issued a notice that he

...had considered most carefully the Transport Users' Consultative Committee's report and other relevant factors. He was satisfied that if certain adjustments to existing bus and rail services were made to improve bus-rail interchange arrangements at Leven, any remaining hardship would be insufficient to justify the retention of the services.

* A fuller account of the activities of this committee and the fight to save the line is given in *The Leven & East of Fife Railway*. Six burghs were named here but Elie and Earlsferry constituted a single burgh, having amalgamated in 1929.

On 19th April, 1965 the British Railways Board announced that, given various representations that had been made to them, they would keep the line open until the end of the tourist season in August and that train connections for the replacement buses at Leven would be improved. The closure date was announced as Monday 6th September, 1965, the last trains between St Andrews and Crail running on Saturday 4th, there never having been a Sunday service between those points. A final attempt was made by the Five Burghs Committee to persuade the Board that the service could be saved by the inauguration of savings such as the de-manning of stations and the sale of tickets on board trains and the reduction of the whole section between Leven and St Andrews to a single line operated by a single dmu with open level crossings, but this argument fell upon stony ground.

### Fatal Dose

On Saturday 21st August, 1965 the last public steam-hauled passenger service was operated over the section of line between St Andrews and Crail when the 2.28 pm St Andrews to Glasgow train - a summer only service - made its final run; from then onwards all remaining public passenger services on this section were operated by the ubiquitous multiple-units, although on the following Saturday, August 28th, a steam-hauled RCTS enthusiasts' special, hauled by 'J37' No. 64569, traversed the whole of the line. Westwards from Crail there were still a couple of daily steam services, the most noted of which was the 2.35 pm Crail to Thornton train that conveyed a fish van but, with the withdrawal of the seasonal extras,* the dmu was destined to reign almost supreme!

On Saturday 4th September, 1965 the 10.35 am (Saturdays Only) Crail to Glasgow and 2.35 pm Crail to Thornton trains had the honour of being the last regular steam passenger services over any section of the Anstruther & St Andrews Railway. Several enthusiasts made their final journey on these trains rather than by the true last up passenger train between St Andrews and Crail (and the last daylight service) namely the 5.05 pm Dundee to Glasgow service which left St Andrews at 5.38 and reached Crail at 6.02. The train finally arrived at Queen Street station at 8.51, at which time the final northbound service to St Andrews via Crail, the 7.41 pm from Edinburgh Waverley, was approaching Cameron Bridge; by the time that Crail was reached the train was well-filled with passengers wishing to make a final sentimental journey over this section of the Anstruther & St Andrews Railway. These included Colonel R.W.B. Purvis, grandson of the John Purvis of Kinaldy who had been Chairman of the Anstruther & St Andrews Railway. Colonel Purvis was accompanied by his son John and by the dented silver spade that his grandmother had used to cut the first sod on that line 83 years before and, according to the local press :

> When the train pulled into St Andrews just after 10 pm about 50 people were waiting on the platform to give the passengers a cheer. The diesel was driven by Mr James Davidson, Dundee, who has worked on the railway for 47 years, and the guard was Mr A. Donaldson, Freddie Tait Street, St Andrews. Provost Braid had the last ticket issued from Leven to St Andrews, but if the Provost has his way it won't be the last ticket sold for the East Neuk trip.

---

* It should be noted that the main tourist season coincides with the Scottish school holidays which both begin earlier and end earlier than those in England.

# THORNTON JUNCTION TO LEUCHARS JUNCTION via ST. ANDREWS

**E78 WEEKDAYS** — **WEEKDAYS E79**

## DOWN

Stations (reading down):

THORNTON JN. • Cameron Bridge • LEVEN • Lundin Links • Largo • Kilconquhar • Elie • St. Monans • Pittenweem • ANSTRUTHER • Crail • Kingsbarns • ST. ANDREWS • Guard Bridge • LEUCHARS JN.

Mileage: 0, 3, 5, 7, 8, 9, 11, 13, 15, 16, 18, 22, 25, 33, 37, 39...

Extract from the BR Working Timetable for Passenger Trains, Winter 1964-65.

## UP — WEEKDAYS (E80 / E81)

| Mileage M C | Station | 2 F | 2 F | 2 C | 2 C | 2 E | 2 E | 2 C | 2 C | 2 C | 2 C | 2 C | 2 C | 2 C | 2 F | 2 C | 2 C | 2 C | 2 |
|---|---|---|---|---|---|---|---|---|---|---|---|---|---|---|---|---|---|---|---|
| 0 0 | LEUCHARS JN. |  |  |  |  |  |  |  |  |  |  |  |  |  |  |  |  | Diesel |  |
| 0 14 / 1 05 | Guard Bridge / ST. ANDREWS |  |  |  |  |  |  |  |  |  |  |  |  |  |  |  |  |  |  |
| 13 / 16 / 20 | Kingsbarns / Crail / ANSTRUTHER |  |  |  |  |  |  |  |  |  |  |  |  |  |  |  |  |  |  |
| 21 / 23 / 25 | Pittenweem / St. Monance / Elie |  |  |  |  |  |  |  |  |  |  |  |  |  |  |  |  |  |  |
| 26 / 30 / 31 | Kilconquhar / Largo / Lundin Links |  |  |  |  |  |  |  |  |  |  |  |  |  |  |  |  |  |  |
| 33 04 | LEVEN |  |  |  |  |  |  |  |  |  |  |  |  |  |  |  |  |  |  |
| 35 20 / 39 01 | Cameron Bridge / THORNTON JN. |  |  |  |  |  |  |  |  |  |  |  |  |  |  |  |  |  |  |

## UP — SUNDAYS

| Station | 2 F | 2 C | 2 C | 2 E | 2 C | 2 C | 2 C | 2 F | 2 C | 2 C | 3 S | 2 C | 2 C | 2 |
|---|---|---|---|---|---|---|---|---|---|---|---|---|---|---|
| LEUCHARS JN. |  |  |  |  |  |  |  |  |  |  |  |  |  |  |
| Guard Bridge / ST. ANDREWS |  |  |  |  |  |  |  |  |  |  |  |  |  |  |
| Kingsbarns / Crail / ANSTRUTHER |  |  |  |  |  |  |  |  |  |  |  |  |  |  |
| Pittenweem / St. Monance / Elie |  |  |  |  |  |  |  |  |  |  |  |  |  |  |
| Kilconquhar / Largo / Lundin Links / LEVEN |  |  |  |  |  |  |  |  |  |  |  |  |  |  |
| Cameron Bridge / THORNTON JN. |  |  |  |  |  |  |  |  |  |  |  |  |  |  |

Extract from the BR Working Timetable for Passenger Trains, Winter 1964-65.

# Withdrawal of passenger train services and closing of stations between Thornton Junction and Dundee (Tay Bridge) via Crail on and from Monday, 6th Sept., 1965

## *Alterations to Passenger Train Services*

## *and*

## *Alternative Road Services*

The Scottish Region of British Railways announce that ALL passenger train services will be withdrawn from the line between

### LEVEN and ST. ANDREWS

and that the following stations will be closed to passenger traffic on and from

### MONDAY, 6TH SEPTEMBER, 1965

| | |
|---|---|
| LUNDIN LINKS | LARGO |
| KILCONQUHAR | ELIE |
| ST. MONANCE | PITTENWEEM |
| ANSTRUTHER | CRAIL |
| GUARDBRIDGE | ST. FORT |

This pamphlet contains details of the revised train services which will operate to LEVEN and ST. ANDREWS and substitutes what is shown in the time table.

Particulars are also given of alternative road services and a time table of bus services covering the route is reproduced.

Front cover of the pamphlet distributed to local households in the summer of 1965.

An enthusiast discusses the march of history with the driver of the last scheduled steam train to St Andrews from the south, the 9.08 am Saturdays-only from Glasgow on 21st August, 1965, while an incoming dmu, the 1.38 pm from Leuchars, arrives from the north.    *C.C. Thornburn*

The last steam-hauled service over any part of the Anstruther & St Andrews, the 2.35 pm Crail to Thornton prepares to leave Crail on Saturday 4th September, 1965 - note the Thompson-pattern stock. The coach in the foreground, No. SC88610E, was the last of its pattern to be delivered to the Scottish Region in 1952 and was built at the Birmingham Railway Carriage & Wagon Co.    *Norman Turnbull*

The last southbound service from St Andrews, the 5.05 pm Dundee Tay Bridge to Glasgow Queen Street via Crail, prepares for a muted departure on Saturday 4th September, 1965.

*Norman Turnbull*

Five hours later, the 7.40 pm Edinburgh Waverley to St Andrews service arrives with the final passenger train over the line from Crail.

*C.C. Thornburn*

The following day, Sunday 5th September, the two final down services to Crail via Anstruther were operated in the morning - the 10.10 am Sundays Only from Glasgow Queen Street and the 10.15 Sundays Only from Edinburgh Waverley. The honour of being the very last passenger service over any part of the Anstruther & St Andrews Railway (and, incidentally, the very last passenger train over the greater part of the Leven & East of Fife Railway) was the 6.20 pm Crail to Glasgow Queen Street diesel multiple unit. A large crowd turned out to travel on this train, some of them having made the journey to Crail on a special 60-seater bus put on from Leven as a result of numerous enquiries at local bus depots. The booking office at Crail was so overwhelmed that the harassed ticket clerk lost count of the number of passengers booked on the train and his stock of tickets ran out; paper Excess Fare tickets had to be issued instead.

On Monday 6th September the buses took over with a nominally hourly bus from Newport and St Andrews to Leven station, or more accurately somewhere near to Leven station. Within days public protests were being made about the poor service provided and of the failure of the buses to maintain any proper connections - hardly a surprise, given the attitude towards rail passengers exhibited by the management of Alexanders.

## Until Further Notice

Special arrangements were put in place at Crail station in respect of goods traffic which had previously been dealt with by passenger trains with newspapers now being forwarded by bus from Leven while forwarded crab traffic continued to be loaded and taken by rail from Crail; all other passenger-rated traffic was to be collected and delivered from St Andrews. The crab traffic was lost almost immediately as BR announced that they would be discontinuing the special preferential rates for boxes of crabs and that thereafter they would only be carrying full wagon loads at the standard rate - this was a clear indication that BR were expecting the crab traffic to move by road as rail had, by this simple ruling, become highly uncompetitive. The signal box at Crail was closed, despite the station still having a sporadic service operating between there and Kirkland Yard. On 26th February, 1966 a Supplementary Operating Instruction in the following terms was issued.

CRAIL/KINGSBARNS - UNTIL FURTHER NOTICE
Electric token block working between Crail and St Andrews has been discontinued. The line has been cut at a point 250 yards on the Kingsbarns side of St Andrews Down Inner Home Signal and at a point 200 yards on the Kingsbarns side of the Down loop points at Crail. Buffer stops have been erected at the points of severance.
The line, Leven to Crail, is worked under the 'one engine in steam' regulations, and a travelling signalman accompanies each train to operate points and signals en route and Kilconquhar level crossing gates. Third Part level crossing gates lie normally across the railway and are operated by trainmen from British Railways.

In May 1966 posters were erected at Crail station announcing that, with effect from 18th July of that year, Crail and all the remaining intermediate stations on

British Railways — Scottish Region

# CLOSING OF

## CRAIL

# GOODS STATION

On and from

## MONDAY, 18 JULY 1966

CRAIL Goods Station

will be CLOSED

Alternative rail facilities are available at METHIL GOODS STATION (Leven Dock)

End of the line at Crail - this photograph is dated 4th December, 1966, almost six months after the line died.

*J.L. Stevenson*

the East of Fife line were to be closed entirely with any goods traffic thereafter to be handled at Methil Goods station. All services were withdrawn on the due date and the line between Crail and Leven was officially declared out of use with effect from 18th December, 1966; the grass-grown rails were now left to await their fate at the hands of the demolition gangs although there was one more revenue-earning load carried over the line when, in the following year, the LNER-built 'A4' Pacific locomotive, No. 60009 *Union of South Africa* was hauled dead by a diesel locomotive as far as Crail where it was then put onto a road low-loader and taken to a new home on the Lochty Private Railway.*

## The Railway Vanishes

On the day that the line to Crail was officially closed and before the corpse was cold, the St Andrews Town Council passed a resolution to enquire of the British Railways Board if they could have first refusal on any railway property within the burgh boundaries that had or might become redundant as a result of the closure of the East Fife line. This application, however, was somewhat premature in that although all services had been withdrawn over that section, and buffer stops placed at both St Andrews and Crail to prevent any movements over it, the line lay derelict pending a decision by the Ministry of Transport as to whether or not the trackbed was to be kept intact for strategic purposes or not - a rare example of forethought on the part of the Government who might have been having second thoughts, or not. Eventually it was decided that the route of the railway had no such value and permission to dispose of the lands concerned was given to BR in March 1967; thereafter the Board agreed to sell through their subsidiary, Railway Sites Ltd (later the BR Property Board), for a mere £500 a fraction of its market value, the whole of the railway lands within the town to the Council, it being made a condition of sale that the Council became immediately responsible for all the overbridges and other redundant structures. Whether the sale at such a price was typical of the defeatist attitude of BR at the time is a moot point but it is noticeable that the estimate of all materials recovered from the closure of the whole of the line from Leven to St Andrews via Crail was officially said to be only £34,534 or an average of only £1,233 per mile.†

By December of that year demolition of the Canongate bridge had taken place in order, it was said, to eliminate a dangerous traffic hazard and this was followed by the complete removal of the track elsewhere along the route and the demolition of several bridges in order that the girders and other salvageable metalwork could be recovered. The cutting between Argyle Street and Doubledykes Road was completely filled in by the end of 1968, the Council-appointed contractors being Bett Brothers, although preparations were being made to save at least some of the route, including the section over the Kinness Burn viaduct, for inclusion in a new public right of way. Had a little more insight been employed by the Council the route might have been retained as a right-of-way suitable as a bridle path and cycleway to Crail and thus providing a recreational opportunity to locals and tourists alike. However, in those now far-off days of small councils and parochialism, elected representatives were

---

* For more details see *The East of Fife Central Railway (The Lochty Branch)*.
† See A.J. Mullay, *Scottish Region: A History 1948-1973*, (2006).

Kingsbarns awaiting the demolition gang on 4th December, 1966 - in the upper picture the signal box and main building have both gone while in the lower picture, looking towards Crail, the track and water tower will follow shortly although the crossing gates and line on the crossing survived in place for a further 15 years.                    *J.L. Stevenson*

often blinkered and obsessed more with immediate money-saving than with considering how future generations might benefit.

Much controversy surrounded the replacement of the trains by the buses, it has to be admitted that the hourly St Andrews-Crail-Anstruther-Leven service, together with local services between St Andrews and Anstruther via Dunino, are a lot more convenient than the trains which they replaced. It is, however, unfortunate that a true rail replacement service, connecting with trains at Leuchars and Kirkcaldy, was never implemented and this was a real shortcoming of the railway closure legislation of the 1960s or indeed since. The trains may have been infrequent and only marginally quicker than the buses, but they were and still are much missed, the majority of those travelling to the East Neuk now do so by private car but there are still through buses between Glasgow and Anstruther; a similar seasonal service to Edinburgh was withdrawn through lack of patronage. The railway has, for the travelling public, not been wholly forgotten for Leuchars, Cupar, Markinch and Kirkcaldy all remain local railheads, particularly for journeys to Edinburgh or the South.

## Remains of the Day

South from St Andrews there are many visible remains of the Anstruther & St Andrews Railway. The Kinness Burn viaduct survives intact and can be walked across since the trackbed here forms part of a footpath. A cutting, stone overbridge and section of embankment remain at Cairnsmill (known locally as Spinkie Den) but at Mount Melville the station has disappeared under a realignment of the A915 although the original stone bridge remains and now carries a minor road to Lumbo, Balone and Craigtoun. At Lamboletham a short distance of rail survives on the deck of the level crossing here, albeit that it is often covered by mud and the solum of the railway can be followed right up to Allanhill as it is now used as a private roadway. The trackbed re-emerges at Prior Muir and not only does the bridge carrying the B9131 over the line survive but so does Stravithie station. Now in the guise of the 'Old Station' guesthouse, complete with a hanging sign reminiscent in style of a Southern Railway station target, the main buildings, which were lived in as a private dwelling for many years after the closure of the line, were transformed and extended in 1999-2000 by the Briggs family and, in a nice touch, a former BR Mark I coach, has been placed alongside the platform and now forms the superior guest accommodation.* Whether any newly-married couple from Cellardyke have ever spent their wedding night here since 1906 is unknown to the authors! The station master's house still survives and is now named Homelands.

The girder bridge at Bonnytown has been dismantled but the stone abutments remain. At Boarhills the station buildings were demolished in 1966 but the Kenly Burn viaduct stands virtually unaltered although both ends are now blocked off to prevent access and it is very difficult to get a real impression of this impressive structure. At Kilduncan the bridge over the burn and a short section of the trackbed remains. The site of Kingsbarns station is somewhat desolate and overgrown with brambles but the platforms and loading bank can

* The coach is No. 70859 (York, 1966), a trailer first corridor vehicle which formed part of a Southern Region unpowered 4-TC set.

The bridge that carries the B9171 over the line at Sypsies near Crail in April 2006 - like many other bridges on the line, it was a solid and well-built structure. *A.M. Hajducki*

Third Part level crossing, between Anstruther and Crail, April 2006 - this is one of several buildings of the Anstruther & St Andrews Railway which still survives as a private residence. *A.M. Hajducki*

*Right:* The nameboard of Stravithie Old Station guesthouse, December 2006 - the sign is somewhat reminiscent of a Southern Railway target! *A.M. Hajducki*

*Below:* Stravithie station showing the main building in December 2006 and, on the down line, a Southern Region Mark I coach from a 4TC set which now forms the superior accommodation at the guest house. *A.M. Hajducki*

still be traced. The buildings here were demolished in 1966 although the crossing gates and a short section of track remained *in situ* until about 15 years ago. The road from here to the village is still, appropriately, named Station Road. A section of about 2 miles south of Kingsbarns station is walkable and forms a bridle path and farm track. A stone occupation bridge and the bridge over the Kippo or Cambo burn can still be seen and at Chance Inn the bridge over which the B9171 road crossed the line is still intact as is the impressive skew bridge at Sypsies, which carried the B940 over the line.

Crail station, albeit in a rather mutilated form, still stands and forms part of the buildings of a garden centre.* West of Crail, Kirkmay and Thirdpart crossing keeper's houses are still lived in and very obviously betray their railway origins. At Kilrenny Common, the public footpath from the village to Muiredge crosses the line over the stone bridge which was the scene of the 1910 tragedy involving a locomotive driver. Much of the trackbed has disappeared here and elsewhere but at Anstruther, although the new station has been completely demolished, the Dreel Burn viaduct is still there and can be walked both over and under, although the bracketed footbridge has been removed, and the site of Anstruther Junction and part of the Old station here form a landscaped public park; this is a good place to sit and to consider the sad fate of the Anstruther & St Andrews Railway!

* At the time of writing (2008) the garden centre had closed down and the future of the station building and its surroundings hangs in the balance.

NBR Reid class 'J' 4-4-0 No. 359 *Dirk Hatteraick* with the stock of the Glasgow portion of the 'Fife Coast Express' passing Cadder down yard, *c.*1920 On the footplate are driver Robert Fearns and fireman Alex Watt while the name of the locomotive comes from a Dutch pirate who features in a Walter Scott novel.

*NBRSG Hennigan Collection*

# Chapter Nine

# The Long Way Round: Passenger Traffic
# on the Anstruther & St Andrews Railway

*'The large party was conveyed by train and spent a most enjoyable day
on Sauchope and Roome Bay Links'*
East of Fife Record, 1908

In this Chapter, the individual passenger stations between St Andrews and
Anstruther and the traffic that they handled are dealt with in turn, followed by
a more general survey of passenger train services on the line.

## St Andrews

The majority of passengers from St Andrews alighted from and joined trains
to Leuchars and Dundee and were either bound for Dundee itself or for main
line connections at Leuchars. This traffic, which consisted of tourists, golfers,
townspeople on business and pleasure, schoolgirls, servicemen and university
undergraduates and staff, was at times a heavy one and is detailed in greater
detail in *The St Andrews Railway*; the present volume is principally concerned
with those passengers who travelled from St Andrews southwards over the line
to Crail, Anstruther and beyond. The line was never regarded by either the
North British or the LNER as a true through route and although one could
travel from, say, Dundee, to Edinburgh via Crail at the same fare as via the
main-line through Cupar, the Fife Coast line was rarely used for this purpose
other than by those wishing to sample its scenic delights or, more usually, by
those with more than a passing interest in railways. The LNER did, however,
encourage holidaymakers to buy Rover tickets and traverse this most pleasing
of routes. Most journeys between St Andrews and Crail were local ones and St
Andrews station tended to cater for those who had business in the town either
of a commercial or shopping nature or of an academic or professional nature. It
has, however, to be remembered that the roundabout route that the railway
took and the sparse nature of the train service, militated against much in the
way of regular commuter traffic and the reluctance of the NBR to grant reduced
rate fares to University students discouraged local students from living at home
and attending classes in St Andrews, or from students from elsewhere seeking
lodgings in the East Neuk towns. If these discouragements to local traffic were
not enough, the rise of the local motor bus put paid to much of the remaining
traffic and the St Andrews to Crail section became one of the quietest sections
of in Fife, only coming to life at the height of the season, during the annual
Lammas Fair, or on Saturdays when shoppers and pleasure-makers tended to
use its trains. The absence of a Sunday service did not help, particularly in an
age when the local buses were all to happy to oblige the public in a way that the
railway company was not.

NBR Reid class 'K' 4-4-0 No. 885 at Craigentinny Sidings with the stock of an Edinburgh via Crail service, June 1922.
*Robert McCulloch, W. Hennigan Collection*

## Mount Melville

This rather isolated station, situated beside the Largo to St Andrews road a couple of miles south of the city, had been built to serve the Mount Melville estate and the scattered farms and cottages in the area around Wester Balrymonth Hill and at the turn of the century a weekly total of some 100 or so passengers were booked to travel on trains from here. Many of these were shoppers travelling to St Andrews at a minimal third-class fare and therefore the station passenger receipts were, unsurprisingly, the lowest on the entire line, and managed to average a grand total of £3 per week, barely enough to cover the staff costs here let alone the additional fuel costs of stopping and starting trains here. A brief period of prosperity occurred in 1908 when the Royal Highland Show,* Scotland's premier agricultural event even now, was held on the Mount Melville estate and the station was so busy with additional traffic that spare passenger coaches had to be berthed at nearby stations. The station was temporarily closed during the latter half of World War I and in reopening in 1919 never managed to regain more than a portion of its pre-war passenger numbers. With the advent of a bus service on the main road passenger figures continued to plummet so that by 1929, the last complete year of passenger services, less than three passenger bookings per day were being made at the station and receipts had slumped to a mere 18s. 6d. per week.

## Stravithie

An even-more isolated station than Mount Melville, Stravithie was situated on the St Andrews to Anstruther via Dunino road and served a wide rural area including Brigton, Stravithie, Dunino and Bonnytown. Rather more successful than Mount Melville, at least from a revenue point of view, the station never really justified its two platforms and footbridge but nevertheless managed to serve as the local post and telegraph office and as a small local shop serving the immediate area; it also handled a considerable traffic in parcels and other passenger-rated traffic. Much of the passenger traffic handled was that of persons visiting and having business at the local estates and farms and there was no season ticket traffic. Remaining open during World War I for operational reasons (it being the intermediate block post between Kingsbarns and St Andrews), it does not seem to have attracted any traffic from the temporarily closed Mount Melville and Boarhills stations. Like Mount Melville the establishment of a direct bus service, in this case between Anstruther and St Andrews, deprived the station of much of its remaining traffic and by 1929 its passenger bookings had sunk to an annual total of just over 1,000 with receipts from passengers and parcels of just over £200. A handful of special and excursion trains called at the station after its closure to regular traffic in 1930 but the existence of RAF Stravithie from 1941 to 1946 does not appear to have engendered any passenger traffic.

---

* The show was originally peripatetic, only settling in its permanent home at Ingliston, near Edinburgh, in 1965. An interesting coda to the Mount Melville show occurred in the 1950s when a porter clearing out a desk at the station found an outward half of an NBR one-day special excursion ticket from Edinburgh; the ticket was subsequently sent to the Museum of British Transport.

## Boarhills

The original temporary terminus of the Anstruther & St Andrews Railway between 1883 and 1887, from where passengers were served by a horse bus service to and from St Andrews, Boarhills served the village of that name as well as the farms and houses of the Kenly Burn valley and surrounding area. In common with Mount Melville and Stravithie, it never thereafter achieved more than moderate passenger figures and by 1900 was handling just under 120 passengers a week. Closed temporarily in the First War as an economy measure, the establishment of the Crail to St Andrews bus service, which ran closer to the village than the railway did, contributed to the eventual demise of the station in 1930. Prior to closure most of the traffic from the station had been long-distance or to the south and bookings to St Andrews fell dramatically as soon as one could travel by bus on a journey of less than 4 miles as opposed to the 6½ by rail.

Before the charabanc removed local excursion traffic, the station at Boarhills handled extra traffic, mainly as a result of the pleasures of the Kenly Burn den and the generosity of the owners of the estate of Kenly Green. Typical examples were the excursion by rail in June 1909 from Anstruther to Boarhills of the children and teachers of the Anstruther parish Church Sunday Schools when 'the park at Kenly was put at their disposal and a very enjoyable day was spent in games and amusements' and a day in 1913 when a special train for some 70 persons was run from Anstruther to Boarhills on behalf of the Cellardyke branch of the YMCA. After the closure of Boarhills to passengers a limited amount of excursion traffic continued to depart from the station and these included, in 1938, a trip to the Empire Exhibition in Glasgow and when a local schoolmaster managed to persuade the LNER to stop an excursion train at the station to allow school pupils to attend a Scotland v England Schoolboy Football International held at Cowdenbeath.

## Kingsbarns

As befitted the largest settlement between St Andrews and Crail, Kingsbarns was also the busiest station, although the term 'busiest' was a relative one as neither passenger or goods receipts were, even at the height of the station's prosperity, anything other than a mere fraction of those at Anstruther or Crail. Nevertheless the station remained both as a place where local journeys began and ended and also as a holiday destination, it being said in the *East of Fife Record* in August 1908 that:

> During the last month Kingsbarns has been favoured with the presence of a large number of visitors, fully 150 finding residence there for the month. Although not the happy possessors of many of the usual seaside attractions, the town is evidently able to attract a good many strangers. This month but few visitors have made their appearance.

The principal attraction of Kingsbarns of course being, then as now, its wonderful beach at Cambo Sands although golfers and country lovers also found it a suitable place for a quiet break. The principal drawback, however, of

Kingsbarns station was its isolated situation, being well over a mile from the village by a winding and unlit country lane and a good two miles from the Cambo Sands. Once the competing bus services from Crail to St Andrews ran straight through the village, the fate of the station was sealed and passenger bookings fell dramatically until the station was closed in 1930. It enjoyed a brief reprise for passengers during World War II when personnel working at the nearby RAF Kilduncan airfield resulted in trains stopping at Kingsbarns on an intermittent basis.

## Crail

Throughout the period that passenger trains served Crail the majority of the traffic was always in a westwards direction towards Anstruther, Leven and Thornton. From the operating point of view the station was more seen as the eastern extremity of the Leven & East of Fife section with several trains terminating there rather than being seen as the first station on the Anstruther & St Andrews line. Loadings towards St Andrews were light and this imbalance between eastwards and westwards traffic became particularly marked after the coastal bus service improved and began to abstract passengers. Nevertheless Crail had a good basic traffic with schoolchildren for the Waid Academy, shoppers bound for Anstruther and Leven, and locals wishing to travel to visit friends or conduct business at the other East Neuk burghs. The town always had a greater than average number of retired people living there and they were often dependent on public transport - an advantage which the railway managed to exploit until the situation of the station at the edge of the burgh became a liability when the bus services ran along the main coast road which passed right through the town. Another intermittent source of traffic was the airfield situated to the north-east of the town which drew many additional passengers, both in its construction stage and from aircrews and ground staff. Between 1956 and 1960 the Joint Services School for Linguistics, whose students were encamped at the airfield, generated a limited amount of traffic and a recent history of that organization* recalls that when the School transferred its quarters from Cornwall to Crail, 'its people and paraphernalia, blackboards, dictionaries, typewriters and desks, were crammed into one special train, with urns of tea and sandwiches provided by the Catering Corps'. Travelling via Crewe, the train eventually entered into East Fife with 'some of its students dozing in the luggage racks' when one of the older gentlemen, a Russian exile, 'was heard to murmur dolefully as he peered out of the windows, *prostory, prostory'* (nothing but empty space) - presumably a reference to the somewhat bleak section of line between Largo and Kilconquhar.

Crail, however, grew as a holiday centre towards the end of the 19th century and it was not long before the local population began to clamour for the extension of the Anstruther express services to their town. This came and the fortunes of the ancient burgh began to revive with a healthy Easter and summer trade in visitors, mainly from Edinburgh and Glasgow; additional trains served golfers and daytrippers although the latter were not encouraged at a place which regarded itself as catering more for 'select' persons, i.e. golfers and 'artistic' types, which latter category

* Elliott and Shukman, *Secret Classrooms – An Untold History of the Cold War* (2002).

included genteel persons of little talent but definitely not bohemians! Incoming excursions from all parts of Fife and beyond were frequent and a typical entry in the *East of Fife Record* for July 1910 reported that:

> The Sunday Schools in connection with Guardbridge and Leuchars United Free Church had their annual excursion to Crail on Saturday. The large party was conveyed by train and spent a most enjoyable day on Sauchope and Roome Bay Links.

Sunday trains were introduced after the war and these proved popular, especially with excursionists who were, in changing times, no longer discouraged. The annual passenger figures at Crail averaged 23,000 until the 1920s but thereafter there was a decline in the number of passengers booked so that by the 1930s it had fallen to less than 10,000. However, for many years the holiday trade boomed and Crail still relied on the railway as the means of transport for many of its visitors despite the rise of the private car. In the 1950s the rising affluence of those who had traditionally holidayed at Crail was drawing them to more exotic locations elsewhere in the British Isles and by the 1960s, however, cheap foreign holidays and changing tastes made further significant inroads into this once lucrative market. To many in the town, the closure of Crail station was merely the final straw so far as the tourist trade was concerned. Like Cellardyke and the burghs to the east, Crail was increasingly becoming a haven for retired folk and second homers and, apart from daytrippers, its heyday as a seasonal holiday resort was over.

### Anstruther

Although the greatest part of the passenger traffic at Anstruther was bound for the west and will be dealt with in detail in the Leven & East of Fife volume, there was nevertheless some not insignificant traffic eastwards to Crail and St Andrews, the bulk of which was bound for the latter destination. Apart from schoolchildren attending the Waid Academy, most local passengers consisted of shoppers from Crail, business and professional men travelling to St Andrews and farmers returning from the markets at Thornton and elsewhere. Longer distance passengers included holidaymakers travelling from the west to Crail and fishermen, crews and others associated with the trade who were travelling up to Aberdeen and other east coast ports via Leuchars. Much excursion traffic originated at Anstruther, much of it associated with the local development and merchants' associations, and several excursions to destinations more distant than St Andrews via Crail were organized to begin at Anstruther. The advent of the motor bus dealt a fatal blow to this local traffic with buses serving directly the coast road and major parts of both Anstruther Easter and Anstruther Wester with a direct service between Anstruther and St Andrews via Dunino, which journey was completed in a shorter time and at a much cheaper fare, as by road the mileage was halved. Many trains from the west terminated at Anstruther or Crail and the service beyond those points was poor, a direct reflection of the lack of potential traffic rather than a reflection on the level of service provided.

## Train Services

The initial passenger train service on the Anstruther & St Andrews Railway consisted of Pittenweem to Boarhills shuttle services, some of which conveyed a through coach from the Leven & East of Fife line. In the summer of 1884 the passenger service was as follows:

|              |      |       | A     | A     | A    | A    |
|--------------|------|-------|-------|-------|------|------|
|              |      | am    | am    | pm    | pm   | pm   |
| Anstruther   | dep. | 7.55  | 9.25  | 12.50 | 4.20 | 7.20 |
| Crail        | dep. | 8.06  | 9.36  | 1.01  | 4.31 | 7.31 |
| Kingsbarns   | dep. | 8.14  | 9.44  | 1.09  | 4.39 | 7.39 |
| Boarhills    | arr. | 8.20  | 9.50  | 1.15  | 4.45 | 7.45 |
| St Andrews   | arr. |       | 10b55 |       | 5b50 |      |

|              |      | C     | C     | C     | C     | E    |
|--------------|------|-------|-------|-------|-------|------|
|              |      | am    | am    | pm    | pm    | pm   |
| St.Andrews   | dep. |       | 7b40  |       | 2b25  |      |
| Boarhils     | dep. | 5.55  | 8.45  | 12.10 | 3.30  | 6.40 |
| Kingsbarns   | dep. | 6.00  | 8.50  | 12.15 | 3.35  | 6.45 |
| Crail        | dep. | 6.08  | 8.58  | 12.23 | 3.48  | 6.53 |
| Anstruther   | arr. | 6.20  | 9.10  | 12.35 | 4.05  | 7.05 |

*Notes:* A - Through train from Thornton Junction; b - bus connection, C- Through train to Thornton Junction; E - Through train Anstruther to Thornton on Saturdays Only.

When the line to St Andrews came into use certain services from Glasgow, Edinburgh and Thornton terminated at Anstruther while others were extended to Crail and a handful to St Andrews, especially after the opening of the Forth Bridge in 1890. The service beyond Crail was never a plentiful one and in the winter although Crail enjoyed a service of some eight trains a day to the west, only four of these had come from St Andrews. It is perhaps remarkable that on the whole of the Fife Coast Line the timetable of the 1950s was in many ways virtually identical to that of the first decade of the century.

The Summer 1964 up passenger service on weekdays was as follows:

|            |      | AD    | BD    | CS    | ES    | FG    | H     | IS    | J     | DK    | DL    |
|------------|------|-------|-------|-------|-------|-------|-------|-------|-------|-------|-------|
| St Andrews | dep. | 06.25 | 08.40 | ...... | ...... | ...... | ...... | 14.28 | ...... | 15.15 | 17.38 |
| Crail      | dep. | 06.47 | 09.05 | 10.35 | 12.30 | 12.40 | 14.35 | 14.52 | 15.25 | 15.41 | 18.02 |
| Anstruther | arr. | 06.57 | 09.14 | 10.44 | 12.40 | 12.51 | 14.45 | 15.00 | 15.35 | 15.48 | 18.10 |

*Notes:* A - to Edinburgh Waverley, arr. 08.45; B - through train from Leuchars Jn (dep. 08.25) to Glasgow Queen St, arr. 11.51; C - to Edinburgh Waverley, arr. 12.46; D - diesel service; E - to Edinburgh Waverley, arr. 14.34, 27/6 to 15/8 only; F - Fridays Only; G - to Edinburgh Waverley, arr. 14.44, 26/6 to 14/8 only; H - to Thornton Jn, arr. 15.36, does not run when E and G run; I - to Glasgow Queen St, arr. 17.48, 27/6-22/8 only; J - to Glasgow Queen St, arr. 18.16, Fridays and Saturdays 26/6-22/8 only; K - from Dundee Tay Bridge dep. 14.42 to Edinburgh Waverley arr. 17.48; L - from Dundee Tay Bridge, dep. 17.05 to Glasgow Queen Street, arr. 20.51; S - Saturdays Only).

On Sundays there was an 18.20 dmu from Crail to Glasgow Queen Street, arr. 21.10, and a 19.55 Crail to Edinburgh Waverley steam train, arr. 22.16.

The 'Fife Coast Express' in its latter days with (*above*) 'B1' class No. 61172 approaching Crail with the down train composed of Gresley teak stock painted in the BR 'blood and custard' livery and (*below*) No. 61180 showing the former 'Silver Jubilee' streamlined stock in the same livery.

*(Both) A.G. Ellis*

As for passenger comforts, the NBR rolling stock in the independent days of the A&StAR was the subject of much criticism but the line never seems to have been favoured with the most modern or comfortable of stock with the possible exception of the Fife Coast Express with its tea car in the early days and the use, after the war, of the streamlined stock from the 'Silver Jubilee'. This consisted of coaches SC1581/2E and SC 1586/7/8, articulated twin- and triple-sets which ran in a modified grey livery until, in 1951, being repainted into the first BR main line red and cream livery and, later on, all-over maroon. When the 'Express' was withdrawn, the sets were employed elsewhere on the Scottish Region. In the 1950s the majority of the stock used on the line was still either ex-LNER (Gresley or Thompson) design but from 1957 onwards ex-London, Midland & Scottish Railway (LMS) stock appeared on through services from Glasgow Buchanan Street. A handful of BR Mark I carriages appeared on the line but, due to the tight curvature of the line north of Crail, restrictions were placed on the speeds that this stock could work. With the advent of diesel multiple units in 1959-1960, some steam workings remained but the basic pattern of services was not altered and the last southbound train from St Andrews departed at tea-time leaving no late working from that city to Crail.

When the Anstruther & St Andrews Railway was opened, the Thornton Junction to Anstruther trains carried through coaches to Crail and Boarhills and, from 1887, to St Andrews. By 1892 trains conveyed first and third class passengers only and were the subject of continual complaints by local passengers who thought that East Fife was the graveyard of ancient and unsatisfactory stock deemed too poor and decrepit to be used elsewhere; although it would have to be admitted that the North British was not generally noted for treating its passengers well. The opening of the Forth Bridge in 1890 brought through Glasgow and Edinburgh to Anstruther services, a handful of which were eventually extended to Crail and eventually to St Andrews (and, in one case, to Dundee) but the North British preferred its passengers for St Andrews to travel via Leuchars rather than by the coast line, although tickets were valid by either route.

The 20th century saw the widespread introduction of bogie carriages, eventually lit by electricity, but their state was often still the subject of controversy particularly in winter when train compartments were said to be cold and miserable. Foot warmers were provided in first class compartments between Leuchars and St Andrews but none were provided between Anstruther and St Andrews after their initial use between Anstruther and Boarhills and the later advent of steam-heating of carriages must have been welcomed by the hardy Fifers and their winter visitors. The 'Fife Coast Express' brought corridor stock and, for a period between the wars, refreshment cars. On ordinary trains ex-North British stock was augmented by newer carriages and, after 1945, by corridor and non-corridor stock of Gresley and Thompson origin. A few years later new suburban-type coaches of Thompson and BR standard design (but all built after nationalisation) appeared on local trains while BR Mark I main line stock regularly appeared after 1956. This stock, which was built on 63 ft 6 in. frames as opposed to the former 57 ft frames, necessitated the imposition of a special speed limit on all trains containing such stock of 15 mph between Stravithie and St Andrews and of 10 mph through St Andrews itself.

# THE FIFE COAST EXPRESS

## WEEK DAYS
### 29th June until 5th September

| | | | | p.m. | | | | | | a.m. |
|---|---|---|---|---|---|---|---|---|---|---|
| Glasgow (Buchanan St.) | | dep. | | 3 50 | St. Andrews | ... | ... | dep. | | 7 10 |
| Aberdour | ... | ... | arr. | 5 10 | Crail | ... | ... | ... | ,, | 7 34 |
| Burntisland | ... | ... | ,, | 5 16 | Anstruther | ... | ... | ,, | 7 41 |
| Kinghorn | ... | ... | ,, | 5 22 | Elie | ... | ... | ... | ,, | 7 56 |
| Kirkcaldy | ... | ... | ,, | 5 29 | Leven | ... | ... | ... | ,, | 8 11 |
| Leven | ... | ... | ,, | 6 1 | Kirkcaldy | ... | ... | ,, | 8 37 |
| Elie | ... | ... | ,, | 6 18 | Glasgow (Queen St.) | | arr. | | 9 51 |
| Anstruther | ... | ... | ,, | 6 30 | | | | | | |
| Crail | ... | ... | ,, | 6 39 | | | | | | |
| St. Andrews | ... | ... | ,, | 7 4 | | | | | | |

**For other Services between Glasgow and St. Andrews, etc.—See Table 27**

The last ever timetable for the 'Fife Coast Express', 1959.

'D34' class 4-4-0 No. 62496 *Glen Loy* and 'B1' class 4-6-0 No. 61108 with a BR Doncaster-built non-gangwayed brake second No. SC43318 on a train of empty coaching stock leaving Crail on 18th July, 1959.     *J.L. Stevenson*

The pattern of passenger services altered little on the coast line and indeed the timetable of 1955 was remarkably similar to that of 50 years earlier even though social conditions were beginning to change out of all recognition. The number of Leuchars to St Andrews trains had doubled by World War II and through trains ran from Dundee, mostly via St Fort but with a handful via Tayport and a few continued southwards to Edinburgh via Crail.

The advent of dieselisation brought a radical overhaul to parts of the timetable and for a time some St Andrews services operated through Dundee to Arbroath and Broughty Ferry for operational reasons. Although all regular St Andrews branch services were run by dmus a Saturdays-only summer service south from St Andrews continued to be steam-hauled until 1965 as did a daily service from Crail to Thornton consisting of a brake third, a composite coach and a fish van. For a period Glasgow services at the weekends ran from the former Caledonian Railway's Buchanan Street station rather than the North British Queen Street and this led to ex-LMS carriages appearing on these trains. When the Anstruther & St Andrews line was closed the diesel shuttles continued but no longer called at Guardbridge and although small alterations were made this timetable continued until the St Andrews branch was closed in 1969; the driving cars of the diesel multiple units had small first-class saloons but this class of travel was little used in later years. There were no regular through carriages to destinations south of Edinburgh or Glasgow via the coast line.

A group of holidaymakers await the 12.30 pm Crail to Edinburgh service arrive at Anstruther, 10th August, 1963.
*C.C. Thornburn*

The 8.25 am Leuchars Junction to Glasgow Queen Street crosses the 7.20 am Dunfermline Upper to Arbroath service at Kingsbarns on 4th July, 1964 - the only scheduled crossing of trains at Kingsbarns. *C.C. Thornburn*

The last run of the 2.35 pm Crail to Thornton service characteristically hauling its fish van of crabs from Crail, 4th September, 1965. *Norman Turnbull*

*Excursion Traffic*

Regular excursion traffic to the East Neuk from both the Dundee and Leven direction was encouraged by the NBR both by the use of special trains and by reduced fares on ordinary trains from specified destinations. Most of this traffic originated from the east and usually terminated at Crail, but there were instances of specials run over the whole length of the Anstruther & St Andrews line, including a regular series of excursions to the north organised by local merchants' organisations. The LNER sought to retain this traffic with special fares and additional services when required and they also provided special trains for cinema goers, day trippers on bank holidays such as Easter Monday, Victoria Day and the Autumn Holiday and those attending special events such as the Lammas Fair and golfing events at St Andrews. Much of the earlier competition with local bus proprietors died away after the passing of the Road Traffic Act 1930 and its subsequent effect on the ownership of the buses passed to the partially railway-owned combines, but it was notable that with the ending of fuel rationing in the 1940s few special trains were run over the Anstruther & St Andrews section. There were, however, exceptions to this rule and particularly from about 1960 onwards specials began to appear again on the line and on occasions diesel haulage (and even on occasions mixed steam and diesel haulage) was used. One notable train was the Scottish Region television train, a dedicated rake of carriages fitted up with a television camera and screens used to relay close circuit television to the passengers. Mainly deployed for schoolchildren, the television train was seen several times between Anstruther and St Andrews.

Documented appearances of the television train included 1st June, 1962, 22nd May, 1963 (Hunters Tryst school, Edinburgh), 31st May, 1963 (West Calder and Juniper Green schools, Midlothian) and 13th and 14th June, 1963 - on all occasions the trains were double-headed by a pair of 'B1s' and were in excess of 10 carriages in length, making them excessively long for any of the local station platforms.

By 1960 a number of special trains for enthusiasts were being run over the Anstruther & St Andrews, largely because appreciation of this quiet rural backwater was increasing and there was a realisation that it probably would not remain open for much longer. Among these notable specials was the RCTS/SLS 'Scottish Railtour' of 12th June, 1960 drawn by NBR 'K' class 4-4-0 *Glen Douglas*, which the previous year had been restored by British Railways to running order carrying its North British livery and original number of 256. Now preserved at the Glasgow Transport Museum, the journey of *Glen Douglas* from Thornton to Leuchars via St Andrews was the last time that the NBR locomotive livery was seen on the Anstruther & St Andrews line and, presumably, the first time for almost 40 years! Unusually this train passed through St Andrews without stopping, having previously called at Crail and Mount Melville. *

Later that year the great-grandson of the Chairman of the Anstruther & St Andrews company organized an excursion that travelled over the line. Hauled by 'B1' class 4-6-0 No. 61172, and consisting of a curious mixture of coaches including Gresley stock and a BR Mark I, the train achieved a notable first in that it called at Stravithie station which had been closed to passengers some 30 years before and it must have been a strange sight to see students wearing Edwardian dress alighting

---

* An account of the tour by Robin Nelson and Stuart Sellar appears in *Steam Days*, March 2008.

Preserved NBR 4-4-0 No. 256 *Glen Douglas* with the RCTS/SLS Scottish Rail Tour at Mount Melville, 12th June, 1960. *Roy Hamilton*

at this ghost station. The *Courier* carried a report of this train in its edition of 31st October, 1960 under the heading 'Only Three Minutes Late':

Heavy rain on Saturday failed to dampen the enthusiasm of 150 St Andrews University students who toured Fife's less frequented railway lines in old-fashioned coaches. The journey covered over 120 miles of lines, many of them now closed to ordinary passenger traffic. These included the old Leslie, the Abernethy-Perth and the Lindores [lines]. The excursion was organised by a third-year arts student, John Purvis, of Kinaldy near St Andrews. Mr Purvis said that the train arrived in St Andrews station only three minutes after the scheduled time. 'I think that the whole thing was a great success.' Girl students, who were collecting for the World University Service, did the catering and gave the profits to that organisation.

When closure of the line was imminent further specials were run, the last of which was the RCTS excursion of 28th August, 1965.

The St Andrews University special calls at Stravithie on 25th October, 1960 - the first passenger train to officially call there for just over 30 years! *Authors' Collection*

# Chapter Ten

# Crabs and Corn: Freight Traffic on the Anstruther & St Andrews Railway

*'Freight trains must stop at the places*
*specified in the timetable'*
*Rule 144, British Railways Rule Book*

Although the vast bulk of traffic on the Anstruther & St Andrews Railways was agricultural in nature, other items were also handled and these included coal (for both household and industrial uses), building materials, sand and gravel, fish and shellfish and a plethora of sundry goods such as parcels, golf clubs, stock for local shops, beer, wine and spirits and almost every other variety of miscellaneous traffic that comes to mind. In this chapter agricultural and fish traffic is dealt with first of all, followed by a station-by-station account of each station or siding running from Anstruther to St Andrews.

## Agricultural Goods

The best farmland in Fife lies along the coastal fringe and also in the valley of the River Eden (known locally as 'the Howe of Fife'), with light, well-drained clay and loam soils and this area also has a lower rainfall than in other parts of the county. Barley, potatoes, turnips and sugar beet all prefer such light soils and thrive in the East Neuk which enjoys comparatively longer periods of sunshine than in the west. Other crops regularly grown include oats, grass and wheat, the latter generally of indifferent quality and often used as feed for chickens and, latterly, in the production of gin and vodka at the Cameron Bridge distillery. Although the farms of the region were predominantly arable some livestock was kept, particularly dairy cattle in the vicinity of St Andrews. The average size of landholdings varied considerably but in 1876 a quarter of all farms in Fife were less than 5 acres in size, while just over a third were greater than 100 acres; in 1947 the equivalent figures were 18 per cent and 37 per cent respectively. Not only was this ratio maintained but, for almost the whole period of the railway's existence, there was a notable stability in local land use and in many cases farmers in the post-war period were growing the same crops as their predecessors two or three generations before. Farm buildings tended to be traditional in look and many dated from the brief period of agricultural prosperity between the Napoleonic Wars and the repeal of the Corn Laws.

Until World War II many farms were run on time-honoured lines and were reasonably profitable, the area never suffering from the extreme depths of trade depression that were found in other parts of the country, but continual outbreaks of swine fever and foot and mouth disease provided severe restrictions on the carriage of livestock by rail to and from Fife, particularly in the period from 1908 to 1917. An increase in wartime production, a stabilisation

NBR Drummond class 'C' 0-6-0 No. 1310 on the 'Coast Goods' running tender first out of St Andrews towards the north; note the NBR 'road van'. This photograph was taken in 1922 and the locomotive was withdrawn from service the following year.

*H. Stirling Everard; NBRSG W. Hennigan Collection*

NBR 'C' class No. 173 crosses the Petheram bridge with the 'Coast Goods' returning to Thornton, *c.*1920.                *NBRSG Collection*

of markets and the introduction of subsidies took East Fife farms into new heights of prosperity and into an era of mechanisation and general improvement. Unfortunately for the railway, this also coincided with farmers having access to their own transport and to the poaching of much trade by local carriers and larger organizations such as the Milk Marketing Board. In 1947 agricultural workers were paid a minimum wage of £4 10s. for a 48-hour week but their total number was in steady decline throughout the period.

The two main crops handled by the railway in its later years were potatoes and sugar beet, the latter being destined for the factory at Cupar. Situated at Prestonhall near to the county town, the beet factory had a direct connection with the main line; opened in 1926 it was the only beet refining facility in Scotland and took beet in that had been grown in the counties of Fife, Angus, Moray, Perth and East Lothian. The beet was conveyed in open mineral wagons with side doors which were important because the beet was 'washed out', i.e. unloaded by being propelled out by high-pressure jets of water, at the factory. Each farmer was given a permit by the factory which stated the time at which the crop was to be delivered to them and these time slots were to be strictly adhered to. The farmer would then contact the railway and inform them of what transport he required and he was then responsible for delivering the beet to the goods yard at the appointed time.

Potatoes, mainly seed, were often bound for East Anglia and were dispatched in bags packed in straw in railway vans without ventilators to avoid the possibility of damage by cold air entering the van via open ventilators; much of the local crop was bought by J.D. Maxwell, a potato merchant based in the Scottish 'tattie capital' of Forfar.

Both beet and potatoes were autumn and winter crops, potatoes being lifted in September and October and the beet being harvested and loaded for processing during the annual intensive 'beet campaign' which lasted from mid-October to the end of December.

### Fruits of the Sea

In fishing terms the coast between St Andrews and Crail has never been of any great significance as far as fishing is concerned, the East Neuk ports of Anstruther and Pittenweem being of far greater importance as the principal landing places for herring and varieties of whitefish. Since the principal markets for locally-caught fish have always been in the South, any fish traffic which was conveyed over the East Fife lines was usually that carried westwards from Anstruther and accordingly is not covered in this volume. A significant traffic was, however, that of lobsters and crabs ('partans' in Scots) landed at Crail harbour and conveyed by rail from Crail station to the markets in the South right up to the eventual closure of the line. This was a seasonal traffic, which at times could be a heavy one, was destined almost exclusively for Billingsgate fish market in London and in latter days was conveyed in a former LMS six-wheeled fish van attached to the 2.35 pm passenger train from Crail to Thornton Junction. At the latter place the van would be attached to the Aberdeen-London

Ivatt Mogul No. 46464 at St Andrews with a trip working from the south, 11th April, 1963. This locomotive, the famed 'Carmyllie Pilot', was later preserved by the late Ian Fraser.

*C.C. Thornburn*

Gresley 'J39' class 0-6-0 No. 64790 passes Mount Melville with a pick-up goods train in 1961.

*D.J. Paul*

overnight fish train and would reach Billingsgate in time for the early morning market the following day. On occasions an additional van destined for Leeds or Manchester would also be attached and, since fish vans could not be attached to diesel multiple units (which could not cope with the extra weight), this perpetuated a regular steam-hauled passenger train until closure of the line. According to Duncan Fraser's *Historic Fife*, published in 1982, the partan season 'came to a height in the early spring and after the crabs have gone creeping out to deeper waters, the lobsters come to the best in the harvest time'.

### St Andrews

A very busy general goods yard, situated at the old station at the Links, St Andrews contributed little traffic to the line south of the city and there is nothing that the authors can add to the account of the yard already given in *The St Andrews Railway*.

### Mount Melville

Mount Melville station was originally built to convey agricultural traffic to and from local farms and to the Mount Melville estate and was, at least in its early years, a busy spot. Inward traffic consisted principally of fertilisers, household coal and cattle feed, including distillery draff (spent grain left as waste after the distilling process and used as a winter cattle feed) from Cameron Bridge. Outward traffic included sugar beet, potatoes, grain, limestone from the Denhead and Ladeddie district, livestock and coal brought by motor lorry from the Radernie pit. This last-mentioned traffic was not, however, great in quantity and an LNER General Manager's report covering the period between March and May 1933 comments that the pit 'is now producing from 50 to 60 tons per day. Owing to a carriage of about 1½ miles to Mount Melville station, the major portion of the output is going by road. We had, however, 263 tons by rail during the period under review'. The station also dealt with a limited amount of horse and carriage traffic - the 1922 NBR General Appendix containing the advice that 'Carriages, but only those for Mr Younger, can be loaded and unloaded at Mount Melville, and these must be conveyed to and from the loading bank by special train only'. In 1925 the station came under the control of St Andrews and was the first to be unstaffed, traffic having dwindled greatly from its one-time peak.

### Stravithie

The station master at Strathvithie had the distinction of also being the local postmaster of the rural district served by the station and the station also doubled up as the post office. Inward traffic consisted of coal, fertilisers (often from Central Farmers Ltd of Methil) and sundries such as parts for farm

Mount Melville in the 1930s showing the yard's Glasgow derrick crane and a hy-bar wagon labelled 'G.W.'
*NBRSG Collection*

Activity at Boarhills as locally-grown potatoes are being off-loaded from a farm trailer into an open wagon on 18th April, 1953.
*J.L. Stevenson*

machinery, animal feeds and cases of wine and spirits while the outward traffic consisted of sugar beet, potatoes, grain and livestock. The station was used by local farms and landed estates including Kinaldy, Gilmerton and Stravithie. For a period in the late 1880s and up to the end of the 19th century the Stravithie Quarry, situated just west of the station, had its own siding and this was used to convey stone away from the quarry.

## Boarhills

Boarhills station had an inwards goods traffic of fertilisers, animal feeds and four or five wagonloads of coal per month and outward traffic in season consisted of agricultural produce, mainly sugar beet bound for Cupar, oats and potatoes, both 'ware' (i.e. for human consumption) and seed. In addition there was a certain amount of livestock, principally cattle being sent to market, and also oatmeal dispatched to Glasgow from the nearby Park Meal Mill of Messrs Rogers. In common with the other stations between Crail and St Andrews, the amount of potatoes and sugar beet increased significantly during World War II and this resulted in a temporary increase in traffic in phosphate fertilisers; in addition there was also an increase in coal traffic handled at Boarhills during this period due to its having been selected as an official strategic storage point for the St Andrews district. The sidings here were shunted by tow-ropes due to the layout of the track; almost all traffic originating from Boarhills, with the exception of seed potatoes, was sent southwards via Anstruther.

## Kingsbarns

Freight traffic at Kingsbarns consisted principally of grain, potatoes, sugar beet, fertilisers and several wagons of coal per month. The area was one of importance for the growing of potatoes, with a trade in seed potatoes to England being a speciality. Prior to the opening of the railway seed potatoes were dispatched to English ports via the small harbour on the shore just to the east of the village; this fell into disuse after the railway had captured the traffic. The estate of Cambo House, seat of the Erskine family, lay to the south-east and provided additional agricultural and horse traffic and for a short period during World War II the Royal Naval Air Service base at Kilduncan/Dunino provided additional traffic. A local coal merchant, Mrs A. Brown of Kingsbarns, had a solitary private owner wagon. This was an 8-ton oak-framed example from R.Y. Pickering of Wishaw and was fitted with spring buffers. The NBR register plate number was 14484 and the Pickering records stated that it was painted in a chocolate colour and that the wagon bore the fleet number '1'. The wagon was leased from the Scottish Wagon Company, and bore that finance company's plate 66683. It is noted as having been 'delivered free of charge to the Michael Pit, West Wemyss* by 6th June, 1902 to the order of Mrs A. Brown, Kingsbarns.

After the withdrawal of passenger services in 1930 a single member of staff sufficed and, in common with Mount Melville, Stravithie and Boarhills, the station was latterly reduced to an unstaffed public siding and closed to all traffic with effect from 5th October, 1964.

---

* The Michael Pit, owned by the Wemyss Coal Company, was, in fact, situated at East Wemyss – see Alan Brotchie, *The Wemyss Private Railway* (Oakwood Press).

The loading gauge and yard at Crail, 18th April, 1953.        *J.L. Stevenson*

This hardy survivor from the NBR era was pictured at Crail on 30th August, 1956 - fortunately it is now in the collection of the Scottish Railway Preservation Society at Bo'ness.     *A.G. Ellis*

## Crail

Crail was a busy station in freight terms, receiving 30 or so wagons of coal per month and with a constant agricultural traffic which included potatoes, straw (both loose and baled), fertilisers and animal feedstuffs. Local traders included R. Hutchinson & Co., corn merchants, flour and provender millers, maltsters and grain traders based in Kirkcaldy but with a local agency, Peattie's coal merchants and Invercauld Industries, homespun tweed manufacturers. Although there was a small gas works in the town it was, for most of its life, served by seaborne coal. Crail received one railway van per day from Anstruther, that is a covered van conveying sundry goods that could not be taken by passenger trains and this was taken in a daily trip working between Anstruther and Mount Melville, the 'coast goods' terminating at the former station. During the wars additional traffic ran to Crail Airfield and HMS *Jackdaw* and at the height of the 'Cold War', between 1959 and 1963, large quantities of sugar were conveyed by rail to Crail to be stockpiled at a Ministry of Agriculture intervention store there, trains often comprising of up to 30 wagons at a time. Additional help to unload these trains and to load the sugar sacks on to the lorries for onward transmission to the store was required and it was the practice of the Anstruther station master to arrange this by hiring unemployed fishermen in that town to act as casual labourers.

A description of Crail goods yard in the 1960s given to the authors by Brian Malaws included the following:

> By then the freight traffic had dwindled away and I don't remember any goods, other than parcels, being handled at the station, although small quantities of crabs and lobsters were sent out in a van attached to the one remaining steam-hauled daily passenger train. There was a cattle pen near the signal box and a small brick-built coal merchant's office at the other end of the yard, but I never saw either in use. Behind the ticket office was an old coach body containing scales, with an old iron weighing platform outside where large parcels and other items, and I think the boxes of shellfish, were weighed. Between the yard tracks and the stone boundary wall was a large corrugated-iron shed, which we were told housed the delivery lorry, but we never saw it.

The goods yard was closed on 18th July, 1966 but, before the line was lifted, the last item dealt with was in 1967 when the steam locomotive *Union of South Africa* was unloaded at Crail prior to being transported by road to the Lochty Private Railway.

## Anstruther

The goods yard at Anstruther, situated at the former terminus of the Leven & East of Fife Railway, was extremely busy but, like St Andrews, contributed little to the goods traffic over the Anstruther & St Andrews line. Accordingly it is fully dealt with in *The Leven & East of Fife Railway*.

*Goods Trains*

The Leven & East of Fife goods trains terminated at Anstruther (Old) and the yards at Crail and beyond were served by local trip workings from Anstruther. By 1925 the Anstruther & St Andrews line was being served by the 'Coast Goods', a single return working between those points and all intermediate stations were called at while a Mondays-only cattle train ran between Stravthie and Thornton Junction via Crail calling at intermediate stations 'when required to lift livestock traffic' with the proviso that 'Stations between Stravithie and Crail to advise Agent, Anstruther, on Saturday forenoon, number of wagons to lift'.

By the summer of 1946 the Monday livestock train had been suspended but on that day the 8.05 am Dundee to Glasgow via Crail ordinary passenger train, if required, would uplift fitted cattle wagons from Stravithie and Kingsbarns for Thornton Junction while the 7.55 am Thornton to Dundee passenger train similarly served Boarhills. A further pair of passenger trains were noted in the working timetable thus:

> When horse box traffic is offered for Mount Melville, Stravithie, Boarhills and Kingsbarns for these trains, District Superintendent, Burntisland, will arrange service. When stop is made to lift Horse Box traffic five minutes will be allowed and train will run correspondingly later.

The sidings between Crail and Mount Melville were all served by a trip working from Anstruther to St Andrews Links, serving Crail, Kingsbarns, Boarhills and Mount Melville on the outward journey and Mount Melville, Stravithie, Boarhills and Kingsbarns in the opposite direction; this service delivered drinking water to Kingsbarns station. Goods depots on the northern section of the line were served by trip workings from Leuchars by a Dundee-based locomotive. As the working timetables put it 'Fish Specials and Extra Goods Trains will be run when the Traffic requires it', but apart from Anstruther (Old) such additional services were rarely required. An odd feature of goods operations on the Anstruther & St Andrews line was found at Mount Melville and Stravithie stations where, due to the somewhat restricted nature of the layout of the sidings there, tow roping (i.e. the moving or shunting of wagons by towing with a rope or chain attached to a locomotive or vehicle moving on the adjacent 'main line') was permitted - a rather unusual practice on an NBR passenger line.

In 1962 a Thornton 'D11/2' class was booked to run the 5.05 am newspaper train from Edinburgh to Crail. The locomotive and crew then ran light engine to Anstruther and formed a trip working departing from Anstruther (Old) at 7.55, arriving at Crail 15 minutes later. At Crail wagons were shunted and on Fridays the train took the station cash from there. In addition full cans of drinking water for Kingsbarns station 'if required' were collected at Crail and the train then waited until 9.05 am. Kingsbarns was reached at 9.15, where there was a 12 minute stop so that shunting and loading operations could be carried out and the full water cans were unloaded, any empty cans being uplifted for eventual delivery back to Crail. Boarhills was reached at 9.32 (departing at 9.46), and Mount Melville reached at 10.09. The final stop was made at St Andrews Links, where arrival was made at 10.20. The southward journey commenced at 10.40 and there was then a lengthy stop at St Andrews (New) station where the engine took on water and there was a crew changeover. The train left St Andrews (New) at 11.15, calling at Mount Melville at 11.28, Stravithie at 11.47, Boarhills at 12 noon, Kingsbarns at 12.15 with arrival at Crail at 12.25 pm. The engine and crew then worked the 2.35 pm passenger train from Crail to Thornton, complete with fish van 'if required'. Crail was also served by a Thornton 'J37' class locomotive on the 6.25 am Kirkland Yard to Anstruther goods service which left the latter place at 9.45 am, with a return working leaving Crail at 10.15. The third working of the day was the 3 pm Anstruther to Boarhills working, also in the hands of a Thornton 'J37'. This ran light engine to Crail, leaving there 'if required' and not on Saturdays, at 4.15 with a van, arriving at Boarhills at 4.26 pm. Leaving Boarhills at 4.35, the locomotive then propelled its train back to Kingsbarns, arriving at 4.41. The engine then ran-round its train and departure was at 5 pm, reaching Crail 10 minutes later. Departure from Crail was at 5.10 with arrival at Thornton at 7.52 pm, having picked up goods and passenger-rated traffic *en route*.

By 1963 Kingsbarns and Boarhills were served by a Thornton 'J37' trip working which worked light engine to Crail, leaving there at 4.05 pm for Boarhills where, after a short stop, the locomotive then propelled the train back to Kingsbarns. Here it used the loop as a run-round, arriving at Anstruther for a lengthy stop before setting off for the various sidings and yards and arriving back at Thornton. The Leuchars No. 1 pilot, a 'J36' based at Dundee (Tay Bridge) shed, served Mount Melville and Stravithie from St Andrews 'if required'.

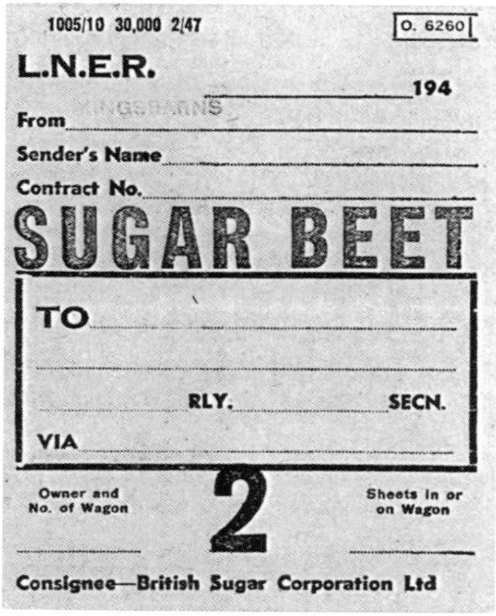

1005/10 30,000 2/47      O. 6260

**L.N.E.R.** _____ 194

From KINGSBARNS _____

Sender's Name _____

Contract No. _____

# SUGAR BEET

TO _____

_____ RLY. _____ SECN.

VIA _____

Owner and No. of Wagon     **2**     Sheets in or on Wagon

**Consignee—British Sugar Corporation Ltd**

NBR 'C' class 0-6-0 No. 774 at the north end of the down platform at St Andrews, flanked by the impressive penny weighing machine, c.1920.　　　　*NBRSG Hennigan Collection*

'Scottish Director' 'D11' class 4-4-0 No. 62694 *James Fitzjames* passes Mount Melville with the 3.18 pm St Andrews to Edinburgh service, 4th February, 1955.　　　　*D.J. Paul*

# Chapter Eleven

# Working the Line:
# Locomotives, Signalling and Staff

*'It is becoming more and more difficult every day to understand the wants*
*and requirements of the travelling public.'*
*Speaker at Anstruther Railwaymen's Dinner, 1899*

### Locomotives

Prior to the official opening of the Anstruther & St Andrews line, it would appear that a regular goods service between Anstruther and Crail was operated using the contractor's own locomotives. When services commenced to Boarhills, the North British initially used Drummond 0-6-0 tank locomotives (LNER class 'J82') and Drummond 4-4-0T (LNER 'D51') locomotives, including No. 1010 *Anstruther*. Within a short period of time the operating restrictions on the line were lifted and tender locomotives began to appear and oust the tank engines with the end result that few, if any, tanks were then seen south of St Andrews. In the 20th century Reid 4-4-0s ('D30') 'Scotts' and ('D34') 'Glens' were seen on passenger services, while goods were in the hands of 0-6-0s, the coast goods being worked by 'J34' class engines. In LNER days the ex-NBR 4-4-0s continued to work the line and examples in classes 'D29', 'D30', 'D32', 'D33' and 'D34', together with 0-6-0s of 'J35' and 'J37' classes were all seen, along with LNER 'D11/2' class 'Scottish Directors' which, unlike their title suggested, were not named after company directors as the Great Central locomotives upon which they were based had been, but were named after characters in Sir Walter Scott's 'Waverley' novels. On through trains from Glasgow Eastfield 'K2' and 'B1' locomotives appeared, the later also working through trains to and from Dundee (Tay Bridge). In BR days the Crail trains continued to be hauled primarily by 'Scotts', 'Glens' and 'Directors' although BR class '4' 2-6-0s, '4MT' 2-6-4T and BR Standard class '5' 4-6-0 were also seen on these services along with several other classes of ex-LNER locomotives such as 'K3s', 'J38s' and 'J39s' and, particularly on through services from Glasgow Buchanan Street, LMS locomotives principally 'Black Fives'. The 'Fife Coast Express' was in BR days regularly hauled by 'B1s' but, in summer months particularly, 'Black Fives' were also regularly seen on this service. Goods services continued to be hauled by 'J35s', and occasionally 'J36s', although the final goods services west of Crail were in the hands of 'B1s'. In the 1950s a class 'K4' 2-6-0 with a cargo of sugar for the food strorage base at Crail is thought to have worked the heaviest-ever train over the East Fife line, conveying 30 wagons of 13 tons each; the train had to divide the load at Anstruther in order to make it up the incline to Crail. The Thornton trip working to Crail, Kingsbarns and Boarhills was undertaken by a 'J37' - as late as May 1964 No. 64595 was observed at Anstruther on this duty.

The route availability of the line was 6, but in addition 'J37', 'J38' and 'L1' locomotives were also permitted. Locomotives seen on the line normally came from either Dundee, Perth or Thornton sheds and, on occasions, the small sub-shed of the

Gresley 'J38' class No. 65921 passes the Waid Academy on its way in to Anstruther with the 12.30 Saturdays-only Crail to Edinburgh working, 13th July, 1963.
*C.C. Thornburn*

latter at Anstruther provided engines for Crail trains. Through trains were hauled by locomotives from Edinburgh and Glasgow sheds but at the height of the summer Saturday traffic 'foreign' locomotives were found on the line and had come from such exotic locations as Fort William or, on at least one occasion, Bolton in Lancashire. The latter had taken a Manchester service up to Glasgow and had then been pressed into service to take a Glasgow to St Andrews via Anstruther infill working before heading once again for the South. The last steam locomotive to travel over any part of the Anstruther & St Andrews section was No. 60009 *Union of South Africa*, the preserved 'A4' that was hauled dead by a class '08' diesel shunter to Crail, *en route* for Lochty, by which time the line was officially out of use. Diesel locomotives were rarely seen on the line and hauled no regular services, passenger or goods, but locomotives from classes '20', '21', '24','25', '26', '27' and '29' were all occasionally seen on excursion or special traffic in the 1960s. Diesel multiple units became common after 1960, but were almost entirely confined to the ubiquitous Metro-Cammell class '101' twin-units based at Thornton and Dundee three-car Derby-built class '107' three-car units and, to a much lesser extent, Gloucester class '100' twin units.

The only locomotive turntable on the line was situated at the old Leven & East of Fife station at Anstruther, close to the small engine shed there. Originally constructed with a 48 ft deck, in the post-war era the turntable was lengthened to 52 ft to cope with the LNER 'B1' locomotives - ironically the similar-sized LMS 'Black Fives' seen on the line in the 1950s were too long for the turntable and accordingly were only allocated to through services to and from Dundee. All trains from the west which were scheduled to terminate at Anstruther were propelled by their locomotive into the loop between the 'new' station and Anstruther Junction and the locomotive then ran round and, after turning, was backed on to the train again and propelled back into the platform. The locomotives that hauled passenger trains which terminated at Crail had to run round and then run light engine tender-first back to Anstruther where they were turned and then run back to Crail tender-first before reversing on to their train - a particularly wasteful form of working which resulted in 10 'dead miles' on each working. Incidentally there is no mention in the working timetable of any such light engine workings, despite the fact that each journey meant that the Anstruther to Crail single line section would be occupied for several minutes and thus those responsible for pathing additional trains would have to be aware of such movements and take them into account - however the absence of documentation of such workings was a common practice and that there was nothing unique to the Anstruther & St Andrews line in omissions of this nature.

All locomotives, whether running light or hauling a train, were required to observe the following permanent speed limits: 30 mph (up) and 15 mph (down) while travelling through the facing crossover at Anstruther, 35 mph over Boarhills viaduct or through the station there, 25 mph on the whole section between Stravithie and Mount Melville with the exception of Lambolethan crossing where a 15 mph limit was in force, and 25 mph on the whole steeply-graded section between Mount Melville and St Andrews although in the up direction such a limit was probably unnecessary as many trains struggled to reach even half that speed! As noted earlier additional speed restrictions were imposed where trains included coaches of BR Mark I design.

Stanier 'Black Five' class 4-6-0 No. 44977 leaves Crail with the 2.15 pm Dundee to Edinburgh service on 3rd October, 1959 - note the 65J shed plate showing that this Fort William locomotive was far from home.

*Roy Hamilton*

'K2' class 2-6-0 No. 61755 working 'wrong line' through Crail, *c.*1955.    *R.W. Lynn Collection*

BR Standard class '4MT' 2-6-0 No. 76111 leaves Anstruther for the east on 13th July, 1963.
*C.C. Thornburn*

Diesels on the junction line between St Andrews Links and New stations - (*above*) an excursion double-headed by two English Electric type '1s' (later class '20') has just crossed the Petheram bridge while (below) Birmingham Railway Carriage & Wagon Co. type '2' No. D5308 departs from St Andrews for the north on a special on 15th September, 1964.

(*Both*) *C.C. Thornburn*

An anonymous 'B1' class 4-6-0 from Crail works tender-first past the Anstruther upside station garden *en route* to the turntable, *c.*1960.                                    *J. Stormonth*

Ex-NBR 'K' class 4-4-0, running as LNER 'D33' No. 9333, being turned at Anstruther in July 1930.
*Alan Brotchie Collection*

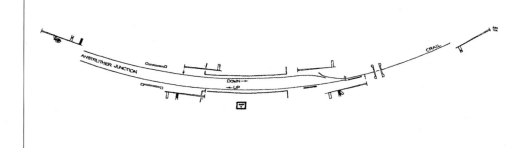

Signalling diagrams for Anstruther station (1900) and Crail (1930).

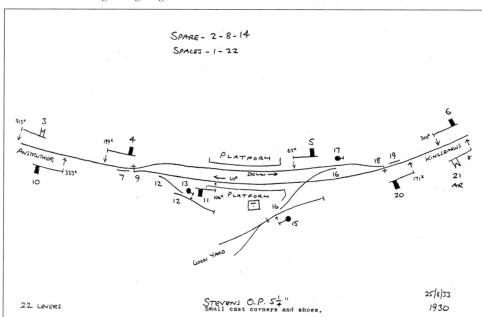

## Signalling

The first section of the Anstruther & St Andrews line, from Anstruther Junction to Boarhills, was worked by train staff and ticket with signal boxes being provided at Anstruther Junction and Boarhills. Upon the extension of the line to St Andrews additional signal boxes were provided at Stravithie, Mount Melville, St Andrews (New) and St Andrews (Links); all signals and boxes were to the design of the contractors, the Railway Signalling Company of Fazakerly, Liverpool.

The North British era saw many changes to signalling including the installation of fully interlocked points and signals (made compulsory by the Regulation of Railways Act 1889), the installation of semaphore signalling along the line and the installation by the late 1890s of the Tyer's electric tablet instruments at each signal cabin; this replaced the older train staff system for controlling single lines and thereafter all cabins between Largo and St Andrews Links were worked by this method with the exception of the short double-track section between Anstruther station and Anstruther Junction which was worked by block telegraph. Most of the signals were of a pattern supplied by Stevens & Sons of Glasgow and London, the signal boxes being also largely of their design. Among the alterations carried out towards the end of the century were the construction of new boxes at Guardbridge, Stravithie, Kingsbarns and Crail and the reduction to ground frames of the signal boxes at Mount Melville and Boarhills; in 1926 the signal boxes at Stravithie and Anstruther Station were closed. Some of the original NBR lower quadrant signals survived up until closure but some were replaced by BR upper quadrant signals in the 1950s; by 1960 the latter were commonplace, Crail being the prolific location for them. In 1966 the line was breached at Crail and St Andrews, the southern section then being worked as 'one engine in steam'.

A chronology of the opening and closing dates of all signal boxes between Anstruther Junction and St Andrews Links is given in *Appendix One*. The original block sections on the Anstruther & St Andrews Railway were Anstruther Junction to Anstruther Station (0 m. 16 ch.), Anstruther Junction to Kingsbarns (6 m. 31 ch.), Kingsbarns to Boarhills (2 m. 37 ch.), Boarhills to Stravithie (1 m. 54 ch.), Stravithie to Mount Melville (2 m. 38 ch.), Mount Melville to St Andrews Station (1 m. 75 ch.) and St Andrews Station to St Andrews Links (0 m. 28 ch.). In 1898 these were altered when Crail box was constructed and new sections Anstruther Station to Crail (4 m. 43 ch.) and Crail to Kingsbarns (2 m. 68 ch.) were created, while with the closure of Mount Melville and Boarhills cabins new sections from St Andrews Station to Stravithie (3 m. 68 ch.) and Stravithie to Kingsbarns (4 m. 20 ch.) were created. In 1926, with the closure of Stravithie box, one long section was created between St Andrews Station and Kingsbarns (8 m. 8 ch.), while the abolition of Anstruther Station box made a new section Anstruther Junction to Crail (4 m. 59 ch.). The closure of St Andrews Links box in 1957 left the most northerly block section on the line as St Andrews Station to Guardbridge (3 m. 40 ch.).

The opening hours of the signal boxes in 1926 (after the abolition of Anstruther Station and Stravithie) were Anstruther [Junction] 6.30 am to 9.00 pm, Crail 6.30 am to 8 pm, Kingsbarns 8.30 am to 8.00 pm, St Andrews Station 6.50 am to 10.15 pm (Saturdays 11 pm) and St Andrews Links 5.30 am to 10.15 pm (Saturdays 11 pm). All were closed on Sundays. By 1959 these had been

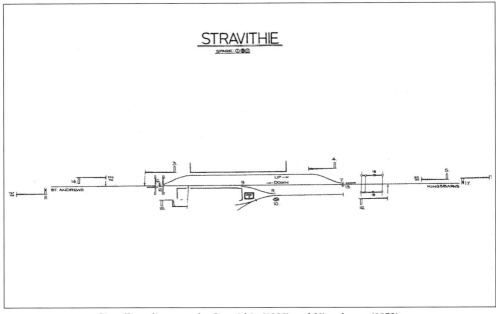

Signalling diagrams for Stravithie (1900) and Kingsbarns (1952).

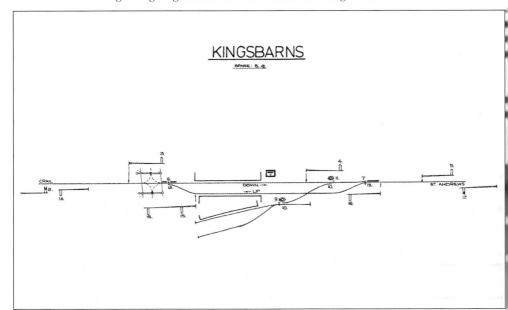

The two signal boxes of Anstruther - (*above*) the Junction signal box (plain Anstruther from 1926) seen in the 1960s - this impressive box marked the physical junction between the Leven & East of Fife and Anstruther & St Andrews line. *Below*, 'D24' class Reid 4-4-0 No. 4896 *Dandie Dinmont* (a Walter Scott character after whom the breed of terrier dog was named) on a westbound working passes through Anstruther in 1924 - the only known photograph showing Anstruther Station box which was closed some two years later.                    *Author's Collection & J.F.Gairns*

An NBR ground signal at St Andrews Links.                    *John Hurst Collection*

The two signal boxes of St Andrews: (*upper*) the Station box – a curious structure situated on the down side adjacent to the footbridge and open from 1888 to 1967 and (*lower*) Exchanging the token at St Andrews Links box in 1954 – this was the most northerly structure paid for by the Anstruther & St Andrews company.

*Both: Nigel Dyckhoff*

Signalman J. Anderson exchanges the tokens at Kingsbarns on the last day of services, Saturday 4th September, 1965.

*Norman Turnbull*

Approaching Kingsbarns to exchange the tokens on the up platform, 28th August, 1965 - a week before the line closed. The locomotive is 'J37' class 0-6-0 No. 64569.        *(Both) J.L. Stevenson*

An LNER upper quadrant signal at the north end of Kingsbarns with a passing Edinburgh-bound dmu, 11th July, 1964.
*C.C. Thornburn*

Crail signal box, from a1996 drawing by Brian Malaws.

altered to: Anstruther - split shifts 6 am to 1.20 pm and 2.20 to 10.20 pm, Crail 6 am to 9 pm ('or the passing of the 7.35 pm from Edinburgh if run'), Kingsbarns 7 am to 8.45 pm and St Andrews Station 5.15 am to 11.30 pm. Once again, all boxes were closed on Sundays with special arrangements being made at Anstruther and Crail when the summer Sunday passenger workings were in operation.

### Staff

The station master's lot was not always an easy one and, in the words of a speaker at a railwaymen's dinner held at Anstruther Town Hall in 1899:

The close observation of little things is the secret of success in business and in every pursuit in life. Human knowledge is but an accumulation of small facts. It requires a fund of patience and good humour not readily meant with in human beings to be a successful railway official. Some people fancy then when they have purchased a ticket that they have subsidised the entire railway system of the United Kingdom. Of course there are exceptions but what I wish to convey, that it is becoming more and more difficult every day to understand the wants and requirements of the travelling public.

A sentiment, no doubt, echoed by present-day railway officials. The status, and pay, of the station master, and the nature of his duties, was defined by the grading of the station. Locally Anstruther (Old) and (New) were a joint appointment (i.e. only one station master between them) and was classified as '2' by the NBR, LNER and BR; Crail was a class '3' station, whereas the remaining four were all in the lowest classification, '5'. At the very end of the North British period the local station masters were William Reid (Mount Melville), John Nicholson (Stravithie), David Brown (Boarhills and Kingsbarns), William Grahamslaw (Crail) and Richard Livingston (Anstruther). At one time Anstruther (Old) and (New), had a combined staff of 15, while Crail had a staff complement of four or five and even Mount Melville and Boarhills had a staff of three, namely a station master, porter and clerk, the duties of which were often interchangeable. After their closure to passengers a clerk and porter were still employed but by the early 1960s a single winter-only porter covered both Stravithie and Mount Melville with a similar porter covering Boarhills and Kingsbarns. The duties of clerks included book-keeping, the calculation of through fares and rates to other companies using the Railway Clearing House manuals, and generally sales, enquiries and ticketing of passengers and goods. Although two girls were employed as booking clerks at Edinburgh Waverley station as far back as 1857, few women were employed on the railway until World War I when several local stations had female clerks. A few remained in their positions after the servicemen returned, although many were dismissed; in any event women were not expected to retain their railway employment upon marriage. An entry in the *East Fife Observer* of 24th November, 1921 recalls one of these women:

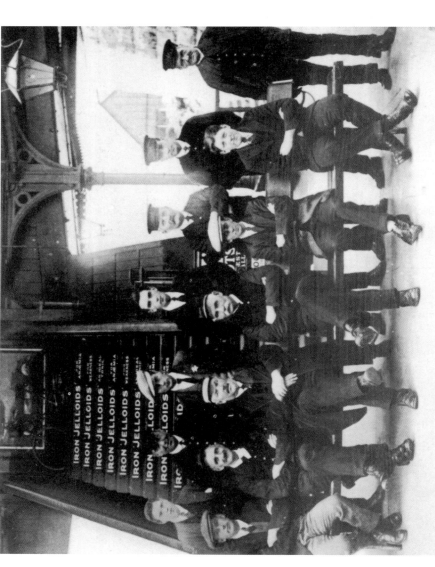

The station staff at St Andrews, c.1920. Those present on the occasion have been identified as (*left to right*) *back row:* clerk A. Mitchell, goods porter W. Gordon, clerk T.F.Currie, clerk J. Robb, signalman W. Roberts, porter J. Proudfoot, who was apparently on a visit from Cupar, and hoistman T. Anderson. *Front row:* chief booking clerk D. Valentine, station foreman J. Currie, station master J. Docherty, station foreman J. Haddow, clerk J. Crowe and junior clerk J.H. Thompson.

*BR Scottish Region*

To mark the occasion of her retiring from the position of clerkess at Crail station, Miss Annie Duncan is being presented with a handsome silver-backed mirror, brush and comb, and a hand-bag subscribed for her by the shopkeepers, traders and railway staff. The articles are at present on view in the window of Mr Milne, jeweller.

During World War II female clerks and porters were again seen but the number of women employed on the East Fife railways was never large, possibly due to the ready employment for women in the fishing industry. By the time the line closed the staff complement of Crail had been reduced to two porters who attended to all duties except those of the signalmen.

When the Anstruther & St Andrews stations fell under the auspices of the North British the staff became eligible to take part in the NBR Best Kept Stations scheme. Following upon annual inspections, stations were awarded cash prizes to be distributed according to the dictates of the relevant station master and in 1897 Mr Henderson at Mount Melville was awarded a rare £5 first prize, while Mr Stenhouse at Anstruther received a £1 fourth prize. In 1917 more local stations were successful, despite the privations of war, and £3 was awarded to Mr Brown for Boarhills and Mr Reid of Mount Melville (despite the temporary closure of both stations) and the same amount to Mr Grahamslaw at Crail while Mr Wotherspoon of Anstruther received a fourth prize of £1.

Local railwaymen seem to have been a sociable lot and their annual dinner dances held in Anstruther remained popular for more than half a century. A typical example was that held at the end of February 1927:

The Town Hall of East Anstruther was brilliantly decorated on the occasion of the annual staff dance of the district railwaymen, held last Friday night. The company of over 70 couples, including not only Anstruther but the surrounding districts, tripped it merrily until 3 o'clock in the morning to the spritely music of Baxter's Orchestra from Lochgelly. The MCs were Mr James Jollie and Mr James Watson, while the catering arrangements were carried through by Mrs Balck, were all that could be desired. Organised by an enthusiastic committee of nine under the convenorship of Mr D Burrell, the dance, like its predecessors, was a great success.

Level crossings on the line were situated at Lamboletham (worked by a gate keeper), Stravithie (worked by the signalman until 1926 and thereafter by a gate keeper), Kilduncan and Kingsbarns both worked by the station staff at Kingsbarns, and West Newhall, Kirkmay and Thirdpart, all worked by resident crossing keepers. All other gated crossings were occupation crossings worked by the user. In the case of Thirdpart, the North British 1922 General Appendix stated that:

Telephonic communication has been provided between Thirdpart level crossing and Crail. All trains and engines must be signalled from Crail to the crossing as follows: When leaving Crail: 2 rings; when leaving Anstruther: 3 rings - the number of rings to be repeated by the level crossing keeper in every case.

The station garden on the down platform in the 1920s - note the 'LNER' written in whitewashed pebbles; unfortunately no photographs have been found of Mr Harrow's Forth Bridge model.

*Authors' Collection*

The arrival of the stores train hauled by a 'J35' class 0-6-0 at Mount Melville, *c.*1922 - note the presence of the St Andrews station master Mr Currie!        *NBRSG Hennigan Collection*

## Well-Kent Faces

In Edwardian times the station masters at both Kingsbarns and Crail were the Browns, father and son, and they were noted not only for their excellent honey (which could be bought at Kingsbarns booking office for one shilling a jar) but also for their sheepdogs which collected for railway charities by carrying a money box strapped to their backs - when trains stopped, the collie dogs entered each compartment in turn, giving passengers the opportunity of responding to their appeal. When David Brown, by now station master in charge of Kingsbarns, Boarhills and Stravithie, retired in December 1932 after some 42 years of service he was presented with a gold watch and chain.

An illustration of how railway employees were required to travel throughout the NBR system in order to gain promotion appeared in the *East Fife Observer* of 30th June, 1927 under the heading 'Anstruther - Stationmaster's Appointment':

Mr William Johnston, stationmaster at Anstruther, has been promoted to the stationmastership of Dundee East Joint Station. Entering the service of the railway company as a clerk at Yoker station, Mr Johnston soon set out on the road for promotion and served as a booking clerk at Glasgow High Street and Lennoxtown. Leaving there he went to Kirkintilloch and later to the parcels department at Glasgow Queen Street. For three summers he served as a purser on the Clyde steamers, and spent a winter in the booking office at Dundee Tay Bridge. As chief clerk he then went to Polmont, and after two and a half years stay there was transferred to Bellgrove and Partick in the capacity as chief clerk. Mr Johnston was then promoted to the relief staff and was attached to the office of the Relief Staff District Superintendent, his duties there giving him an opportunity of gaining valuable experience throughout the entire Western Area. Some thirteen years later he was promoted to Garthill, Coatbridge and then Anstruther, where he has carried in his duties for the past two and a half years. The first year of Mr Johnston's stay at Anstruther was marked by the station gaining first prize for the best kept station, and last year the premier award (special prize) was secured by Anstruther. Preparations for the inspection in July are at present being made.

At Anstruther the station gardens were always noted for their fine floral displays rivalling St Andrews, but in June 1931 a new attraction appeared when porter David Harrow was responsible for 'another grand improvement which it may be said to surpass, if possible, all the novelties which have preceded it during the past few years, fashioned by the same hand', namely a sizeable model of the Forth Bridge which was placed above the name of the station written in shells behind the up platform. Mr Swinton, station master at Anstruther, was quoted as saying that Mr Harrow's works contributed to the station winning prizes for its best-kept awards and that, although six award certificates were hanging around the walls of the booking office - 'There is plenty of room for more!' The last station master at Anstruther was William Walker who, by time of closure, was also in charge of Crail, Kingsbarns, Pittenweem, St Monance, Elie and Kilconquhar stations.

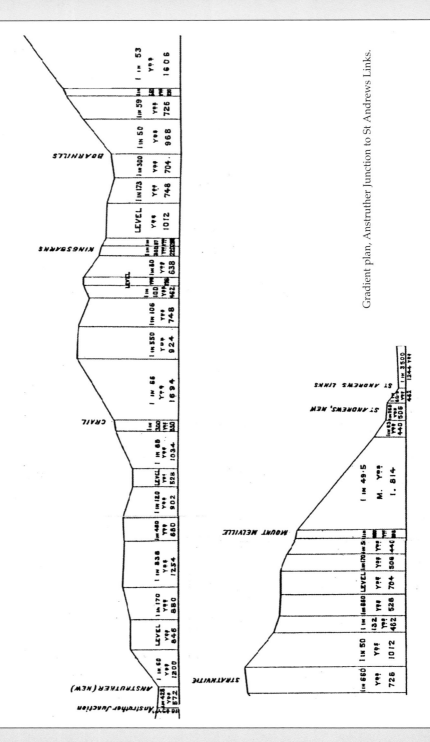

Gradient plan, Anstruther Junction to St Andrews Links.

# Chapter Twelve

# Sixteen Miles and One Chain:
# The Line Described

*'The world has changed, and with it,
the Fringes of Fife'*

John Geddie

## Skirting the Fringe

This chapter attempts to describe what the Anstruther & St Andrews Railway looked like from the point of view of a traveller and follows an imaginary journey from north to south beginning at St Andrews Links, the point at which the line joined up with the original St Andrews Railway, to Anstruther Junction, where the line made a link up with the Leven & East of Fife Railway. All distances are given in the familiar measurements used by railway and canal surveyors, namely miles and chains, miles being equivalent to about 1.61 km and being divided into 80 chains (a chain being equivalent to 20.11 metres or 22 yards) and begin at the goods platform at St Andrews Links station. The designations 'up' and 'down' are used, respectively, to describe the Anstruther and St Andrews directions and correspond to the designations given by the North British Railway and its successors.

## The St Andrews Junction Line

The journey begins at **St Andrews Links** (00.00), the former passenger station of the St Andrews Railway, which was opened in 1852 and rebuilt after a fire in 1901. The station ceased to be used by passengers on the opening of the Anstruther & St Andrews line and thereafter became the city's principal goods depot, remaining open until June 1966. Its site is now incorporated into the formerly railway-owned Old Course Hotel. Passing the site of the level crossing on what was once the main road from St Andrews to Leuchars (Old Station Road, replaced as a through route by the diverted main road in 1887), the line began a climb at 1 in 60 in order to cross the new road by the **Petheram bridge**, emerging on to an embankment that had been built to double-track standards. **St Andrews (New) Station** (00.28).* Situated in a deep cutting, the single island platform was linked to the world by two footbridges on the up side. Graced by wooden buildings that were the 1902 replacement for the original Anstruther & St Andrews structures damaged by fire the year before, the station boasted waiting and refreshment rooms, ticket and parcels offices, lavatories and a bookstall and the main footbridge was supplemented by a luggage hoist. A small wooden signal box, St Andrews Station, was perched up against the main footbridge on the down side of the line. Although the site was somewhat

---

* The two St Andrews stations are more fully dealt with in *The St Andrews Railway*.

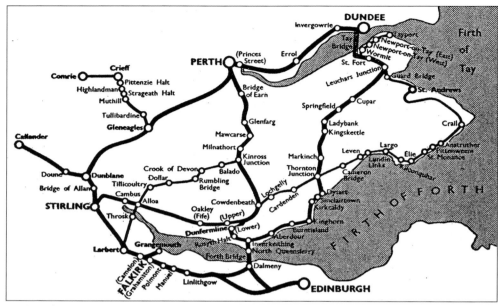

Map from BR Day Rover leaflet.

A Leuchars to St Andrews dmu passes by the Links station and is about to enter the Anstruther & St Andrews line from the north, 22nd January, 1965 .          *C.C. Thornburn*

constrained by retaining walls and the sides of the cutting, the platform seemed to be remarkably spacious and this effect was enhanced by the glass and iron canopies which often sported hanging flower baskets. Flowers were, indeed, always a feature of St Andrews station, right up until its eventual closure. Anstruther trains normally used the up face of the platform and would arrive at the down face; after the closure of the Anstruther & St Andews line the down face of the platform was taken out of use and all trains used the up face. The main dimensions of the station were platform length 400 feet, and main buildings 120 feet. Other facilities included a carriage dock and water tank.

## South of St Andrews

Leaving St Andrews (New) the line passed beneath Doubledykes Road, which crossed it on a single-arch brick bridge, and then continued in a cutting before being crossed first by Argyle Street and then by the Lade Braes Walk on an attractive but narrow hump-backed stone bridge. There then followed the **Kinness Burn viaduct** (00.49), a large freestone structure of three arches each of which had a span of 30 feet. A short distance further on was the Canongate bridge, where the line crossed over what had been a quiet country road but one which, with creeping suburbanisation, had become busier; by the 1950s the bridge had become something of a traffic hazard. The line then began a stiff quarter-mile climb at 1 in 63 as the line swung abruptly to the south and this was immediately followed by what train crews regarded as a horrendous climb of 1 in 49 on a steeply curving course. This gradient was so severe that trains, especially heavily loaded holiday trains or the first steam-hauled services on a wet Monday morning, struggled to surmount the hill and the sound of labouring locomotives with their wheels slipping furiously was an everyday feature and not infrequently trains had to be banked or divided on this section. A great sweep to the west now took place as the line joined the route of the Cairnsmill Burn, a confluent of the Kinness Burn, and passing Cairnsmill itself the route then skirted the bulwark of Wester Balrymonth Hill.

A temporary relief to the reverse curves and steep gradient was now afforded as the line passed beneath the St Andrews to Largo A915 road and entered **Mount Melville station**, (02.20). The curving platform of this wayside station was situated on the up side, the main building being a neat rectangular single-storey building of rubble construction with a dressed stone frontage, distinctive tall chimneys and a hipped slate roof 60 feet in length. The central bay of the building had a recessed waiting room with a glass and wood frontage and a slave clock on the platform side was connected to the main clock in the booking office. The style of building was virtually identical to that at Stravithie, Boarhills and Kingsbarns and was unique to the Anstruther & St Andrews Railway. Behind the platform, and served by the access road, was a standard-pattern NBR station master's house which, after the post was abolished in 1925, was occupied by other railway staff. On the down side and opposite the platform was the yard with three sidings, a weighing machine and crane with a capacity of 1 ton 5 cwt. Two unusual features of the yard were the horse-box dock,

'B1s' Nos. 61146 and 61244 double-head the Scottish Region television train southbound in the cutting between Doubledykes Road and Argyle Street bridges on 31st May, 1965 with a party of Midlothian schoolchildren and teachers from West Calder and Juniper Green schools. *C.C. Thornburn*

reserved for the use of the inhabitants of Mount Melville House, and the notice board detailing the unusual working arrangements in force. In passenger days the station was well-kept and ornamental shrubs were planted on the platform and between the running line and the goods yard; in later years these grew unchecked so that by the end they all but obscured the sidings. A small signal box was provided when the line was opened but this was replaced by a ground frame in 1898 when the original signalling was removed.

From Mount Melville the line ran in a generally eastwards direction, the 1 in 50 gradually easing out to 1 in 170 and then there followed a half-mile of level track which passed a prominent wind-pump before reaching **Lamboletham level crossing** (03.02), where the line was crossed by a by-road leading southwards to the differently-spelt farms of North and South Lambieletham; the crossing was gated and worked by a resident crossing keeper. Then the line began to climb again, the ascent becoming 1 in 50 for nearly three-quarters of a mile until, at a point where it would have been joined at a trailing junction by the proposed East of Fife Central branch from Lochty, the summit of the line was reached at a height of 318 feet above sea level. There was now some relief for train crews as half a mile on a downward gradient of 1 in 660 followed and at **Allanhill bridge** (03.72) the line was crossed by the Grange to Kinaldy road before the railway turned north-eastwards to cross Prior Muir.

Siberian scenes at Cairnsmill on the outskirts of St Andrews with the 9.08 am Glasgow to Dundee service battling through the snowy landscape, 29th January, 1965. *(Both) C.C. Thornburn*

The Scottish Region TV train, double-headed by 'B1s' Nos. 61292 and 61293, heads into St Andrews on 1st June, 1962. *C.C. Thorburn*

Tackling the climb to Mount Melville: (*above*) 'B1' class No. 61132 on the 4.53 pm Dundee to Edinburgh service in June 1958 and (*below*) No. 61244 on the same service two years later.

*(Both) Douglas Paul*

'B1s' Nos. 61118 and 61130 double-heading the Scottish Region TV train filled with pupils of Hunter's Tryst school in Edinburgh, head south in a sylvan setting at Mount Melville, 22nd May, 1963.
*C.C. Thornburn*

### Stravithie to the Kenly Burn

On the Muir a farm road crossed over the railway on a bridge and the railway entered a cutting where, on the down side, was **Stravithie Quarry Siding** (04.16), a single siding which served the adjacent freestone quarry and was joined to the main-line by a trailing junction; this siding was opened in about 1888 and extended in 1896 but went out of use by 1902. The line was then crossed on a hump-backed bridge by the B9131 Anstruther to Dunino and St Andrews direct road before entering **Stravithie station** (04.31), an establishment with two platforms and a passing loop; the original main building of Mount Melville-pattern was half-way along the down platform. In 1898 the passing loop and second (up) platform were added, together with a footbridge and small wooden shelter of NBR pattern opposite the main building and a new signal box was built in the angle between the goods sidings and down line. But in 1926 the loop, footbridge and signal box were all removed and the station ceased to be a passing place - the marooned up platform shelter survived disused until the war. In 1930 the station was closed to passengers and the waiting rooms and public post office situated in the main building were closed. To the south of the station lay two goods sidings, linked to the running line by a trailing junction while in the Crail direction was **Stravithie level crossing** (04.35) where a by-road crossed the line; the gates here were worked by the Stravithie signalman until the closure of the signal box and thereafter by a member of the station staff there who was in telephonic communication with the St Andrews Station signalman.

The late-running 2.28 pm St Andrews to Glasgow service approaches Allanhill bridge near Stravithie on Saturday 17th August, 1963 - the poor timekeeping was due to the locomotive, 'B1' class No. 61262, having stalled on the gradient at Mount Melville for almost an hour and a half.

*C.C. Thornburn*

The driver of a 'B1' class locomotive on a southbound working exchanges words with the permanent way crew at Lambolethan crossing, *c*.1955.      *Nigel Dyckhoff*

The 4.08 pm St Andrews to Glasgow service, hauled by 'Black Five' class No. 44970 and with a light loading of Mark I stock, passes by the photographer on the way to Boarhills, 6th July, 1963.

*C.C. Thornburn*

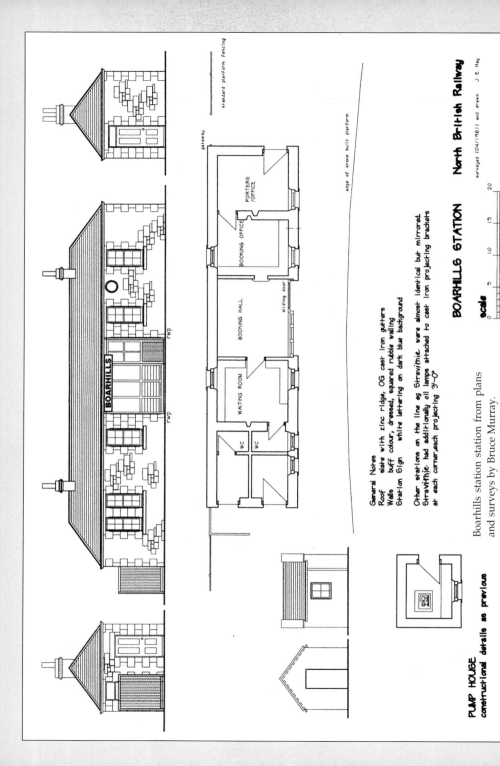

**BOARHILLS**

**PUMP HOUSE**
constructional details as previous

**General Notes**
Roof     slate with zinc ridge, OG cast iron gutters
Walls    buff colour, dressed, squared rubble walling
Station Sign   white lettering on dark blue background

Other stations on the line eg Stravithie were almost identical but mirrored.
Stravithie had additionally oil lamps attached to cast iron projecting brackets
at each corner, each projecting 3'-0"

WC
WC
WAITING ROOM
sliding door
BOOKING HALL
BOOKING OFFICE
PORTERS /OFFICE

gateway
standard platform fencing
edge of stone built platform

**BOARHILLS STATION**     North British Railway

Scale
0    5    10    15    20

surveyed (04/1981) and drawn    J E May

Boarhills station station from plans
and surveys by Bruce Murray.

After passing through the distinctive V-shaped wooded windbreak of Easter Balrymonth, the line now turned south-eastwards and fell steadily on a ruling gradient of 1 in 50 which continued on for almost the whole of the two miles to Boarhills - this gradient caused some not inconsiderable grief to enginemen travelling in the opposite direction! Passing by one of the plentiful ancient standing stones in the district the line then crossed the **Bonnytown Road bridge** (05.26), a single-span plate-girder affair carried on freestone abutments before swinging again to the north-east close to the site of the proposed Kenly Quarry Siding and entering the den or valley of the Kenly Burn, otherwise the Kenly Water. **Boarhills station** (05.78) was now reached. The temporary terminus of the Anstruther & St Andrews Railway between 1883 and 1887, this station had a curved platform on the up side complete with a Mount Melville-style building behind which were two goods sidings. There were no remains of the original wooden engine shed built on the site later occupied by the running line and demolished after the extension of the railway to St Andrews but the pump-house survived intact long after it had gone out of use. The steam-worked pump had been used to raise water from the Kenly Burn and pump it into an iron tank by the line where it could be used to replenish the tanks and tenders of locomotives; the pump-house oil-lamp survives in a private collection. Originally there was a small wooden signal box at the down end of the passenger platform but this, together with its associated signalling, was abolished in 1898. Leaving the station, the line swung through an arc over the **Kenly Burn viaduct** where it crossed, at a height of 60 feet, the stream on a curved structure consisting of five spans of 40 feet with masonry piers, coursed rubble spandrels and blue-brick arch rings with corbelled refuges on each pier.

## Parish of Kingsbarns

A gently undulating section, with wide seaward views towards the distant Bell Rock lighthouse,* followed until **Kilduncan Level Crossing** (07.14) a gated crossing which carried the link road between the house at Kilduncan and the farm of that name. Never a busy crossing (probably because both house and farm were independently served by separate access routes), the gates at Kilduncan were operated as required by the Kingsbarns station staff. The line then crossed the Kilduncan Burn, dammed at that point by a local farmer to provide irrigation for his potato crop, on a freestone single-arched bridge. Adjacent to the down side was the wartime RAF airfield of Kilduncan where passenger trains were known to have stopped on demand although no temporary platform was, apparently, ever provided there. The line then ran southwards at a ruling gradient of 1 in 87 to **Kingsbarns station** (08.51), a station which, after 1926, was the only remaining passing place between St Andrews (New) and Crail. On the up platform was yet another Anstruther & St Andrews Railway standard-pattern building while on the down platform there

---

* The Bell or Inchcape Rock is a long sandstone ridge situated off-shore some 12 miles south-east of Arbroath and in the path of shipping entering the Firth of Tay. Made famous by Southey's poem *Ralph the Rover*, the rock is surmounted by Stevenson's lighthouse, built between 1807 and 1811 which, being 117 feet tall, can be clearly seen from many a vantage point in Fife.

'Black Five' No. 45153 with the 2.28 pm Saturdays-only St Andrews to Glasgow Queen Street service approaches Crail from the north, 13th July, 1963.                    *C.C. Thornburn*

Signalman Sam Myles holds out the token to the driver of 'B1' class No. 61396 heading a Glasgow train into Crail, 13th July, 1963.                    *C.C. Thornburn*

was a small shelter and, at the northern end, a wooden signal box. The platforms were linked by a footbridge but after closure of the station to passengers in 1930 the footbridge and down shelter were removed but the platform, albeit overgrown, remained. At the south end of the down platform was a large water tank, a rather ungainly stone tower topped by a rectangular iron tank; in later years the tank was removed and the stone tower fitted with a shallow pitched roof. Clean drinking water was always a problem at this station and goods trains delivered daily cans of water from Crail for domestic purposes - a practice which was continued in later years by the trip-workings from Anstruther. Behind the up platform were two goods sidings and a loading bank with a wooden crane of 1 ton capacity while, adjacent to the road, was the NBR-pattern station master's house. Then followed **Kingsbarns level crossing**, which carried the Dunino to Kingsbarns road (appropriately named Station Road) across the line; this gated crossing was worked by the Kingsbarns station staff. Travelling southwards on another climb which included a 1 in 60 section, the line now crossed the Cambo or Kippo Burn and a farm track on the double-arched freestone **Cambo bridge** before continuing on a straight course to **West Newhall level crossing** (09.74), a gated public crossing named after the adjacent farm with its handsome Georgian house; this crossing, despite its quiet location was looked after by a crossing keeper.

*Farthest East*

The line now reached its second summit at a height above sea level of just over 200 feet before embarking upon a downwards ruling gradient of 1 in 66 which, in the reverse direction, was a stiff climb out of Crail lasting for almost a mile. On this section two overbridges were then met at Chance Inn and Sypsies, carrying respectively the B9171 Crail to Colinsburgh and B940 Crail to Cupar roads, the latter being banked up so that the road could cross the line without needing the main road to be raised but which resulted in an expensive and difficult to build skew-angled structure, something which Victorian engineers were, understandably, keen to avoid where possible. The line now entered **Crail station** (11.41).

This busy station was made a passing place in 1898. The up platform was 400 feet in length and contained the main building, which was of an unusual pattern, being 75 feet in length and built out of local sandstone with twin gables each topped by a stone ball finial in a vaguely Jacobean-style style; the northern gable somewhat confusingly displayed the carved date '1881'. The middle bay between the gables was fronted by a low stone wall surmounted by a glazed wooden screen and originally contained the booking hall and waiting room. To the north of the main building was the general waiting room, a small wooden strucure added in 1898 when the former waiting room in the original building became the parcels office. At the same time an incongruous brick-built lean-to extension was added to the southern gable. In 1919 this extension was replaced by a wood and glass structure which served as the station entrance and gave some shelter to those using the booking and parcels office; the original street frontage was then

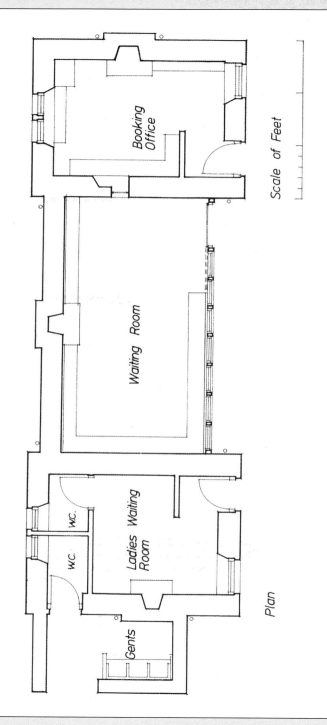

Booking Office

Waiting Room

Ladies Waiting Room

W.C.

W.C.

Gents

Scale of Feet

Plan

*Crail Station · North British Railway*

Crail station from plans and surveys by Bruce Murray.

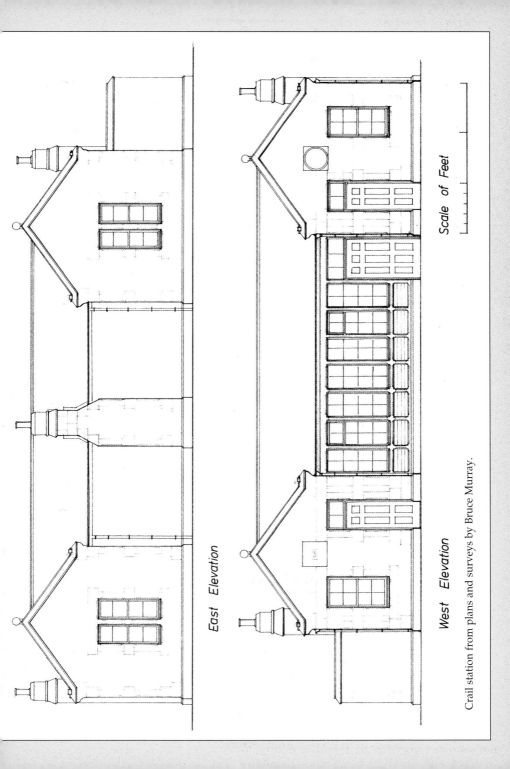

East Elevation

West Elevation

Scale of Feet

Crail station from plans and surveys by Bruce Murray.

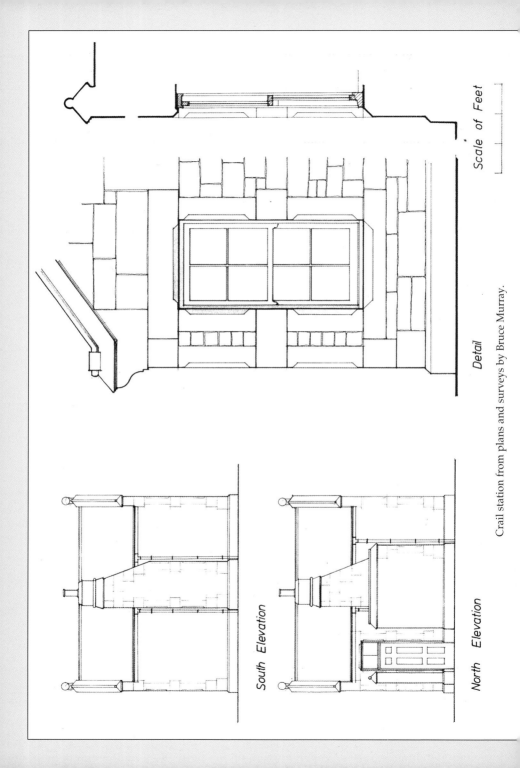

Scale of Feet

Detail

Crail station from plans and surveys by Bruce Murray.

South Elevation

North Elevation

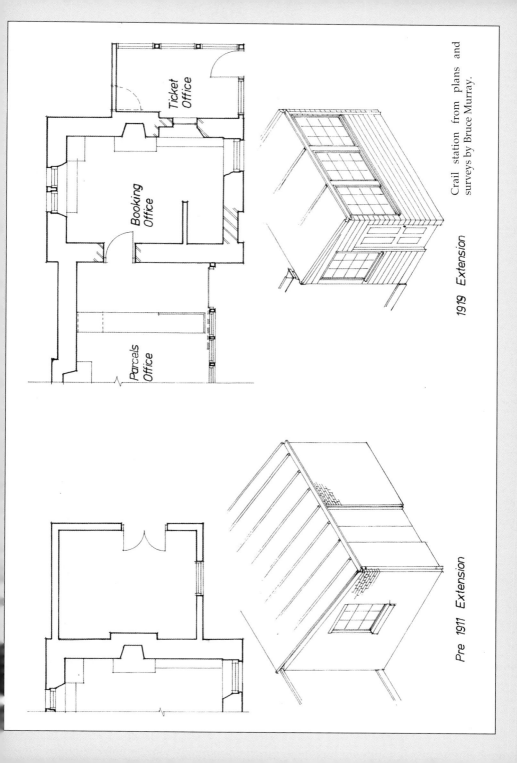

Ticket Office

Booking Office

Parcels Office

1919 Extension

Crail station from plans and surveys by Bruce Murray.

Pre 1911 Extension

'B1' class No. 61342 with a special train of ex-LMS empty coaching stock unusually works tender-first past the bowling green at Crail, 13th July, 1963.          *C.C. Thornburn*

A 'B1' approaches Crail station from the south on the penultimate day of services on that section of the line, 4th September, 1965.          *Norman Turnbull*

obscured by a wooden screen fence and a couple of old coach bodies which were used as additional shed accommodation; at the same time the ball finials were removed from the gables. On the down platform, which was 385 feet in length, a small wooden NBR shelter was placed facing the main buildings. The platforms were initially linked by a wood and iron footbridge which was in about 1930 replaced by a lattice steel bridge. The signal box, dating from 1898, was a neat brick and timber structure and was situated at the St Andrews end of the up platform. Three sidings and a loading bank with a 1 ton capacity crane were situated to the east of the signal box. The colour scheme at Crail in BR days (which was similar to that of the other stations on the line) was as follows: timberwork - Scottish Region standard brown and cream; footbridge - black, concrete flower tubs on platform - grass green and white; platform lamp-posts, the old coach bodies serving as sheds and coal merchant's office - all eggshell-blue (and, possibly, originally Scottish Region 'Caledonian' blue but faded with time).

## Following the Forth

Leaving Crail station the line skirted the town and, falling for over half a mile on a gradient of 1 in 65, turned west to parallel the coast which, at Fife Ness, had also turned west and now formed the northern shore of the Firth of Forth; extensive views across to the May Island and East Lothian coast were to be had from this stretch of line. There then followed a gated and manned crossing at **Kirkmay level crossing** (12.49) where a network of lanes joined the A917 main coast road close by. A noted feature here in later years was the crossing keeper's garden where a number of unusual plants, including tobacco plants, were grown. A short climb at 1 in 120 led to **Thirdpart level crossing** (13.52), where a by-road was crossed and which, like Kirkmay, was provided with a crossing keeper's cottage. The line then passed under the Cornceres to Backfield road before passing behind Kilrenny Common where there was another stone overbridge of standard Anstruther & St Andrews railway pattern carrying the Muiredge to Kilrenny right of way. This bridge was the scene of a particularly gruesome accident in 1910 when a locomotive driver struck his head on the bridge with fatal results. After passing the site of a proposed halt, the line bridged the Renny Burn and passed under the Kilrenny to Pitkierie by-road near to the farm at Rennyhill before falling on a gentle gradient which soon became a formidable 1 in 60 for nearly ¾ mile and, like the Mount Melville gradients 13 miles to the north, were the bane of many an engine driver's life. On this steeply falling section the railway swung south-westwards towards Anstruther and entering the burgh of Anstruther Easter, passed the Waid Academy on the up side and, travelling under the Anstruther to Dunino and St Andrews road, entered **Anstruther (New) station** (15.65).

This station was the second busiest on the line after St Andrews and was altered significantly during its lifetime. The original platform (later the up platform) was 380 feet in length and contained the main station building, a handsome single-storey freestone building some 110 feet in length with a small projecting canopy on the platform side with valancing and barge boards. In true

'B1' class No. 61343 enters the burgh of Crail on 13th July, 1963. Note the view of the Isle of May between the houses. The gates of the occupation crossing now are seeing further service at a house in Wales!        *C.C. Thornburn*

'B1' class No. 61103 heads the 8.45 am Glasgow Queen Street to Dundee service at Kirkmay Crossing near Crail, 18th April, 1953.        *J.L. Stevenson*

Anstruther & St Andrews Railway style tall chimneys were provided and a bookstall was situated under the canopy. The roadside elevation was similar in style to Crail, with two projecting bays with tall gable ends at right angles to the running line finished in dressed stone and topped with stone ball finials and a recessed entrance bay parallel to the running lines and sheltered by a continuation of the slated pitched roof which formed a canopy over the door. An eastern extension of the building housed a parcels room and the station lavatories. It is, however, curious that there were so many detail differences between the stations at Anstruther and Crail despite them having been built within a year of each other and this is perhaps suggestive of the fact that their local builders were responsible for a rather loose interpretation of the railway engineer's plans. A signal box, named Anstruther Station, was placed on the platform immediately to the south of the main building. In 1900-1 a second (down) platform 480 feet in length was added and, linked by a footbridge, had a brick-built NBR-pattern building some 40 feet in length with a projecting valanced canopy. At the same time the passing loop was upgraded to comply with Board of Trade regulations as a consequence of the 1896 accident so that the section between the east end of the station and Anstruther Junction was worked as a double line. In 1926, the box at Anstruther Station was abolished and the block section became Anstruther Junction to Crail; as a consequence the cross-over was moved westwards and the down running line was truncated with buffer stops at the east end of the down platform so that the up platform became bi-directional and the down platform was thereafter only used for trains to and from the Leven direction which were starting or terminating at Anstruther. The station never handled goods and, from December 1933 onwards, was officially known as 'Anstruther for Cellardyke'.

From Anstruther (New) the line now crossed the Dreel Burn, which separated Anstruther Easter from Anstruther Wester, on the **Dreel Burn viaduct**, a large freestone structure with two arches which carried the line over both the burn and a road. Alongside the double track on the up side of the deck of the viaduct was a narrow attached footbridge with a latticed parapet which dated from 1901 and carried a footpath between the station and goods yard. Then, passing on the up side the former Leven & East of Fife Railway terminus at **Anstruther (Old)**, which continued in use as the town's goods and locomotive depot, the line reached **Anstruther Junction** (16.01). Here the double-track section ended next to the tall signal box which marked the end of the Anstruther & St Andrews Railway and the beginning of the Leven & East of Fife Section, which is covered in a subsequent volume.

A child is nearly deafened by the blast of ex-LMS 'Black Five' No. 44969 storming up the bank towards Mount Melville on 27th August, 1960. In the distance are the towers of St Salvator's and Holy Trinity churches. *Douglas Paul Collection*

'Each a glimpse and gone forever!' - a Metro-Cammell triple-set passes Kingsbarns with the 2.42 pm Dundee to Edinburgh service on 27th March, 1965. *W.A.C. Smith*

# Chapter Thirteen

## Gone but not Forgotten: The Line Remembered

*'To me it was one of the most fascinating lines,
even if I am prejudiced.'*

John Purvis, MEP

### East Fifers Abroad

The pages of the *East Fife Observer* related some interesting examples of train excursions made by the inhabitants of the East Neuk in the years between the wars. On 31st May, 1934 the paper reported that,

There was great excitement among the Crail Brownies last week when their long-looked-forward-to visit to Edinburgh and the zoo drew near. They had been saving for it since September, and with the help of a few kind friends, were able to have a tremendous treat that will long be spoken of. On arrival at Waverley, a short visit was made to Woolworths, before proceeding to Renton's for lunch, and then by train to the zoo.* The time seemed all too short, but they were able to see all the animals, reptiles and birds. The chimpanzees' tea party was a great attraction, also feeding time at the sealions' pool. It was a tired but happy pack that arrived at Crail that night, which made a special run from Anstruther.

A few weeks later it was announced that,

Residents in Anstruther and district will soon be able to see the 'His Master's Voice' National Show Train. This unique combination of rolling stock was named and inspected by the Prime Minister at Paddington recently. It was built by HMV in order to promote the trade in radio and gramophones throughout the country thus keeping the 10,000 workers at the Hayes factory in employment during the year. The train is of ultra-modern construction and besides having a special acoustically designed showroom, it has a café, mobile power station and sleeping accommodation for the crew of three. Arrangements have been made to have it open for inspection from 11 am to 8.45 pm at Dundee West station, number 4 bay, on Thursday 28th June. Admission will be by ticket only, obtainable from Gray & Pringle Ltd., Anstruther. It will be possible for visitors to the train to see for the first time any of the latest developments of radio research. More than 30 types of radio and gramophone instruments will be able to be heard in operation on board and interesting technical radio and gramophone features, such as fluid-light tuning, may be inspected at leisure.

A less happy group of travellers were those who were left stranded by the LNER at St Andrews in June 1936:

A party of eight passengers, including six from Pittenweem, had an unfortunate experience last Thursday. After having spent the day in Dundee they made for Tay Bridge station, intending to catch the 5.40 pm train. This train is the Aberdeen express, East Fife passengers changing at Leuchars. The express arrived in Dundee at the

---

* They presumably travelled from Waverley to Pinkhill station on the Corstorphine branch.

scheduled time, but owing to the fact that it was 15 minutes late in leaving, the East Fife passengers failed to catch their connection at Leuchars. Unaware that their train had left, they boarded a waiting train at Leuchars station. This, however, went no further than St Andrews, where the party of eight were stranded so far as their journey by train was concerned. An official at St Andrews station explained the circumstances to us and suggested that we should complete the remainder of the journey by bus. He denied that we were stranded as we had the alternative of going home by road. I do not think that this is fair treatment for passengers who were left at a railway station through no fault of their own. Is this where the Railway Company's responsibility ends? We ultimately had to travel the remainder of our journey by bus. This caused considerable inconvenience and delay and it is hoped that closer supervision will ensure that we have no cause for another complaint in the future'.

Finally a lively account of 'Anstruther at Waverley: Fife Invasion at Waverley' appeared in the *Observer* of 6th October, 1927.

'Whaurs the Anster train?' 'Whit platform for the Fife train?' - These and sundry other questions of an equally anxious nature were all that one heard at Waverley station, Edinburgh, on Monday night when crowds of East Fife folks made ready to depart after their autumn jaunt to the capital. They were asked in no uncertain terms by harassed mothers and parcel laden fathers, but despite a continual fire of these questions, porters and other railway officials maintained their equanimity and good humour and guided those in doubt to their correct platforms and trains.

One happy little family had just got safely ensconced in a comfy carriage after a temper trying jostle through the seething crowds, and were enjoying a little rest when a mother made a startled discovery. 'Whaur's wee Tammy?', she cried and jumped up to scan the platform and adjacent carriages for the truant member of the family. No where to be seen. Mother then left the train and ran along the platform in the direction of the engine. A minute or so elapsed, during which time Pa had added his efforts to the search, and stood, pipe in mouth, surveying the streaming platform and soliloquising that it was 'Just like Tammy to get wonnered.' Bearing a sorrowful looking infant in her arms mother then appeared. A few minutes later the family had again resumed a normal state of calm and mother explained that 'Tammy, the wee gouk, had just gaen up the platform tae hae a keek at the engine'. Tommy here interrupted with a delightful gurgle and an impressive 'Choo Choo' in imitation of the engine. 'Ahve a guid mind tae smack ye' said mother, but Tommy put on such a beautiful air of injured innocence that mother, remembering it was a holiday, forebode to carry out her intention.

At different portions of the train families were packing themselves in and exchanging news of the day's adventures. By the time that the shores of Fife had been reached, delinquent children were fast asleep, and generally everyone was tired but happy, for the weather clerk had been on his best behaviour and the sights of Edinburgh had been enjoyed.

### The Railway Children

Brian Malaws, now resident in Wales, used to make an annual family visit to Crail in the early 1960s and has contributed the following account of how he haunted the station there.

Between about 1960 and the closure of the station to passengers in 1965, my young sister Wendy and I spent many a happy hour in and around the signal box at Crail during the school summer holidays. We were only allowed in the box when one signalman in particular, Sam Myles, was in duty. He showed us how the trains were signalled and the route was set, how the circular brass tablets were collected and issued for the sections between Crail and Kingsbarns, and Crail and Anstruther, strapped into a leather pouch attached to a white leather-covered wire loop so that the locomotive fireman and signalman could exchange tablets with the train on the move. We were introduced to the principles of interlocking, and patient explanations of the intricacies of the Tyer's No. 6 tablet machines were forthcoming in response to our many questions, although sadly were not retained in our young memories for long.

There were twenty-one levers in total, painted red for the home signals, yellow for the distant, black for points and blue for point locks with three spare ones painted white. Under close supervision we were allowed to pull the levers when a train was expected. There was, however, one lever that defeated us; we could just not shift lever No. 9 (the down loop points), no matter how we tried - even with both of us together. Mr Myles made it look so easy and teased us as weaklings, which was not far from the truth. He ascertained that we had porridge for breakfast, but was horrified to learn that we put sugar and cream on it, whereas of course it should always be taken with salt. So for the next few days my sister and I doggedly sprinkled salt on our porage; I don't know why, but after that No. 9 lever posed no problem at all. To this day I can only eat porridge with salt on it.

The evening treat (if we were allowed to stay up late) towards the end of the evening shift - being slipped a few shillings by Mr Myles and told to run down to Borella's shop in Crail High Street for three fish suppers. After the last train (only a dmu) had departed at around a quarter to ten, the log was written up, the signal box switched out and, one by one, the various buildings around the station were locked up, culminating with the lights being turned off in turn at the master switchboard in the booking office (the electric platform lamps I remember were particularly ungainly in appearance). Then that door was locked also (a Yale lock, I remember) and we set off in the gloaming, Mr Myles to his home in the grounds of Crail castle and my sister and I to our granny's house (which overlooked the famous harbour, but more importantly also overlooked the railway). We had great respect for Mr Myles and appreciated that he allowed us into his 'office'. Although we enjoyed enormously our times in the box, being there was always slightly tempered with the feeling that we were strictly breaking the rules - young respectable middle-class children from the Home Counties like us did not do that sort of things in those days. After all, Mr Myles was 'Authority' - he wore a hat with a peak! On occasions Wendy would pull the up starter (No.11) lever up-and-down repeatedly, and my great worry was that it would be noticed and reported to the 'polis' since the police house was in St Andrews Road directly behind the signal box.

On one of our last visits, Mr Myles gave me an oil-lamp with revolving tri-coloured glasses - which I still have - and upon cleaning it I uncovered a painted over brass plate bearing the initials 'NER'. How I wished, even then, that they had been 'NBR'! Sights, smells and sounds experienced nowadays will bring back instant memories of being in the box at Crail; a lofty, oil-lit semaphore signal box at dusk, the smell of creosote, the aroma of Mr Myles pipe tobacco, the smell of polish used on the linoleum floor (naturally the box was always kept scrupulously clean), the sharp sound of the bell and the deeper more relaxed chime of the gong of the tablet instruments and the sharp, acrid smoke from the coal fire which was burning even in summer. To my eternal regret, after the line closed and Mr Myles had retired, I never visited him at home, although I heard that he was always asking for me when we made our annual visit to Crail (our family persisted with railway travel for just one year, 1966, then bought our first car). I don't know why I never visited and by the time I 'came back' to railways a few years later, Mr Myles had sadly passed away.

## A Wicked Climb

Whatever physical remains of the line survive, the Anstruther & St Andrews Railway is still remembered as being one of the most characteristic of Scotland's railway byways and the final sections of this book contain some reminiscences about the line and the way it was operated. The first of these deals with the steep gradients on the line south of St Andrews station, and the frequent trouble that train crews found themselves in at this spot. An anonymous member of the Angus Railway Group wrote that, in the 1930s:

> The usual four-coach train was invariably hauled by a 'Scott', but occasionally a 'Glen' or a 'Director'. Sometimes the first southbound train from St Andrews on a Monday morning in winter, when frost covered the rail surfaces, would slip to a standstill on the 1 in 49. The position would be aggravated by the fact that no train had passed over the section since the last northbound train from Crail on the previous Saturday evening. Considerable delay could ensue while the unfortunate engine strove to progress at a walking pace, aided by liberal amounts of sand between the driving wheels. An awe-inspiring audible and visual display of steam-power in difficulties!

Shortly before the closure of the Anstruther & St Andrews line, John Purvis, dealing with the same location, wrote:

> The climb from St Andrews to Stravithie ... must be one of the more wicked ones in Britain, particularly the first 1½ miles to Mount Melville. From a standstill at St Andrews one is launched almost immediately on to the 1 in 49 climb with two very tight-angled reverse curves and a curve through the station which is sustained through nearly two-thirds of a circle. It is not surprising engine and driver find it too much sometimes, especially when greasy, as the curves limit the size of engine used – usually a B1. Nowadays what service there is, is provided mostly by diesel units, but in the summer there is a 4.18 steam train from St Andrews to Glasgow, Saturdays only ... There are, however, some unadvertised holiday specials, usually just running through after unloading on the Fife coast, to St Andrews, Leuchars or Dundee. Most adventurous of all, the Scottish Region television train negotiates this climb periodically with a load of school-children on educational excursions. It really is a sight watching this double-headed train belching smoke and spinning its wheels as it tries to gain adhesion on these 1 in 49 curves. So far as I know a banking engine is never used. The time-table allowance from St Andrews to Crail is very liberal, but in the days of steam operation allowance had to be made for exigencies. Several drivers have told me of the days when they could get no further and had to split their train and reassemble it at Mount Melville. Some of the trains were not that light either - for instance the 'Fife Coast Express', which included First Class coaches with arm-chairs for a while.
>
> There are also hair-raising stories of shunting operations at Mount Melville. Being single-track there are, of course, no switch-points, and if something went awry, trucks were liable to roar down the mile or two of incline, through St Andrews station at full-speed and end somewhere on the links on the way to Leuchars. Certainly at both Mount Melville and Stravithie there are large sign-boards, contemporary with the building of the line, exhorting the greatest caution in shunting. Even nowadays shunting at Mount Melville is done by placing the brake-vans apparently securely braked, on the downhill grade of the main line and using it as a buffer.

Similar sentiments were expressed by the late Douglas Brown who, in a letter published in the *St Andrews Citizen* in January 1966 said that:

As a small boy I frequently visited St Andrews station, on occasions with others who were similarly interested in locomotive matters. No mere number takers, we would discourse on saturated and superheated steam, vacuum and Westinghouse brakes and kindred subjects. Blessed with residence in a house whose rear windows overlooked the line, I was able to watch both its operation and its varying fortunes. According to my recollections, the locomotive designs of Matthew Holmes, William Reid, Nigel Gresley and Edward Thompson fought their way up to Mount Melville and beyond. Since these early years I have travelled on the line many times. Generally speaking the North British Railway, who took over from the original promoters of the line, had no station as beautiful as the Caledonian Railway's Wemyss Bay, Gleneagles or Strathyre, for example. The East Fife line was a glorious exception. The exquisite beauty of all its station gardens betokened the loving care of the true railwayman: it would be invidious to mention any one station as being superior to another in this respect. It was all the more sad, therefore, to note on my last visit the forlorn condition of the intermediate stations between St Andrews and Crail since the cessation of the freight service. The substitution of steam hauled stock by diesel multiple units resulted in a more comfortable journey and the enthralling spectacle of 'Glen', 'Scott' and 'Director' class steam engines making prodigious efforts up to Mount Melville is now only a nostalgic memory ... The charm of its well-kept stations, the natural beauty of its location and the friendly courtesy of its staff will be remembered when other lines are forgotten. It is deeply regretted that it was not able to survive.

### Goodbye to All That

Much reminiscing took place in the last years of the existence of the Anstruther & St Andrews line and typical of these was an article which appeared in the *Sunday Times* in 1965 and which was written by a Mrs J. Donington-Smith of St Andrews. After describing a sentimental last journey between Thornton and Crail she went on to recount that,

Kingsbarns station still has two oil-lamps hanging on their posts as they did in the days when a watering halt delivered a day's supply to the station master's house. In Boarhills the clock had stopped and grass is springing through the chinks in the platform. Along the single track to Stravithie and Mount Melville we pounded relentlessly without even a courtesy hoot in passing. How often in the past we had filled baskets with wild strawberries gathered on these sheltered banks. Now we were approaching St Andrews and an old familiar sound was missing - the grinding, churning noise of brakes applied on a steep gradient. Here we were at the spot where we used to look for the white pencil on the horizon that is the Bell Rock Lighthouse. Here is the slaughterhouse, once a far flung outpost of the town now partially submerged in an acre of new housing. Here we snapped the hat elastic under our chin, donned the white gloves again and snatched up our pail and spades with happy expectations. We drew into St Andrews station and, thank goodness, it is still the same, banks with flowers and with splendid blooming baskets acrawl with nasturtiums suspended like blossoming stalactites from the roof. The hanging gardens of Babylon would have found competition here. The station master no longer wears the frock-tails of our youth, but he is still a personage, believe me. Unfortunately this happy state of affairs is unlikely to continue much longer ...

## A Brave Venture

The Anstruther & St Andrews Railway was a brave venture which ultimately failed but performed a valuable service to the folk of the East Neuk during the 80 years that it was in operation. With only a handful of trains each way and little intermediate traffic worth bothering about, the LNER was perhaps right to consider closing the major portion of the line when it did and the only surprising thing is that the line between Crail and St Andrews survived as long as it did. Perhaps the Crail to Anstruther section, bound up as it was with the fortunes of the Leven and East of Fife line would have had a different future had a more sympathetic government been in power, but the tide of economic forces and the new world forged in the white heat of the technological revolution made even this coastal branch line look increasingly like a beached whale foundering on the sands. There were many, however, who welcomed the fact that the Anstruther & St Andrews did manage to survive into their lifetimes. The stretch north of Crail was, particularly, the epitome of a country branch line that reached the seaside after meandering through nowhere in particular. In the words of John Purvis, the great-grandson of the Chairman of the Anstruther & St Andrews Railway who recounted, in 1965, that:

> I shall never forget my last run on this line, which was last September at the front of the 6.26 am diesel from St Andrews to Edinburgh (Waverley). The sun was just coming out of the North Sea dead-ahead as we came down the hill from Stravithie to Boarhills and the partridges and pheasants flushed in front of us. To me it was one of the most fascinating lines, even if I am prejudiced … Alas, perhaps there will not be another chance.

He had another chance, but only on the last train which ran barely a year later and now the line has gone; the East Neuk will never again vibrate to the rumble of a dmu forming an unhurried local train to 'St Andrews by the Northern Sea'.

## Journey's End

Perhaps it would not be over-indulgent to end this book with another personal reminiscence from a more innocent age as a small boy awaits, with his mother and brother, the arrival on a sunny August morning of the 9.08 am Glasgow Buchanan Street to Dundee train at the quiet country station of Pittenweem. They are, uncharacteristically, a few minutes early and the boy strikes up a conversation with the sole railway functionary at the station, a resigned looking individual who produces with a flourish a blue Scottish Region timetable and hands it to the boy, commenting that the summer season is nearly at an end and 'the book's nae guid the noo and anywa' the line's to be shut soon enough'. Little stirs except the long grass at the side of the track and then a faint humming sound is heard in the distance. As it grows louder, the boy's anticipation begins to build up and he cheers when, eventually, the green multiple-unit bursts from under the bridge in a cloud of diesel fumes and comes to a halt at the single platform. The boy and his brother race to the front of the train in order to gain the seats with the view through the cab and the driver looks amused as their mother, flustered, follows them. But there was no need to hurry as competition is all but absent - the train has few passengers and the boy imagines that, even if it ever was busy, all of the people must already have alighted at the enticing beachside stations of Lundin Links, Largo or Elie.

The train starts off and, after trundling through the ripening fields for a matter of minutes, enters what seems to the boy to be the grandly-named station of Anstruther for Cellardyke, but where Cellardyke is or why this important looking station should be 'for' anywhere else is beyond his powers of imagination. A handful of passengers alight and they now have the front carriage entirely to themselves. On the next section there are views out over farmland towards the sea and the distant Isle of May which looks like the sort of place that the 'Famous Five' might choose to camp upon. The slight drone of the engine is only broken by the regular sound of the klaxon horn warning non-existent road users at the level crossings. Into Crail and the token is exchanged while a couple with a large canvas bag containing unseen treasures struggle along the platform. A solitary collie dog, who may or may not be associated with the goings-on at the station, watches the train with suspicion, his one blue eye and one brown looking in anticipation. Then, deciding that all was in order, he turns tail and slopes off nonchalantly in the way that only a collie dog can while a contented cat, with no apparent interest in the railway or the collie, sleeps in the sun.

The whistle blows and, amidst a crashing of gears, they are underway again. More farms follow one after the other until the train slows down to walking pace for another token exchange at the mysterious and seemingly closed station of Kingsbarns where the clock still tells the right time and the nameboard still tells of where it is - or more accurately perhaps, where it pretends to be. Then, all too soon, the train is gathering speed and travelling, 'over hedges and over ditches'. Soon follows another ghost station - Boarhills - but why? The train swings round the curves, changing direction to the west, and climbs to the summit at Stravithie where in swift succession, 'each a glimpse and gone forever', follow a third and a fourth of these deserted stations which all look as though they have been long forgotten and now exist only in some strange land like Narnia which the boy has never visited but would very much like to. Such musings are, however, brought to an end as the train begins to squeal around tight curves and enters the long descent into St Andrews with an ever-widening view of the city and the sea unfolding through the front windows. Through the houses and under the bridges until the brakes shudder and the train pulls up at the flower-bedecked platform where a small crowd are waiting to board for the trip onwards - oe'r the brig and on to the city of jute, jam and journalism.

But the three J's are of no concern to the boy as he joins his brother and mother as they traipse over the footbridge and into the town. Soon the delights of St Andrews are upon them as they wander through the streets, listen to the bells of the carillon, buy a Puffin book for half-a-crown at Innes' bookshop and dig sandcastles on the windy beach before an early high-tea of egg and chips at Macarthurs and the scurry back to the station. Here the last southbound train of the day (the boy having studied the timetable with great care), the 5.38 to Thornton and Glasgow, is preparing to leave and the boy leans out of the window to watch the green flag flutter as the whistle blows. All too soon they are moving off along the wandering way past Balrymonth and Lamboletham and as the train grinds the weary miles away back to Pittenweem the boy looks out of the window at the sparkling sea on one side and the westering sun on the other and thinks to himself that he likes travelling by train, particularly on this line, and for a moment overlooks the fact that he is tired and that there is still a long walk back from the station to their High Street lodgings. But the memory of that summer journey half a lifetime ago never leaves him and he, too, is now one of the authors of this book.

Farewell to the Anstruther & St Andrews - the 2.28 pm to Glasgow leaves St Andrews with the last scheduled steam train to the south on 21st August, 1965.     *C.C. Thornburn*

# A Brief Chronology

All opening and closing dates are the 'with effect from' dates; the actual date upon which the last train ran may be one or two days before if the closure date was a Monday. In the case of signal boxes closure dates given are when use of box was discontinued.

### Sections of line

St Andrews Links to St Andrews (New) – opened (P&G) 01.07.1887 A&StAR, closed (P&G) 06.01.1969 BR.

St Andrews (New) to Boarhills – opened (P&G) 01.07.1887 A&StAR, closed (P&G) 06.09.1965 BR.

Boarhills to Crail – opened (P&G) 01.09.1883 A&StAR, closed (P&G) 06.09.1965 BR.

Crail to Anstruther Junction – opened (G) 01.05.1883, (P) 01.09.1883 A&StAR, closed (P) 06.09.1965 BR, (G) 18.06.1966 BR; line out of use 18.12.1966

### Passenger Stations

|  | Company | Opened | Closed | Notes |
|---|---|---|---|---|
| Anstruther (New) | A&StAR | 01.09.1883 | 06.09.1965 | a |
| Anstruther (Old) | L&EoFR | 01.09.1863 | 20.12.1883 | b |
| Boarhills | A&StAR | 01.09.1883 | 01.01.1917 | c |
|  |  | 01.02.1919 | 22.09.1930 |  |
| Crail | A&StAR | 01.09.1883 | 06.09.1965 |  |
| Kingsbarns | A&StAR | 01.09.1883 | 22.09.1930 |  |
| Mount Melville | A&StAR | 01.09.1883 | 01.01.1917 | c |
|  |  | 01.02.1919 | 22.09.1930 |  |
| St Andrews (Links) | StAR | 01.07.1852 | 01.07.1887 | d |
| St Andrews (New) | A&StAR | 01.07.1887 | 06.01.1969 |  |
| Stravithie | A&StAR | 01.07.1887 | 22.09.1930 |  |

Notes: a – Anstruther for Cellardyke from 31.12.1933; b – replaced by Anstruther (New) from 21.12.1883; c – Temporary wartime closure; d – replaced by St Andrews (New) from that date; L&EoFR - Leven & East of Fife Railway.

**Goods Stations, Sidings, etc.**

|  | Company | Opened | Closed | Notes |
|---|---|---|---|---|
| Anstruther (Old) | LEoFR | 01.09.1863 | 18.07.1966 | |
| Boarhills | A&StAR | 01.09.1883 | 01.01.1917 | a |
| | | 01.02.1919 | 05.10.1964 | b |
| Crail | A&StAR | 01.05.1883 | 18.07.1966 | b |
| Kingsbarns | A&StAR | 01.09.1883 | 05.10.1964 | |
| Mount Melville | A&StAR | 01.07.1887 | 01.01.1917 | a |
| | | 01.02.1919 | 05.10.1964 | b, c |
| St Andrews Links | StAR | 01.07.1852 | 20.06.1966 | |
| Stravithie | A&StAR | 01.07.1887 | 05.10.1964 | |
| Stravithie Quarry Siding | A&StAR | 06.1887 | c.1914 | d |

Notes
a – Closed to regular traffic for duration of war.
b – Partially re-opened to goods (full wagon loads only) 21.03.1917.
c – Reduced to unstaffed public siding 01.06.1959.
d – Out of use since c.1902.

**Signal Boxes**

|  | Company | Opened | Closed | Notes |
|---|---|---|---|---|
| Anstruther Junction | A&StAR | 01.09.1883 | 05.10.1965 | a |
| Anstruther Station | A&StAR | 20.12.1883 | 12.09.1926 | |
| Boarhills | A&StAR | 01.09.1883 | 31.05.1898 | b |
| Crail | NBR | 07.05.1898 | 18.12.1966 | c |
| Kingsbarns | A&StAR | 01.09.1883 | 04.09.1965 | |
| Mount Melville | A&StAR | 01.07.1887 | 31.05.1898 | d |
| St Andrews Links | A&StAR | 01.07.1887 | 10.02.1957 | d |
| St Andrews Station | A&StAR | 01.07.1887 | 03.09.1967 | |
| Stravithie (first) | A&StAR | 01.07.1887 | 22.04.1898 | e |
| Stravithie (second) | NBR | 31.05.1898 | 22.08.1926 | d |

Notes
a – Renamed Anstruther 12.09.1926.
b – Replaced by ground frame.
c – Reduced to ground frame 05.10.1965.
d – Replaced by ground frame released by token.
e – Replaced by second box.

# Appendix Two

## Station Traffic Statistics 1900-1934

| | Passengers Booked (No.) | Receipts inc. parcels £ | Merchandise & Minerals (tons) | Coal (tons) | Livestock (no.) | Goods £ (A) |
|---|---|---|---|---|---|---|
| **Anstruther (New) and (Old)** | | | | | | |
| 1900 | 49,510 | 3,996 | 14,777 | 13,924 | 2,889 | 2,647 |
| 1901 | 52,794 | 4,012 | 18,553 | 9,628 | 3,004 | 2,893 |
| 1902 | 50,317 | 3,982 | 8,177 | 9,329 | 3,808 | 2,789 |
| 1903 | 54,425 | 4,473 | 15,999 | 8,689 | 3,500 | 3,132 |
| 1904 | 53,844 | 4,537 | 15,822 | 8,948 | 2,538 | 2,658 |
| 1905 | 50,414 | 4,299 | 15,206 | 8,446 | 3,052 | 2,434 |
| 1906 | 49,779 | 4,496 | 15,113 | 8,629 | 3,094 | 2,700 |
| 1907 | 52,737 | 4,459 | 11,700 | 9,719 | 3,389 | 2,719 |
| 1908 | 49,544 | 4,635 | 13,145 | 10,979 | 3,914 | 2,624 |
| 1909 | 42,842 | 4,048 | 11,141 | 12,429 | 3,200 | 2,041 |
| 1910 | 46,212 | 4,289 | 11,699 | 12,019 | 5,339 | 2,904 |
| 1911 | 44,698 | 4,339 | 12,215 | 12,251 | 5,185 | 2,073 |
| 1912 | 42,937 | 4,592 | 12,159 | 11,684 | 4,706 | 2,476 |
| 1913 | 47,986 | 5,034 | 11,257 | 12,470 | 5,037 | 2,287 |
| 1914 | 45,228 | 4,061 | 11,717 | 10,554 | 4,593 | 1,939 |
| 1915 | 38,030 | 3,414 | 9,472 | 7,222 | 4,332 | 1,733 |
| 1916 | 43,433 | 3,937 | 7,820 | 7,529 | 3,721 | 1,463 |
| 1917 | 37,964 | 4,814 | 11,556 | 11,165 | 5,521 | 2,625 |
| 1918 | 52,270 | 5,684 | 14,017 | 11,483 | 6,145 | 4,010 |
| 1919 | 59,058 | 7,833 | 9,928 | 9,237 | 3,772 | 2,835 |
| 1920 | 56,373 | 7,913 | 11,287 | 9,888 | 2,613 | 4,841 |
| 1921 | 44,085 | 6,236 | 14,028 | 7,197 | 2,999 | 4,469 |
| 1922 | 49,683 | 6,612 | 11,801 | 8,423 | 2,636 | 4,028 |
| 1923 | 49,673 | 6,289 | 10,526 | 8,109 | 4,006 | 3,444 |
| 1924 | 46,583 | 6,400 | 10,483 | 7,919 | 3,128 | 3,676 |
| 1925 | 43,781 | 6,610 | 10,249 | 7,161 | 4,834 | 3,498 |
| 1926 | 30,328 | 6,193 | 8,614 | 5,292 | 3,287 | 2,997 |
| 1927 | 37,302 | 5,943 | 9,280 | 6,058 | 4,177 | 3,141 |
| 1928 | 34,471 | 5,741 | 11,775 | 5,767 | 5,281 | 3,918 |
| 1929 | 32,832 | 5,892 | 10,427 | 6,312 | 4,533 | 4,004 |
| 1930 | 29,596 | 5,723 | 2,518 | 6,848 | 3,706 | 4,089 |
| 1931 | 27,928 | 5,330 | 9,036 | 6,180 | 2,924 | 2,848 |
| 1932 | 25,563 | 5,350 | 10,536 | 5,370 | 2,121 | 2,253 |
| 1933 | 26,188 | 5,056 | 8,899 | 4,915 | 2,898 | 1,803 |
| 1934 | 28,505 | 5,673 | 9,235 | 4,514 | 3,537 | 1,863 |
| | | | | | | |
| **Crail** | | | | | | |
| 1900 | 23,311 | 1,445 | 6,989 | 2,757 | 2,909 | 516 |
| 1901 | 23,497 | 1,448 | 6,239 | 2,696 | 4,793 | 667 |
| 1902 | 22,651 | 1,491 | 6,092 | 2,750 | 4,035 | 519 |
| 1903 | 25,925 | 1,568 | 7,108 | 2,643 | 2,027 | 660 |
| 1904 | 23,395 | 1,500 | 7,317 | 2,703 | 1,855 | 668 |
| 1905 | 24,290 | 1,397 | 8,064 | 2,752 | 2,316 | 645 |
| 1906 | 23,486 | 1,522 | 9,646 | 2,950 | 2,848 | 624 |
| 1907 | 23,867 | 1,554 | 9,111 | 2,984 | 2,854 | 647 |
| 1908 | 23,788 | 1,512 | 7,656 | 2,659 | 3,728 | 606 |
| 1909 | 25,076 | 1,611 | 8,852 | 2,848 | 3,212 | 600 |
| 1910 | 23,109 | 1,634 | 7,730 | 2,592 | 2,699 | 593 |
| 1911 | 20,628 | 1,770 | 8,985 | 2,715 | 3,017 | 547 |
| 1912 | 21,579 | 1,666 | 6,767 | 3,512 | 2,250 | 549 |
| 1913 | 22,845 | 1,702 | 11,449 | 2,561 | 4,095 | 684 |

| | Passengers Booked (No.) | Receipts inc. parcels £ | Merchandise & Minerals (tons) | Coal (tons) | Livestock (no.) | Goods £ (A) |
|---|---|---|---|---|---|---|
| Crail (continued) | | | | | | |
| 1914 | 20,294 | 1,577 | 7,587 | 2,461 | 3,047 | 566 |
| 1915 | 17,967 | 1,445 | 9,539 | 2,663 | 2,965 | 400 |
| 1916 | 20,268 | 1,644 | 9,243 | 2,864 | 2,534 | 416 |
| 1917 | 15,786 | 1,732 | 7,456 | 2,836 | 1,685 | 505 |
| 1918 | 99,545 | 8,359 | 35,382 | 4,621 | 4,812 | 1,244 |
| 1919 | 36,749 | 4,055 | 11,427 | 3,692 | 4,474 | 1,436 |
| 1920 | 27,507 | 3,488 | 9,499 | 3,237 | 2,493 | 1,714 |
| 1921 | 23,552 | 3,170 | 11,898 | 2,599 | 2,285 | 3,881 |
| 1922 | 22,185 | 2,974 | 9,222 | 3,492 | 2,771 | 1,679 |
| 1923 | 20,280 | 2,614 | 11,188 | 3,429 | 3,690 | 1,362 |
| 1924 | 20,234 | 2,678 | 9,375 | 3,459 | 2,938 | 1,192 |
| 1925 | 20,033 | 2,777 | 11,687 | 3,445 | 3,896 | 1,213 |
| 1926 | 13,533 | 2,266 | 8,593 | 2,304 | 4,690 | 1,072 |
| 1927 | 15,905 | 2,481 | 10,370 | 3,351 | 6,803 | 1,109 |
| 1928 | 13,702 | 2,236 | 8,687 | 3,406 | 6,586 | 1,071 |
| 1929 | 12,349 | 2,138 | 8,058 | 3,441 | 7,520 | 1,066 |
| 1930 | 10,950 | 1,959 | 8,708 | 3,662 | 7,702 | 1,062 |
| 1931 | 9,831 | 2,026 | 7,775 | 3,312 | 4,723 | 762 |
| 1932 | 8,859 | 1,759 | 5,349 | 3,138 | 4,667 | 644 |
| 1933 | 8,492 | 1,628 | 5,358 | 2,825 | 3,650 | 546 |
| 1934 | 9,554 | 1,737 | 4,859 | 3,034 | 4,211 | 526 |
| Kingsbarns | | | | | | |
| 1900 | 7,616 | 382 | 1,711 | 736 | 1,270 | 129 |
| 1901 | 7,072 | 360 | 2,362 | 715 | 1,335 | 151 |
| 1902 | 6,837 | 353 | 2,559 | 790 | 1,460 | 162 |
| 1903 | 7,423 | 339 | 2,206 | 793 | 1,723 | 148 |
| 1904 | 7,503 | 361 | 2,673 | 888 | 1,265 | 240 |
| 1905 | 7,197 | 357 | 2,563 | 903 | 1,987 | 190 |
| 1906 | 7,299 | 362 | 3,419 | 825 | 2,381 | 204 |
| 1907 | 7,218 | 391 | 2,889 | 712 | 1,871 | 181 |
| 1908 | 6,692 | 384 | 3,678 | 697 | 2,191 | 180 |
| 1909 | 5,964 | 361 | 3,092 | 886 | 1,730 | 140 |
| 1910 | 5,630 | 326 | 2,323 | 788 | 1,490 | 117 |
| 1911 | 6,039 | 438 | 2,872 | 799 | 2,037 | 156 |
| 1912 | 4,779 | 359 | 2,537 | 730 | 1,279 | 136 |
| 1913 | 6,039 | 351 | 3,125 | 688 | 1,591 | 151 |
| 1914 | 6,016 | 363 | 3,022 | 614 | 1,618 | 116 |
| 1915 | 5,607 | 371 | 4,292 | 662 | 1,606 | 156 |
| 1916 | 6,143 | 388 | 3,653 | 684 | 2,774 | 307 |
| 1917 | 3,413 | 324 | 4,948 | 974 | 3,152 | 360 |
| 1918 | 3,759 | 404 | 5,828 | 958 | 4,947 | 487 |
| 1919 | 6,751 | 489 | 3,501 | 717 | 2,296 | 418 |
| 1920 | 7,644 | 612 | 3,769 | 800 | 3,054 | 616 |
| 1921 | 6,577 | 563 | 4,608 | 601 | 2,964 | 620 |
| 1922 | 5,438 | 427 | 3,393 | 718 | 3,288 | 535 |
| 1923 | 4,083 | 321 | 4,325 | 719 | 2,820 | 417 |
| 1924 | 3,474 | 301 | 3,080 | 730 | 3,477 | 421 |
| 1925 | 2,987 | 285 | 3,344 | 730 | 2,980 | 406 |
| 1926 | 1,702 | 207 | 3,509 | 393 | 3,305 | 313 |
| 1927 | 1,940 | 195 | 3,023 | 692 | 3,667 | 375 |
| 1928 | 1,472 | 174 | 2,463 | 727 | 3,809 | 319 |
| 1929 | 1,392 | 198 | 2,725 | 756 | 3,531 | 305 |
| 1930 | 925 | 152 | 1,752 | 502 | 2,441 | 162 |
| 1931 (C) | - | - | - | - | - | - |
| 1932 (D) | 16 | 17 | 1,652 | 623 | 5,304 | 313 |
| 1933 (E) | 42 | 23 | 5,720 | 1,019 | 7,281 | 488 |
| 1934 (E) | 26 | 49 | 5,338 | 1,051 | 9,106 | 588 |

| | Passengers Booked (No.) | Receipts inc. parcels £ | Merchandise & Minerals (tons) | Coal (tons) | Livestock (no.) | Goods £ (A) |
|---|---|---|---|---|---|---|
| **Boarhills** | | | | | | |
| 1900 | 6,236 | 283 | 2,483 | 569 | 1,144 | 115 |
| 1901 | 6,145 | 274 | 2,421 | 540 | 1,588 | 131 |
| 1902 | 6,175 | 292 | 2,913 | 662 | 1,394 | 147 |
| 1903 | 6,643 | 323 | 3,035 | 666 | 2,974 | 131 |
| 1904 | 6,471 | 288 | 2,163 | 602 | 1,232 | 131 |
| 1905 | 6,027 | 290 | 2,951 | 467 | 1,227 | 160 |
| 1906 | 5,816 | 291 | 2,833 | 533 | 1,506 | 142 |
| 1907 | 5,393 | 291 | 2,741 | 447 | 1,630 | 143 |
| 1908 | 5,228 | 300 | 2,713 | 451 | 2,953 | 182 |
| 1909 | 5,248 | 314 | 2,886 | 541 | 1,687 | 130 |
| 1910 | 5,116 | 299 | 3,046 | 480 | 1,784 | 135 |
| 1911 | 5,212 | 316 | 2,581 | 504 | 1,666 | 142 |
| 1912 | 5,056 | 252 | 2,135 | 496 | 1,201 | 131 |
| 1913 | 5,632 | 289 | 2,646 | 543 | 2,496 | 117 |
| 1914 | 5,188 | 216 | 2,587 | 500 | 2,045 | 166 |
| 1915 | 4,990 | 238 | 2,925 | 481 | 2,013 | 149 |
| 1916 | 4,583 | 237 | 3,004 | 466 | 2,527 | 138 |
| 1917 (B ) | - | - | - | | - | - |
| 1918 (B,F) | - | - | - | 14 | - | - |
| 1919 | 3,917 | 299 | 1,509 | 269 | 1,712 | 202 |
| 1920 | 5,413 | 398 | 2,885 | 406 | 1,853 | 391 |
| 1921 | 3,947 | 346 | 3,524 | 413 | 1,403 | 403 |
| 1922 | 3,505 | 310 | 2,814 | 553 | 2,148 | 393 |
| 1923 | 2,217 | 194 | 3,757 | 515 | 3,435 | 295 |
| 1924 | 1,709 | 151 | 4,568 | 520 | 3,214 | 352 |
| 1925 | 1,822 | 180 | 3,388 | 507 | 4,038 | 338 |
| 1926 | 984 | 141 | 2,224 | 262 | 3,666 | 322 |
| 1927 | 1,003 | 125 | 4,038 | 454 | 3,903 | 301 |
| 1928 | 822 | 87 | 3,375 | 431 | 2,922 | 298 |
| 1929 (G) | 633 | 114 | 4,335 | 1,029 | 12,261 | 843 |
| 1930 (H) | 348 | 98 | 5,285 | 1,314 | 10,944 | 681 |
| 1931 (H) | - | 37 | 6,272 | 1,553 | 9,827 | 684 |
| 1932 (I) | 1 | 75 | 2,685 | 662 | 3,956 | 248 |
| 1933 (I) | - | 32 | - | - | - | - |
| 1934 (I) | - | 35 | - | - | - | - |
| | | | | | | |
| **Stravithie** | | | | | | |
| 1900 | 4,689 | 311 | 2,857 | 473 | 2,947 | 275 |
| 1901 | 4,913 | 316 | 2,611 | 464 | 3,238 | 186 |
| 1902 | 4,575 | 337 | 3,380 | 694 | 3,135 | 202 |
| 1903 | 4,719 | 343 | 2,414 | 410 | 3,081 | 156 |
| 1904 | 4,608 | 290 | 2,193 | 266 | 2,874 | 171 |
| 1905 | 5,066 | 415 | 3,472 | 293 | 2,947 | 259 |
| 1906 | 4,897 | 324 | 3,321 | 205 | 4,158 | 224 |
| 1907 | 4,968 | 391 | 3,201 | 235 | 3,603 | 215 |
| 1908 | 4,600 | 303 | 2,747 | 219 | 3,994 | 229 |
| 1909 | 4,969 | 291 | 2,875 | 316 | 3,735 | 233 |
| 1910 | 4,369 | 274 | 2,674 | 318 | 3,227 | 218 |
| 1911 | 4,759 | 282 | 2,836 | 475 | 4,006 | 226 |
| 1912 | 5,001 | 326 | 3,312 | 974 | 3,775 | 252 |
| 1913 | 4,850 | 273 | 4,477 | 971 | 4,876 | 309 |
| 1914 | 4,802 | 411 | 3,009 | 907 | 3,164 | 256 |
| 1915 | 4,634 | 270 | 4,134 | 944 | 3,695 | 282 |
| 1916 | 3,917 | 250 | 3,189 | 920 | 5,640 | 343 |
| 1917 | 2,420 | 260 | 4,566 | 1,904 | 6,637 | 411 |
| 1918 | 3,246 | 351 | 7,309 | 1,985 | 7,094 | 598 |

| | Passengers Booked (No.) | Receipts inc. parcels £ | Merchandise & Minerals (tons) | Coal (tons) | Livestock (no.) | Goods £ (A) |
|---|---|---|---|---|---|---|
| *Stravithie (continued)* | | | | | | |
| 1919 | 4,204 | 390 | 4,783 | 967 | 3,555 | 468 |
| 1920 | 4,116 | 487 | 4,298 | 927 | 3,607 | 896 |
| 1921 | 3,590 | 410 | 5,260 | 701 | 4,292 | 987 |
| 1922 | 3,305 | 323 | 4,571 | 929 | 3,758 | 839 |
| 1923 | 2,815 | 248 | 3,553 | 925 | 5,125 | 617 |
| 1924 | 2,722 | 239 | 2,715 | 1,171 | 4,936 | 577 |
| 1925 | 2,703 | 223 | 3,421 | 959 | 5,745 | 577 |
| 1926 | 2,118 | 261 | 3,691 | 551 | 5,947 | 566 |
| 1927 | 1,747 | 201 | 2,831 | 817 | 6,246 | 517 |
| 1928 | 1,106 | 207 | 2,653 | 780 | 5,981 | 472 |
| 1929 (J) | 1,068 | 205 | 762 | 228 | 1,240 | 111 |
| 1930 (K) | 684 | 177 | - | - | - | - |
| 1931 (K) | - | 123 | - | - | - | - |
| 1932 (K) | 12 | 155 | - | - | - | - |
| 1933 (L) | 14 | 162 | - | - | - | - |
| 1934 (L) | - | 202 | - | - | - | - |
| | | | | | | |
| *Mount Melville* | | | | | | |
| 1900 | 5,491 | 158 | 3,481 | 843 | 857 | 140 |
| 1901 | 5,561 | 162 | 3,738 | 348 | 644 | 168 |
| 1902 | 5,338 | 169 | 5,276 | 691 | 604 | 428 |
| 1903 | 5,394 | 173 | 5,484 | 552 | 893 | 531 |
| 1904 | 5,341 | 165 | 5,838 | 480 | 823 | 264 |
| 1905 | 5,912 | 189 | 4,394 | 534 | 1,386 | 406 |
| 1906 | 5,360 | 168 | 3,155 | 525 | 842 | 138 |
| 1907 | 5,059 | 170 | 2,863 | 470 | 1,083 | 168 |
| 1908 | 4,802 | 163 | 2,954 | 609 | 742 | 141 |
| 1909 | 4,534 | 168 | 3,247 | 629 | 996 | 126 |
| 1910 | 4,474 | 159 | 2,739 | 730 | 888 | 186 |
| 1911 | 5,062 | 182 | 4,884 | 1,018 | 1,270 | 194 |
| 1912 | 4,608 | 190 | 4,701 | 1,332 | 770 | 293 |
| 1913 | 5,186 | 204 | 3,737 | 872 | 1,257 | 180 |
| 1914 | 4,774 | 183 | 3,555 | 1,096 | 1,470 | 221 |
| 1915 | 5,309 | 200 | 5,668 | 1,030 | 1,778 | 251 |
| 1916 | 4,682 | 199 | 3,950 | 1,102 | 2,164 | 246 |
| 1917 (B) | - | - | - | - | - | - |
| 1918 (B) | - | - | - | - | - | - |
| 1919 | 2,431 | 176 | 3,367 | 969 | 1,474 | 316 |
| 1920 | 2,950 | 216 | 4,409 | 1,212 | 1,661 | 793 |
| 1921 | 2,448 | 207 | 5,346 | 1,147 | 877 | 621 |
| 1922 | 2,850 | 203 | 5,107 | 1,188 | 727 | 557 |
| 1923 | 2,481 | 154 | 4,607 | 1,260 | 2,108 | 521 |
| 1924 | 2,160 | 120 | 5,943 | 1,280 | 2,295 | 561 |
| 1925 | 1,826 | 99 | 6,395 | 1,322 | 2,171 | 449 |
| 1926 | 1,259 | 61 | 3,467 | 791 | 2,748 | 49 |
| 1927 | 2,029 | 72 | 2,372 | 1,233 | 2,612 | 251 |
| 1928 | 2,178 | 63 | 2,131 | 397 | 1,536 | 257 |
| 1929 | 1,036 | 48 | 2,807 | 294 | 2,227 | 581 |
| 1930 | 675 | 29 | 1,761 | 200 | 940 | 563 |
| 1931 (M) | - | 12 | - | - | - | - |
| 1932 (M) | - | 9 | - | - | - | - |
| 1933 (M) | - | 3 | - | - | - | - |
| 1934 (M) | - | - | - | - | - | - |

| | Passengers Booked (No.) | Receipts inc. parcels £ | Merchandise & Minerals (tons) | Coal (tons) | Livestock (no.) | Goods £ (A) |
|---|---|---|---|---|---|---|
| *St Andrews (Links) and (New)* | | | | | | |
| 1900 | 131,319 | 13,389 | 16,851 | 17,934 | 7,537 | 3,601 |
| 1901 | 118,856 | 17,706 | 15,369 | 17,314 | 6,458 | 3,231 |
| 1902 | 115,383 | 13,628 | 16,811 | 18,916 | 4,508 | 3,225 |
| 1903 | 126,979 | 14,090 | 18,438 | 18,713 | 5,637 | 3,347 |
| 1904 | 140,456 | 15,174 | 21,279 | 19,922 | 6,809 | 3,525 |
| 1905 | 141,419 | 14,908 | 23,995 | 19,618 | 6,571 | 3,583 |
| 1906 | 134,985 | 14,507 | 25,012 | 20,640 | 8,089 | 3,275 |
| 1907 | 137,781 | 14,906 | 20,676 | 21,291 | 8,127 | 3,463 |
| 1908 | 132,774 | 15,626 | 24,082 | 20,514 | 8,207 | 3,982 |
| 1909 | 129,378 | 15,484 | 21,096 | 21,828 | 6,708 | 3,743 |
| 1910 | 131,995 | 15,268 | 21,431 | 21,054 | 6,998 | 3,318 |
| 1911 | 133,009 | 16,251 | 21,054 | 20,515 | 7,707 | 3,250 |
| 1912 | 128,011 | 15,767 | 21,423 | 21,498 | 7,392 | 3,224 |
| 1913 | 133,519 | 15,068 | 19,230 | 21,566 | 7,996 | 3,056 |
| 1914 | 133,650 | 15,103 | 19,281 | 21,094 | 5,951 | 3,056 |
| 1915 | 112,943 | 13,838 | 12,978 | 21,772 | 5,232 | 1,997 |
| 1916 | 114,588 | 14,824 | 12,285 | 21,274 | 4,675 | 2,638 |
| 1917 | 74,029 | 14,401 | 12,684 | 22,587 | 6,133 | 2,851 |
| 1918 | 94,291 | 17,646 | 12,630 | 21,206 | 3,272 | 2,661 |
| 1919 | 130,481 | 24,399 | 14,749 | 20,643 | 3,495 | 3,495 |
| 1920 | 141,437 | 30,014 | 19,230 | 23,310 | 3,679 | 6,871 |
| 1921 | 128,548 | 31,909 | 20,405 | 19,836 | 5,449 | 7,080 |
| 1922 | 145,947 | 31,213 | 18,563 | 22,723 | 4,231 | 6,490 |
| 1923 | 168,760 | 28,979 | 18,320 | 23,508 | 5,580 | 5,555 |
| 1924 | 169,175 | 29,851 | 18,918 | 24,087 | 6,009 | 4,713 |
| 1925 | 176,884 | 28,547 | 18,003 | 24,076 | 5,866 | 4,684 |
| 1926 | 161,846 | 27,668 | 28,058 | 17,744 | 5,851 | 5,422 |
| 1927 | 176,100 | 29,524 | 19,194 | 23,743 | 5,120 | 4,888 |
| 1928 | 165,599 | 28,761 | 16,996 | 25,063 | 5,344 | 4,558 |
| 1929 | 172,770 | 26,760 | 24,191 | 26,276 | 5,673 | 4,515 |
| 1930 | 162,007 | 25,682 | 15,469 | 27,222 | 5,661 | 4,527 |
| 1931 | 147,810 | 23,240 | 25,656 | 25,415 | 6,656 | 4,417 |
| 1932 | 139,686 | 20,999 | 12,302 | 25,656 | 5,545 | 2,081 |
| 1933 | 137,344 | 21,082 | 12,153 | 24,664 | 3,555 | 3,567 |
| 1934 | 136,360 | 20,581 | 13,481 | 25,282 | 4,064 | 3,736 |

*General Note:* All figures for years up to 1912 are the addition of six-month periods ending 31st July and 31st January of the following years. Owing to a change in the way figures were kept, the year 1912 comprises only of the statistics from 1st February, 1912 to 31st December, 1912. Thereafter figures relate to the actual calendar years.

*Other Notes:* (A) Cash remitted; (B) Station temporarily closed; (C) No figures available; (D) Figures to end of June only, thereafter included with Boarhills; (E) Figures included with Boarhills; (F) Figure refers to July-December only; (G) Figures include those for Stravithie from July 1929; (H) Figures include Stravithie; (I) Figures include Stravithie and are to June 1931 only; thereafter included in Kingsbarns; (J) Figures included in Kingsbarns; (K) Figures to June only; thereafter included in Boarhills; (L) Goods figures included in Kingsbarns; (M) Figures included in St Andrews.

# Appendix Three

## Extract from the NBR Working Timetable, June 1903

88

**NOTES to DOWN TRAINS on pages 84 and 85.**

No. 2 Down.—Engine and Guard turn out at 4·0 a.m. to do shunting work.

No. 7 Down.—Conveys Live Stock for Cupar to be transferred at Leuchars to the *Ladybank Pilot Train. Meets at Kingsbarns No. 5 Up.* No. 8 Down.—*Meets at Crail No. 7 Up.*

No. 11 Down.—Carries Road Wagons, labelled "intermediate between Thornton and St Andrews;" "Leith Walk and St Andrews;" and "Kirkcaldy and St Andrews. Meets at Anstruther "the Van Way-Bills to be delivered to Station Master St Andrews. *Meets at Cameron Bridge Nos. 2 and 3 Up; at Leven Nos. 5, 6, and 8a Up; at Anstruther No. 11 Up, and at Strathvithie No. 19 Up. Shunts at Anstruther for No. 14 Down.*

No. 14 Down.—*Meets at East Fife Central Junction No. 5 Up; at Largo No. 6 Up; at Elie No. 8a Up, and at Crail No. 11 Up. Passes at Anstruther No. 11 Down.*

No. 16 Down.—Engine and men turn out at 8·35 a.m. to marshal Train. Shunts Sidings at Cameron Bridge.

† No. 18 Down.—Calls at Kilconquhar on Thursdays only. On other days it calls only when required to set down Passengers from Edinburgh and Glasgow. *Meets at Cameron Bridge No. 8a Up, and at East of Fife Central Junction No. 11 Up.*

No. 19a Down.—Carries Road Wagon ticketed "St Andrews to Leith Walk." Shunts at Leuchars, and assists from Leuchars to Wormit as required, but the Engine must be at Dundee in good time to work the 5·40 p.m. Passenger Train from Dundee to Thornton.

† No. 21 Down.—*Meets at Elie No. 18 Up and at Anstruther No. 19 Up.*

† No. 23 Down.—Follows Stores Train when required.

† No. 25 Down.—*Meets at Leven No. 18 Up.*

No. 25 Down.—*Meets at St Andrews No. 27 Up.* No. 26.—*Connection from Edinburgh on Saturdays only. Up, and at St Andrews No. 27 Up.* No. 26.—Connection from Edinburgh on Saturdays only.

No. 28 Down.—*Meets at Elie No. 24 Up* † On Saturdays follows from Largo Nos. 29 and 30 Down.

No. 27 Up.

No. 29 Down.—*Passes at Largo No. 28 Down. Meets at Elie No. 24 Up, and at Anstruther No. 27 Up.*

No. 30 Down.—*Passes at Largo No. 28 Down.*

No. 31 Down.—*Meets at Largo No. 24 Up, at Elie No. 27 Up, and at Anstruther No. 29 Up.*

No. 33 Down.—Calls at Cameron Bridge, Leven, Lundin Links, Largo, and Kilconquhar only to leave off Live Stock. Engine turns out at 12·0 noon to shunt in Thornton Yard. *Meets at Elie No. 35 Up, and at Anstruther No. 37 Up. Shunts at Anstruther for Nos. 37 and 39 Down.*

No. 36.—This Train must not be detained for 4·5 p.m. Train from Dundee if latter be late.

† Nos. 36 and 37 Down.—Calls at Kilconquhar when required to set down Passengers from Edinburgh and Glasgow.

No. 37 Down.—*Meets at Elie No. 35 Up. Passes at Anstruther No. 33 Down.*

No. 39 Down.—*Meets at Elie No. 35 Up, and at Anstruther No. 37 Up. Passes at Anstruther No. 33 Down.*

No. 40 and 41 Down.—Connect with 9·50 p.m Goods Train from Dundee to Glasgow.

No. 43 Down.—*Meets at Leven No. 35 Up, and at Largo No. 37 Up.* † On Saturdays meets No. 39 Up at Elie, and on that day runs five minutes later from Elie to Crail.

† No. 44 Down.—Calls at Lundin Links, Largo, and Kilconquhar only when required with Live Stock and Perishable Traffic. ‡ When this Train is preceded by the 9·0 p.m. Passenger Train from Thornton to Anstruther, the former will not call at Pittenweem. *Meets at Cameron Bridge No. 39 Up.*

† No. 45.—This Train may leave Dundee at 7·30 p.m.

**Anstruther and Dundee Passenger Engine.**—This Engine must turn out at 6·20 a.m. to shunt for 30 minutes as required.

**NOTES to UP TRAINS on pages 86 and 87.**    **June 1903.**

No. 2 Up.—Works Live Stock Traffic, and connects at Anstruther with 3·45 a.m. Train from Dundee. *Meets at Leven No. 11 Down.*

† No. 4a Up.—Calls at Kilconquhar on Mondays only. *Meets at Crail No. 11 Down.*

† No. 5 Up.—Calls at St Monans only to pick up Passengers. Calls at East Fife Central Junction No. 14 Down. † Calls at St Monans only to pick up Passengers.    No. 3 Up.—*Meets at Cameron Bridge No. 11 Down.*

No. 6 Up.—Calls at Kilconquhar only when required to pick up Passengers for Glasgow. *Meets at Elie No. 11 Down, and at Largo No. 14 Down, and passes at Elie No. 8a Up.*

No. 7 Up.—*Meets at Crail No. 8 Down.* Engine, with Guard and Van, to work this Train leaves Anstruther at 6·40 a.m.

No. 8a Up.—*Meets at Elie Nos. 11 and 14 Down, and at Cameron Bridge No. 18 Down, and shunts at Elie No. 6 Up, and at Cameron Bridge No. 11 Up.*

No. 11 Up.—*Meets at Crail No. 14 Down, at Anstruther No. 11 Down, and at East of Fife Junction No. 18 Down. Passes No. 8 Up at Cameron Bridge.*

No. 18 Up.—*Meets at Elie No. 21 Down, at Largo No. 24 Down, and at Leven Stores Train*

No. 19 Up.—*Meets at Strathvithie No. 11 Down, at Anstruther No. 21 Down, and at Largo Stores Train.* † Connection to Dundee on Saturdays only.

No. 24 Up.—*Meets at Kingsbarns No. 25 Down, at Elie No. 28 Down, and at Largo No. 31 Down. Waits at Elie the arrival of Nos. 29 and 30 Down.*    [31 Down.

No. 27 Up.—*Meets Stores Train at St Andrews, and at Anstruther No. 29 Down, and at Elie No.*

Nos. 27 and 29 Up.—All Stations sending Fish Traffic by these Trains for South of Edinburgh must wire Station-master and Parcels Agent, Edinburgh, full particulars, giving number of packages and destination of each consignment.

No 29 Up.—Must be worked punctually. Calls at Kilconquhar only when required to pick up Passengers for Edinburgh. *Meets at Anstruther No. 31 Down.*

No. 33 Up.—Engine with Guard and Van only returns to Leuchars immediately.

No. 35 Up.—*Meets at Elie Nos. 33, 37, and 39 Down, also meets at Leven No. 43 Down.* Carries Road Vans ticketed "Anstruther and Sig'whill," and Road Wagons ticketed "Anstruther and Leith Walk" and "Anstruther and Dundee;" the Way-bills to be delivered to Station-Master, Thornton.

No 37 Up.—This Train will not wait at Leuchars Junction for the Train due from the South at 5·57 p.m. if the latter be 15 minutes or more late. *Meets at Anstruther Nos. 33 and 39 Down and at Largo No. 43 Down.*

No. 39 Up.—*Meets at Elie No. 43 Down and at Cameron Bridge No. 44 Down.*

† No. 42 Up.—This train may leave Dundee at 7·30 p.m.

**Speed of Trains and Engines over Leven Brick Works Crossing.**

The Speed of Trains and Engines, Up and Down (by Night and by Day), must not exceed **Four Miles an Hour** when passing over Leven Brick Works Crossing, about 460 yards East of Leven Station. Engine Drivers must always have their Engines and Trains under such control when approaching that they will be able to stop before fouling the Level Crossing.

**Working of Traffic at Mount Melville and Stravithie.**

For special particulars as to the Working of Traffic at Mount Melville and Stravithie Stations, see printed Order, M. 1866, dated 6th July 1887.

**Fish Specials and Extra Goods Trains will be run when the Traffic requires it.**

# LEVEN and EAST OF FIFE, ANSTRUTHER & ST ANDREWS, and ST ANDREWS & LEUCHARS SECTIONS, and MUIREDGE BRANCH.—Down Trains.

June 1903.

## WEEK-DAYS.

| Stations and Sidings. | Distance from Thornton (Miles) | (Chns.) | 1 | 2 Branch Engine Goods a.m. | 3 Pass. a.m. | 4 Pass. a.m. | 5 Pass. a.m. | 6 Pass. a.m. | 7 Cattle Tues. only a.m. | 8 Pass. a.m. | 9 Pass. a.m. | 10 | 11 Thornton and St Andrews Goods a.m. | 12 Pass. a.m. | 13 | 14 Pass. a.m. | 15 Pass. a.m. | 16 East Fife Min. a.m. | 17 Pass. a.m. | 18 Fast Pass. a.m. | 19 East Fife Min. a.m. | 20 Pass. p.m. | 21 Pass. a.m. | 22 Pass. Sat. only p.m. |
|---|---|---|---|---|---|---|---|---|---|---|---|---|---|---|---|---|---|---|---|---|---|---|---|---|
| Dundee ... dep. | | | | | | | | | | | | | | | | | | | | 8 15 / 8 50 | | | 9 0 | 8 50 |
| Edinburgh ... dep. | | | | | | | | | | | | | | | | | | | 9 51 | | | | 10 45 / 10 54 | |
| Thornton Jun. ... dep. | | | | | | | | | | | | | 6 20 | | | 6 40 | | | | | | | | |
| Drumcaldie Distillery Siding | 3 | 45 | | | | | | | | | | | 6 32 | | | | | | | | | | | |
| Cameron Bridge ... arr. | 3 | 61 | | | | | | | | | | | 6 40 | | | 7 56 | | 9 5 / 9 20 / 9 25 / 10 0 / 10 15 | | | | | | |
| Cameron Bridge ... dep. | 3 | 61 | | | | | | | | | | | | | | | | | | | | | | | |
| Pirnie Colliery | 3 | 50 | | | | | | | | | | | | | | | | | | | | | | | |
| Cameron Pit Sidings ... arr. | 4 | 57 | | | | | | | | | | | | | | | | | | | | | | | |
| Cameron Bridge ... dep. | 4 | 61 | | | | | | | | | | | 6 40 | | | 7 57 | | | | | | | | | |
| East Fife Central Junction | 4 | 51 | | | | | | | | | | | 6 47 | | | | | | | | | | | | |
| Leven ... arr. | 5 | 77 | | | | | | | | | | | 7 5 | | | 7 59 | | 10 20 | | 10 4 | 10 45 | | | 11 1 | |
| Do. ... dep. | 5 | 77 | | 4 40 | | | | | | | | | | | | 8 14 | | Stop. | | | 10 52 | | | | |
| Leven Brick Work Siding | 6 | 18 | | | | | | | | | | | 7 10 | | | | | | | 10 8 | Stop. | | | | |
| Silverburn Siding | 7 | 16 | | 4 55 | | | | | | | | | 7 20 | | | 8 19 | | | | | | | | | |
| Lundin Links | 7 | 60 | | 5 0 | | | | | | | | | 7 35 | | | 8 25 | | | | 10 13 | | | | 11 17 | |
| Largo | 8 | 50 | | | | | | | | | | | 7 40 | | | 8 34 | | | | 10 17 | | | | 11 20 | |
| Kilconquhar | 12 | 89 | | | | | | | | | | | | | | 8 38 | | | | 10 14 | | | | 11 24 | |
| Elie ... arr. | 13 | 71 | | | | | | | | | | | | | | | | | | 10 27 | | | | | |
| Do. ... dep. | 13 | 78 | | | | | | | | | | | | | | 8 39 | | | | | | | | 11 26 | |
| St Monan's | 13 | 78 | | | | | | | | | | | | | | 8 46 | | | | 10 29 | | | | 11 33 | |
| Pittenweem | 17 | 42 | | | | | | | | | | | | | | 8 51 | | | | 10 35 | | | | 11 38 | |
| Anstruther (Old Station) ... arr. | 18 | 45 | | | | | | | | | | | | | | | | | | 10 40 | | | | | |
| Anstruther (New Station) ... arr. | 18 | 52 | | | | | | | 6 20 | 7 19 | | | 8 14 | | | 8 54 | | | | 10 43 | | | | 11 43 | |
| Do.   Do. ... dep. | 18 | 52 | | | | | | | 6 22 | 7 30 | | | 8 24 | | | 8 57 | | | | 10 45 | | | | 11 48 | 1 15 |
| Crail | 22 | 74 | | | | | | | 6 35 | 7 36 | | | 8 32 | | | 9 8 | | | | 10 55 | | | | 11 59 | |
| Kingsbarns ... arr. | 25 | 64 | | | | | | | 6 41 | 7 37 | | | 9 35 | | | 9 14 | | | | Stop. | | | | 12 6 | |
| Do. ... dep. | 25 | 64 | | | | | | | 6 50 | 7 42 | | | 9 40 | | | 9 15 | | | | | | | | 12 18 | |
| Boarhills | 27 | 27 | | | | | | | 6 59 | 7 49 | | | 10 0 | | | 9 20 | | | | | | | | 12 18 | |
| Stravithie | 29 | 1 | | | | | | | 7 6 | 7 56 | | | 10 10 | | | 9 27 | | | | | | | | 12 25 | |
| Mount Melville | 32 | 76 | | | | | | | 7 16 | 8 2 | | | 10 23 | | | 9 34 | | | | | | | | 12 29 | |
| St Andrews (New Station) ... arr. | 33 | 1 | | | | | | | | | | | 11 17 | | | 9 38 | | | | | | | | | |
| Do. (New Do.) ... dep. | 33 | 76 | | | | 6 0 | | 7 0 | 7 45 | 8 11 | 8 45 | | 11 30 | | | 9 40 | | | | | 19a | 12 10 | 1 0 | |
| Do. (Links Station) | 37 | 24 | | | | | | | | | | | 11 40 | | | | | | | | Goods | | | | |
| Edenside Brick Work Siding | 37 | 53 | | | | | | | | | | | Stop. | | | | | | | | 11 45 | | 1 10 | 1 24 |
| Guard Bridge | 38 | 67 | | | | 6 9 | 7 9 | | 7 55 | 8 14 | 8 52 | | | | | 9 49 | 9 55 | | 10 46 | | 11 57 | 12 20 | 1 10 | 1 24 |
| Seggie Siding | 38 | 8 | | | | | | | | | | | | | | 9 54 | 10 4 | | 10 49 | | 12 0 / 12 5 | 12 25 | 1 15 | 1 28 |
| Leuchars Junction ... arr. | 39 | 8 | | | | 6 13 | 7 13 | | 8 0 | 8 34 | 8 55 | | | | | 10 8 | 10 8 | | | | 12 8 | | 4 5 | 2 4 |
| Edinburgh ... arr. | 39 | 1 | | | | | | | | | 11 44 | | | | | 12 2 | 12 2 | | 11 18 | | To T'port | 1 57 | 1 38 | |
| Dundee - ... arr. | | | | | | 9 11 | 9 26 | | 9 13 | | 9 18 | | | | | 10 20 | 10 20 | | | | | | | |

# LEVEN and EAST OF FIFE, ANSTRUTHER & ST ANDREWS, and ST ANDREWS & LEUCHARS SECTIONS. and MUIREDGE BRANCH.—Down Trains.

## WEEK-DAYS.

| Stations and Sidings. | 23 Goods, Leuchars and Tayport Pilot, Thurs. only. | 24 Pass. | 25 Stores, Thurs June 18. | 26 Pass. | 27 Pass. Mon. only. | 28 Goods, Thornton and Anstruther. | 29 Pass. Sat. only. | 30 Exp. Pass. Sat. only. From Glasgow. | 31 Pass. | 32 East Fife Min. | 33 Goods Mon. only. | 34 When required. | 35 Goods, Thornton, Leven, and Methil. | 36 ex. Sat. From Glasgow. | 37 Fast Pass. | 38 Pass. | 39 Pass. | 40 Goods, Leuchars and Tayport Pilot, Sat. only. | 41 Branch Goods. ex. Sat. | 42 Pass. Sat. only. | 43 Pass. | 44 Goods, Anstruther and Thornton. | 45 Pass. | 46 Pass. Sat. only. |
|---|---|---|---|---|---|---|---|---|---|---|---|---|---|---|---|---|---|---|---|---|---|---|---|---|
| | p.m. | a.m. | a.m. | p.m. | p.m. | p.m. | p.m. | p.m. | p.m. | p.m. | p.m. | | p.m. | p.m. | p.m. | p.m. | p.m. | p.m. | p.m. | p.m. | p.m. | p.m. | p.m. | p.m. |
| Dundee ... dep. | … | 10 0 | … | 12 25 | … | … | … | 2 50 | 12 55 | … | … | | … | 4 5 | 4 5 | 4 5 | 4 5 | … | … | … | 5 5 | … | 7 35 | 10 0 |
| Edinburgh ... dep. | … | 9 53 | 11 52 | 12 10 | … | … | 1 35 | … | 12 50 | … | … | | … | 3 50 | 4 55 | 4 55 | 4 55 | … | … | … | … | … | 7 12 | 10 10 |
| **Thornton Jun.** | | | | | | | | | | | | | | | | | | | | | | | | |
| Drumcaldie Distillery Siding dep. | … | 11 23 | … | 1 20 | … | 1 36 | … | … | … | … | 4 46 | | 5 0 | … | … | … | … | … | … | … | … | … | … | Stop. |
| Cameron Bridge arr. | … | 11 23 | … | 1 20 | … | … | 2 31 | 2 57 | 3 0 | … | … | | 5 15 | 5 27 | 5 54 | … | … | … | … | … | 7 17 | … | 9 0 | … |
| Cameron Bridge dep. | … | 11 32 | … | 1 29 | … | 1 45 | … | … | 3 9 | 4 0 | 5 0 | | 5 15 | … | … | 6 1 | 6 10 | … | … | … | … | 8 11 | 9 9 | … |
| Pirnie Colliery | … | … | … | … | … | … | … | … | … | … | … | | … | … | … | … | … | … | … | … | … | … | … | … |
| Cameron Pit Sidings | … | … | … | … | … | … | … | … | … | … | … | | … | … | … | … | … | … | … | … | … | … | … | … |
| Cameron Bridge dep. | … | 11 38 | 12 1 | 1 30 | … | … | 3 9 | … | 3 10 | … | … | | … | … | 6 1 | … | … | … | … | … | … | … | … | … |
| East Fife Central Junction | … | … | … | … | … | 1 48 | … | … | … | … | … | | … | … | … | … | … | … | … | … | 7 24 | … | … | … |
| Leven ... arr. | … | 11 39 | 12 6 | 1 36 | … | 1 48 | … | … | 3 15 | 4 15 | … | | … | … | … | … | … | … | … | … | 7 28 | 8 23 | 9 10 | … |
| Do. ... dep. | … | 11 40 | 12 7 | 1 36 | 1 38 | 1 53 | 2 43 | 3 1 | 3 17 | 4 20 | 5 10 | | 5 25 | 5 38 | 6 5 | 6 11 | 6 11 | … | … | … | 7 30 | 8 25 | 9 17 | … |
| Leven Brick Work Siding | … | … | … | Stop. | … | 1 58 | … | … | … | Stop. | … | | Stop. | 5 40 | 6 7 | … | … | … | … | … | … | 8 32 | … | … |
| Silverburn Siding | … | … | … | … | … | 2 10 | … | … | … | … | … | | … | … | … | … | … | … | … | … | … | 8 35 | … | … |
| Lundin Links | … | … | … | … | 1 43 | 2 15 | … | … | … | … | 5 18 | | … | 5 45 | 6 12 | … | 6 16 | … | … | … | 7 35 | 8 40 | 9 22 | … |
| Largo ... | … | 11 45 | 12 12 | … | 1 43 | 2 20 | … | 3 2 | 3 22 | … | 5 18 | | … | 5 45 | 6 12 | … | 6 16 | … | … | … | 7 35 | 8 40 | 9 22 | … |
| Kilconquhar ... | … | 11 49 | 12 18 | … | 1 47 | 2 25 / 2 30 | 2 48 | 3 7 | 3 26 | … | 5 23 | | … | 5 49 | 6 16 | … | 6 26 | … | … | … | 7 39 | 8 43 | 9 26 | … |
| Elie ... arr. | … | 11 58 | 12 28 | … | 1 56 | 2 44 / 2 49 | 2 52 | 3 11 | 3 35 | … | 5 38 | | … | 5 58 | … | … | 6 35 | … | … | … | 7 48 | 8 54 | 9 35 | … |
| ... dep. | … | 12 2 | 12 32 | … | 2 0 | 2 49 | 2 52 | 3 20 | 3 40 | … | 5 43 | | … | Stop. | 6 25 | … | 6 40 | … | … | … | 7 53 | 8 59 | 9 40 | … |
| Do. ... dep. | … | Stop. | 12 33 | … | 2 0 | 2 49 | … | Stop. | … | … | … | | … | … | … | … | … | … | … | … | … | … | … | … |
| St Monan's | … | … | 12 40 | … | 2 8 | 2 54 | 3 1 | … | 3 42 | … | 6 5 | | … | … | 6 27 | … | 6 42 | … | … | … | 7 55 | 9 10 | 9 42 | … |
| Pittenweem | … | … | 12 46 | … | 2 13 | 3 8 | 3 2 | … | 3 48 | … | 6 22 | | … | … | 6 36 | … | 6 48 | … | … | … | 8 4 | 9 20 | 9 48 | … |
| Anstruther (Old Station) arr. | … | … | 12 46 | … | 2 18 | 3 12 | 3 11 | … | 3 53 | 32a | 6 25 | | 35a | Commences 15th June. | 6 40 | … | 6 53 | … | … | … | … | 9 25 | 9 53 | … |
| Anstruther (New Station) dep. | … | … | 1 0 | … | Stop. | 28a | 3 14 | … | 3 58 | p.m. | 7 20 | | p.m. | | 6 40 | … | 6 58 | … | … | … | 8 10 | Stop. | Stop. | … |
| Crail ( Do. ) arr. | … | … | 1 20 | 26a | 27a | Pass. | 3 29 | … | 4 12 | … | 7 35 | | 6 37 | | 6 42 | … | 7 12 | … | … | … | 8 20 | 44a | … | … |
| Do. ( Do. ) dep. | … | … | 1 30 | Pass. | Pass. | p.m. | Stop. | … | 4 18 | … | 7 45 | | … | | 6 52 | … | 7 18 | … | … | … | … | Pass. | … | … |
| Kingsbarns | … | … | 1 38 | p.m. | p.m. | 4 15 | … | … | 4 19 | … | Stop. | | … | | Stop. | … | 7 24 | … | … | … | … | Sat. only. | … | … |
| Boarhills | … | … | 1 46 | 2 50 | 3 30 | … | … | … | 4 24 | … | … | | … | | … | … | 7 31 | … | … | … | … | p.m. | … | … |
| Stravithie | … | … | 1 51 | … | … | … | … | … | 4 31 | … | … | | … | | … | … | 7 38 | … | … | … | … | … | … | … |
| Mount Melville | … | … | 2 0 | … | … | … | … | … | 4 38 | … | … | | … | | … | … | 7 42 | … | … | … | … | … | … | … |
| St Andrews (New Station) arr. | 2 32 | … | 2 10 | … | … | … | … | … | 4 42 | 5 25 | … | | … | | … | 7 20 | 7 46 | 8 50 | … | 9 15 | … | 10 15 | … | … |
| Do. Do. dep. | 2 42 | … | 2 15 | 2 50 | 3 30 | 4 15 | … | … | 5 0 | 5 25 | … | | 6 37 | | … | 7 20 | 7 46 | 8 50 | 8 50 | 9 15 | 8 10 | 10 15 | … | … |
| Do. (links Station) | 2 42 | … | 2 35 | … | … | … | … | … | … | … | … | | … | | … | 7 29 | 7 56 | … | 9 0 | 9 24 | 8 20 | 10 24 | … | … |
| Edenside Brick Work Siding | … | … | 2 45 | 2 59 | 3 39 | 4 24 | … | … | 5 9 | 5 34 | … | | 6 46 | | … | 7 29 | 7 56 | 9 0 | 9 0 | 9 24 | … | 10 24 | … | … |
| Guard Bridge | 2 47 | … | 2 45 | 2 59 | 3 39 | 4 24 | … | … | 5 9 | 5 34 | … | | 6 46 | | … | 7 29 | 7 56 | 9 0 | 9 5 | 9 24 | … | 10 24 | … | … |
| Seggie Siding | 2 52 | … | 2 50 | 3 3 | 3 43 | 4 28 | … | … | 5 14 | 5 38 | … | | 6 50 | | … | 7 33 | 8 1 | 9 5 | 9 10 | 9 29 | … | 10 29 | … | … |
| Leuchars Junction arr. | 2 56 | … | 3 15 | 3 37 | 5 18 | 5 25 | … | … | 5 40 | 6 15 | … | | 7 38 | | … | 9 16 | 8 42 | 9 10 | 9 10 | 10 3 | … | … | … | … |
| Edinburgh ... arr. | … | … | 3 15 | 3 37 | … | … | … | … | 7 9 | … | … | | … | | … | 9 16 | … | … | … | … | … | … | … | … |
| Dundee arr. | … | … | … | … | … | … | … | … | 6 15 | … | … | | … | | … | 8 2 | … | … | … | … | … | … | … | … |

# LEVEN and EAST OF FIFE, ANSTRUTHER & ST ANDREWS, and ST ANDREWS & LEUCHARS SECTIONS and MUIREDGE BRANCH.—Up Trains.

June 1903.

## WEEK-DAYS.

| Stations and Sidings | Distance from Leuchars Junction (Miles) | (Chains) | 1 Cattle Tues. only. | 2 Cattle Tues. only. | 3 Pass. | 4 Branch Engine Goods | 5 Exp. Pass. | 6 Pass. | 7 Anstruther and Thornton Goods Mon. only. When required. | 8 Pass. | 9 Pass. | 10 Pass. | 11 Pass. | 12 East Fife Min. | 13 Pass. | 14 Goods | 15 | 16 Pass. | 17 East Fife Min. | 18 Anstruther and Thornton Goods ex. Mon. | 19 Pass. | 20 Pass. | 21 Pass. | 22 East Fife Min. |
|---|---|---|---|---|---|---|---|---|---|---|---|---|---|---|---|---|---|---|---|---|---|---|---|---|
| | | | a.m. | a.m. | a.m. | a.m. | a.m. | a.m. | a.m. | a.m | | a.m. | a.m. | a.m. | a.m. | a.m. | | a.m. | a.m. | a.m. | a.m. | a.m. | p.m. | p.m. |
| Dundee ... dep. | ... | ... | | | | | | | | | | | | | | | | 10 0 | 11 20 | | 10 5 | 9 35 | 12 15 | |
| Edinburgh ... dep. | ... | ... | | | | | | | | 6 30 | | 7 24 | 8 0 | | 8 15 | 9 10 | | 10 22 | 11 25 | | 10 49 | 11 20 | 9 53 | |
| —Leuchars Junction ... dep. | ... | ... | 3 45 | | 4 45 | 5 35 | | | | | | 7 29 | 6 25 | | 7 35 | 9 15 | | 10 26 | | | | 12 12 40 | |
| Seggie Siding ... " | ... | 73 | | | 5 3 | 5 40 | | | | 6 34 | | | 8 25 | | 9 0 | 9 20 | | | | | 10 53 | 11 25 | | |
| —Guard Bridge ... " | 1 | 14 | 4 15 | | 5 7 | | | | | | | | | | 9 4 | 9 25 | | | | | | | | |
| Edenside Brick Work Siding ... " | 1 | 28 | 4 19 | | | | | | | | | | 8 29 | | | | | | | | | | | |
| —St Andrews (Links Station) " | 4 | 57 | 4 30 | | 5 14 | 5 50 | | | | 6 41 | | 7 36 | 8 37 | | 9 12 | 9 35 | | 10 34 | | | 11 1 | 11 35 12 50 | | |
| Do. (New Station) arr. | 5 | 5 | | | | Stop. | | | | Stop. 8a | | Stop. | 8 38 | | Stop. | Stop. | | Stop. | | | | Stop. | Stop. | |
| Do. Do. dep. | 5 | 0 | 4 31 | | 5 16 | | | | | | | | 8 45 | | | | | | | | 11 2 | | | |
| Mount Melville ... " | 7 | | 4 38 | | 5 23 | | | | | | | | 8 51 | | | | | | | | 11 9 | | | |
| Stravithie ... " | 9 | 37 | 4 47 | | 5 30 | | | | | | | | 8 57 | | | | | | | | 11 16 | | | |
| Boarhills ... " | 11 | 54 | 4 55 | | 5 35 | | 7 10 | 7 54 | | | | | 9 0 | | | | | | | | 11 21 | | | |
| Kingsbarns ... arr. | 13 | 17 | 5 0 | | 5 38 | | 7 18 | 8 2 | | | | | 9 1 | | | | | | | | 11 25 | | | |
| Do. ... dep. | 13 | 17 | 5 13 | | 5 46 | | 7 22 | 8 4 | | | | | 9 8 | | | | | | | | 11 32 | | | |
| —Crail ... " | 16 | 7 | 5 23 | | 5 54 | | | | 7 20 | | | | 9 16 | | | | | | | | 11 41 | | | |
| —Anstruther (New Station) arr. | 20 | 29 | | | 5 56 | | | | 7 35 | | | | 9 18 | | | | | | | | 11 46 | | | |
| Do. Do. dep. | 20 | 29 | | | 6 0 | | | | 7 45 | | | | | | | | | | | | | | | |
| —Anstruther (Old Station) dep. | 21 | 39 | 5 25 | 5 30 | 6 5 | 4a | 7 26 | 8 8 | 7 47 | 7 50 | | | 9 22 | | | | | | | 10 55 | 11 50 | | | |
| Pittenweem ... " | 23 | 3 | Stop. | 5 40 | 6 9 | | 7 31 | 8 12 | Stop. | 7 55 | | | 9 27 | | | | | | | 11 5 | 11 51 | | | |
| St Monan's ... " | 25 | 10 | | 5 45 | 6 10 | | 7 35 | 8 14 | | 8 0 | | | 9 32 | | | | | | | 11 15 | 11 56 | | | |
| Elie ... " | 25 | | | | 6 11 | | 7 37 | 8 15 | | 8 8 | | | | | | | | | | 11 20 | 12 1 | | | |
| Do. ... dep. | 26 | 42 | | 5 47 | 6 16 | Exp. Pass. | 8 10 | | | 8 40 | | | 9 33 | | | | | | | 11 25 | 12 4 | | | |
| Kilconquhar ... " | 30 | 31 | | 5 53 | 6 24 | 6 45 | 7 40 | 8 25 | | 8 46 | | | 9 38 | | | | | | | 11 35 | 12 9 | | | |
| Largo ... " | 31 | 21 | | 6 6 | 6 28 | 6 48 | 7 47 | 8 29 | | 9 0 | | | 9 46 | | | | | | | 11 50 | 12 17 | | | |
| Lundin Links ... " | 32 | 68 | | 6 6 | | 6 55 | 7 51 | | | 9 10 | | | 9 50 | | | | | | | 11 55 | 12 21 | | | |
| Leven Brick Work Siding ... " | 33 | 4 | | | | 6 59 | | | | | | | | | | | | | | 12 0 | | | | |
| —Leven ... arr. | | | | 6 12 | 6 32 | 7 3 | 7 55 | 8 33 | | 9 20 | | | 9 54 | | | | | | | 12 5 | 12 25 | | | |
| Do. ... dep. | | | | 6 20 | 6 34 | 7 4 | 7 57 | 8 34 | | 9 25 | | | 9 56 | | | | 11 20 | | 12 10 | 12 27 | | 2 0 | 12 35 | 4 5 |
| —East Fife Central Junction ... " | 33 | 4 | | 6 22 | | | 7 59 | 8 40 | | 9 35 | | | 10 2 | | | | 11 25 | | 12 15 | 12 33 | | 2 6 | 12 45 | 3 37 |
| —Cameron Bridge ... arr. | 34 | 30 | | 6 27 | 6 40 | | 8 3 | | | | | | | Stop. | | | | | | 12 18 | | | | |
| Cameron Pit Sidings ... dep. | 35 | 20 | | | | | | | | | | | | 10 25 | | | | | | | | | 2 17 | |
| Pirnie Colliery ... arr. | | | | | | | | | | | | | | 10 30 | | | | | | | | 2 7 | 2 26 | |
| Cameron Bridge ... dep. | 35 | 20 | | 6 32 | 6 42 | 7 17 To Glasgow | 8 4 | 8 41 | | 10 12 | | | 10 3 | 10 35 | | | | | | 12 20 | 12 33 | 2 16 | | |
| —Thornton Junction ... arr. | 39 | 1 | | 6 42 | 6 52 | | 8 14 | 8 52 | | 10 22 | | | 10 12 | Stop. | | | | | | 12 33 | 12 45 | 2 16 | | |
| Edinburgh ... arr. | ... | ... | | Stop. | 8 37 | 9 26 | 10 39 | 10 39 | | | | | 11 44 | | | | | | | | 1 57 | 2 7 | 4 5 | |
| Dundee | ... | ... | | | 8 34 | 10 39 | | | | | | | 11 18 | | | | | | | | 2 14 | 2 16 | 3 37 | |

*From Lochty: 3 5, 3 8, Stop.*

*To Lochty.*

*20a. Sat. Pass. Sat. only.*   *21a. Pass. ex. Sat.*

# LEVEN and EAST OF FIFE, ANSTRUTHER & ST ANDREWS, and ST ANDREWS & LEUCHARS SECTIONS, and MUIREDGE BRANCH.—Up Trains.

**June 1903.**

## WEEK-DAYS.

| Stations and Sidings. | | 23 | 24 | 25 | 26 | 27 | 28 | 29 | 30 | 31 | 32 | 33 | 34 | 35 | 36 | 37 | 38 | 39 | 40 | 41 | 42 | 43 | 44 | 45 | 46 |
|---|---|---|---|---|---|---|---|---|---|---|---|---|---|---|---|---|---|---|---|---|---|---|---|---|---|
| | | Thornton and St Andrews Goods | Thornton and St Andrews Goods | Leuchars & Tayport Pilot. Goods | Pass. Sat. only. | Pass. | Pass. | Exp. Pass. | | East Fife Min. | Pass. | Dundee, Bath, and Kelly. Cattle Tues. only. | Bath, and Kelly. | Anstruther and Thornton. Goods | | Pass. | Pass. | Pass. Sat. only. | Pass. | Goods Mon. only. | Pass. | Leuchars and Tay-port Pilot. Sat. only. Goods | Branch Goods ex. Sat. | Pass. Sat. only. | Pass. Sat. only. |
| | | p.m. | p.m. | p.m. | p.m. | p.m. | p.m. | p.m | | p.m. | p.m. | p.m. | p.m. | p.m. | | p.m. | p.m. | | p.m. | p.m. | p.m. | p.m. | p.m. | p.m. | p.m. |
| Dundee ... ... | dep. | ... | ... | 1 28 | 12 10 | 1 45 | 3 7 | ... | ... | ... | 3 35 | 4 28 | 4 5 | ... | ... | 5 40 | 6 15 | ... | 6 25 | ... | 7 35 | 8 15 | 9 35 | 7 12 | 10 15 |
| Edinburgh ... ... | ,, | ... | ... | 1 33 | 1 52 | 2 20 | 3 12 | ... | ... | ... | 1 50 | ... | ... | ... | ... | 4 25 | 6 20 | ... | 7 3 | ... | 6 40 | 8 20 | 9 40 | 9 45 | 10 40 |
| Leuchars Junction | dep. | ... | 1 5 | 1 38 | 1 57 | 2 24 | ... | ... | ... | ... | 4 0 | 4 40 | 4 40 | ... | ... | 6 8 | ... | ... | 7 8 | ... | 8 10 | 8 25 | 9 45 | 9 50 | 10 45 |
| Seggie Siding | ,, | ... | ... | 1 43 | ... | ... | ... | ... | ... | ... | ... | ... | ... | ... | ... | ... | ... | ... | ... | ... | ... | ... | ... | ... | ... |
| Guard Bridge | ,, | ... | ... | 1 53 | ... | ... | ... | ... | ... | ... | ... | ... | ... | ... | ... | ... | ... | ... | ... | ... | ... | ... | ... | ... | ... |
| Edenside Brick Work Siding | ,, | ... | ... | ... | ... | ... | ... | ... | ... | ... | ... | ... | ... | ... | ... | ... | ... | ... | ... | ... | ... | ... | ... | ... | ... |
| St Andrews (Links Station) | ,, | ... | 1 5 | ... | ... | 2 32 | 3 20 | ... | ... | ... | 4 8 | 4 39 | 4 48 | ... | ... | 6 16 | 6 30 | ... | 7 16 | ... | 8 20 | 8 35 | 9 55 | 10 0 | 10 55 |
| Do. (New Station) | arr. | ... | ... | ... | ... | ... | ... | ... | ... | ... | ... | ... | ... | ... | ... | ... | ... | ... | ... | ... | ... | ... | ... | ... | ... |
| Do. ) do. ( | dep. | ... | 1 17 | ... | Stop. | 2 33 | Stop. | ... | ... | ... | Stop. | Stop. | Stop. | ... | ... | 6 17 | Stop. | 7 35 | Stop. | ... | Stop. | Stop. | Stop. | Stop. | Stop. |
| Mount Melville | ,, | ... | 1 30 | ... | ... | 2 40 | ... | ... | ... | ... | ... | ... | ... | ... | ... | 6 24 | ... | 7 45 | ... | ... | ... | ... | ... | ... | ... |
| Stravithie | ,, | ... | 1 40 | ... | ... | 2 47 | ... | ... | ... | ... | ... | ... | ... | ... | ... | 6 31 | ... | 7 48 | ... | ... | ... | ... | ... | ... | ... |
| Boarhills | ,, | ... | 1 45 | ... | ... | 2 53 | ... | ... | ... | ... | ... | ... | ... | ... | ... | 6 37 | ... | ... | ... | ... | ... | ... | ... | ... | ... |
| Kingsbarns ... ... | arr. | ... | 1 53 | ... | ... | 2 56 | ... | 3 40 | ... | ... | ... | ... | ... | 5 30 | ... | 6 40 | ... | ... | ... | ... | ... | ... | ... | ... | ... |
| Do. ... ... | dep. | ... | 2 10 | ... | ... | 2 57 | ... | 3 50 | ... | ... | ... | ... | ... | 5 40 | ... | 6 41 | ... | ... | 7 50 | ... | ... | ... | ... | ... | ... |
| Crail ... ... | arr. | ... | ... | ... | ... | 3 5 | ... | 4 0 | ... | ... | ... | ... | ... | 5 45 | ... | 6 52 | ... | ... | 8 20 | ... | ... | ... | ... | ... | ... |
| Anstruther (New Station) | ,, | ... | 2 13 | ... | 2 7 | 3 15 | ... | ... | ... | ... | ... | ... | ... | 5 55 | ... | 7 1 | ... | ... | ... | ... | ... | ... | ... | ... | ... |
| Do. ) do. ( | dep. | ... | ... | ... | ... | 3 17 | ... | ... | ... | ... | ... | 33a | ... | ... | ... | 7 7 | ... | ... | ... | 8 35 | ... | ... | ... | ... | ... |
| Anstruther (Old Station) | dep. | ... | 2 30 | ... | ... | 3 21 | ... | 4 4 | ... | ... | ... | ... | ... | 6 40 | ... | 7 11 | ... | 7 52 | ... | ... | ... | ... | ... | ... | ... |
| Pittenweem ... ... | ,, | ... | 2 33 | ... | ... | 3 27 | ... | 4 10 | ... | ... | ... | Thornton, Leven, & Methil. Goods | ... | 6 50 | ... | 7 16 | ... | 7 59 | ... | ... | ... | ... | ... | ... | ... |
| St Monan's ... ... | ,, | ... | 2 39 | ... | ... | 3 32 | ... | ... | ... | ... | ... | ... | ... | 7 5 | ... | 7 21 | ... | ... | ... | ... | ... | ... | ... | ... | ... |
| Elie ... ... | arr. | ... | 2 45 | ... | ... | ... | ... | 4 12 | ... | ... | ... | ... | ... | 7 10 | ... | ... | ... | 8 0 | ... | ... | ... | ... | ... | ... | ... |
| Do. ... ... | dep. | ... | 2 50 | ... | ... | 3 41 | ... | 4 15 | ... | 4 25 | ... | ... | ... | ... | ... | 7 23 | ... | 8 10 | ... | ... | ... | ... | ... | ... | ... |
| Kilconquhar ... ... | ,, | ... | 3 27 | ... | ... | 3 46 | ... | 4 22 | ... | 4 40 | ... | ... | ... | ... | ... | 7 28 | ... | 8 14 | ... | ... | ... | ... | ... | ... | ... |
| Largo ... ... | ,, | ... | ... | ... | ... | 3 54 | ... | 4 26 | ... | 4 45 | ... | ... | ... | ... | ... | 7 39 | ... | ... | ... | ... | ... | ... | ... | ... | ... |
| Lundin Links | ,, | ... | 3 37 | ... | ... | 3 58 | ... | ... | ... | 6 20 | ... | 6 16 | ... | ... | ... | 7 43 | ... | 8 18 | ... | ... | ... | ... | ... | ... | ... |
| Leven Brick Work Siding | ,, | ... | ... | ... | ... | ... | ... | 4 30 | ... | 6 35 | ... | ... | ... | 7 15 | ... | 7 47 | ... | 8 20 | ... | ... | ... | ... | ... | ... | ... |
| Leven ... ... | dep. | ... | 3 40 | ... | ... | 4 2 | ... | 4 32 | ... | ... | ... | 6 26 | ... | ... | ... | 7 48 | ... | ... | ... | ... | ... | ... | ... | ... | ... |
| Do. ... ... | dep. | ... | ... | ... | ... | 4 4 | ... | ... | ... | Stop. | ... | ... | ... | 7 28 | ... | ... | ... | ... | ... | ... | ... | ... | ... | ... | ... |
| East Fife Central Junction | ,, | ... | ... | ... | ... | 4 7 | ... | ... | ... | ... | ... | ... | ... | ... | ... | ... | ... | ... | ... | ... | ... | ... | ... | ... | ... |
| Cameron Bridge ... | arr. | ... | 3 50 | ... | ... | 4 10 | ... | ... | ... | ... | ... | 6 26 | ... | 7 34 | ... | 7 54 | ... | ... | ... | ... | ... | ... | ... | ... | ... |
| Cameron Pit Sidings | dep. | ... | ... | ... | ... | ... | ... | ... | ... | ... | ... | ... | ... | ... | ... | ... | ... | ... | ... | ... | ... | ... | ... | ... | ... |
| Pirnie Colliery | ,, | ... | ... | ... | ... | ... | ... | ... | ... | ... | ... | ... | ... | ... | ... | ... | ... | ... | ... | ... | ... | ... | ... | ... | ... |
| Cameron Bridge | arr. | ... | 3 53 | ... | ... | 4 12 | ... | 4 36 | ... | ... | ... | 6 35 | ... | 7 37 | ... | 7 56 | ... | ... | ... | ... | ... | ... | ... | ... | ... |
| Cameron Bridge ... | dep. | ... | 4 8 | ... | ... | 4 22 | ... | 4 46 | ... | ... | ... | 6 50 | ... | 7 50 | ... | 8 0 | ... | ... | ... | ... | ... | ... | ... | ... | ... |
| Thornton Junction | arr. | ... | ... | ... | ... | ... | ... | ... | ... | ... | ... | ... | ... | ... | ... | ... | ... | ... | ... | ... | ... | ... | ... | ... | ... |
| Edinburgh ... ... | arr. | ... | ... | ... | ... | 5 46 | ... | 5 46 | ... | ... | ... | ... | ... | ... | ... | 9 16 | ... | 9 50 | ... | ... | ... | ... | ... | ... | ... |
| Dundee ... ... | ,, | ... | ... | ... | ... | 6 15 | ... | 6 15 | ... | ... | ... | ... | ... | ... | ... | 10 3 | ... | 10 51 | ... | ... | ... | ... | ... | ... | ... |

*When required.*

# Sources, Bibliography and Acknowledgements

This book has been compiled wherever possible from primary resources which are to be found in the National Archives of Scotland, the National Archives in Kew, the St Andrews University Archives and numerous private collections. Of chief interest were the Minute Books, accounts, cash books and journals and other records of the Anstruther & St Andrews Railway (BR/AST), the Edinburgh, Perth & Dundee Railway (BR/EPD) and the North British, LNER and British Railways Scottish Region and British Transport Hotels, together with timetables (public and working), General Appendices, special traffic notices, Board of Trade inspection and accident reports and a variety of other official documents together with advertising and other materials. In addition much help was derived from the Minute Books of the St Andrews, Crail and Anstruther Town Councils and from local newspapers dating back to 1839 including:

*The Scotsman, The Fifeshire Journal, The Fifeshire Advertiser, The Dundee Courier, The East of Fife Record, The St Andrews Citizen, The Fife News & Coast Chronicle, The Coastal Burghs Observer/East Fife Observer, The Dundee Evening Telegraph, The Edinburgh Evening Despatch* and *The Edinburgh Evening News*. Other publications consulted included the *Railway Magazine, LNER* and *BR Scottish Region Magazines, North British Railway Study Group Journal* and *Railway World*.

Perhaps the most interesting sources of all were the personal reminiscences of those who worked on, used as passengers or merchants or trainspotted on the lines and special thanks are given for their most valuable contributions which helped this book to come to life.

The following works may prove of interest to those who wish to know more about St Andrews and the East Neuk or particular aspects of the line and its workings:

### Local Topography
Dick, S. , *The Pageant of the Forth*, (1911); Farnie, H., *Handbook to the Fife Coast*, (1862); Fife, M., *Crail and Dunino - the story of two Scottish airfields*, (2003); Geddie, J., *The Fringes of Fife*, (1907); Gifford, J., *The Buildings of Scotland: Fife*,(1988); Groome, F.H., *Ordnance Gazetteer of Scotland*,(1892); Jackson, Rev John, *Guide to Crail*, (1896); Leighton, J., *History of the County of Fife*, (1840); Lenman, B., *From Esk to Tweed*, (1975); Smith, A. (ed) *Third Statistical Account of Scotland: Fife*, (1952).

### Local Railways
Batchelor, R., *East Fife Railway Album* (1984); Brotchie, A., *Fife Trams and Buses*, (1990); Corstorphine, J.K., *East of Thornton Junction*, (1995); Hamilton Ellis, C., *The North British Railway*,(1955); Railway Correspondence & Travel Society, *Locomotives of the LNER* (various); Scott Bruce, W., *Railways of Fife*, (1980); Smith, D.J. *Action Stations No. 7: Military Airfields of Scotland, etc.* (1993); Stephenson Locomotive Society, *Locomotives of the NBR (1846-1882)*; Thomas, J., *North British Railway*, 2 vols (1969, 1975) and a multimedia CD: *A Puff of Smoke: Memories of the East of Fife Railway* by R. MacAlindin (2005). A list of magazine articles that have appeared on the Anstruther & St Andrews Railway appears in our companion volume *The St Andrews Railway*.

The authors wish to thank the following who contributed their knowledge, time and, in some cases, documents, photographs and other illustrations and without whose help this book would have been a lot poorer: the late John Bennett, Alan Brotchie, Donald Cattanach, Jim Corstorphine, the late William Docherty, Bruce Ellis, George Fairlie, Jim Hay, L.A.C. Home, J. Hunter, John Hurst, Jeff Hurst, John Langford, Bill Lynn, Bruce Murray, Brian Malaws, Dr D. MacDonald, Alison MacKintosh, Ray Montgomery, Ed. Nicholl, Archie Noble, Jim Page, Douglas Paul, the late Roger Pedrick, Alan Rodgers, John Purvis, Bill Rear, D.P. Rowland, Anna Singer, Martin Smith, Michael B. Smith, W.A.C. Smith, David Stirling, Jim Stormonth, Chris Thornburn, Norman Turnbull, Pete Westwater, D. Woodcock and Douglas Yuill. Thanks are also due to the staff of the Advocates Library, Edinburgh, Anstruther Public Library, Crail Museum, Cupar Public Library, Edinburgh Central Library, Glasgow Museum of Transport, Kirkcaldy Public Library, Glasgow University Business Archives, Leven Public Library, Methil Public Library, National Archives of Scotland, National Archives at Kew, National Library of Scotland including its Map Room, St Andrews Public Library and St Andrews University Library and Archive. With regard to the photographs, to those who might criticise us for a preponderance of 'B1s' and Metro-Cammell dmus we can only say that pictures of the Anstruther & St Andrews photographs pre-1950 seem to be few and far between, a fact that we attribute to the sparse timetable and, in the days before enthusiasts owned cars, the remoteness of many of the locations; we would also add that personally the authors quite like both the 'B1s' and the Metro-Cams! Despite their efforts to trace the original photographers, the provenance of some of the illustrations is unknown to the authors, and apologies are tendered for any ommissions. Once again thanks are given to Kate Hajducka and we hope that *The Anstruther & St Andrews Railway* justifies her, and our, efforts! Lastly we would thank our publishers for their patience and faith in us and particularly Ian Kennedy for his continuing support and encouragement and look forward to working with him on *The Leven & East of Fife Railway*.

Finally, any reader who is especially interested in the North British Railway, its predecessors and successors, is invited to join the North British Railway Study Group, details of which can be found on line at www.nbrstudygroup.co.uk.

# Index